TRUTH AND CONSEQUENCE

ALSO BY DANIEL ELLSBERG

The Doomsday Machine: Confessions of a Nuclear War Planner (2017)

Secrets: A Memoir of Vietnam and the Pentagon Papers (2002)

Risk, Ambiguity and Decision (2001)

Papers on the War (1972)

TRUTH AND CONSEQUENCE

REFLECTIONS ON CATASTROPHE, CIVIL RESISTANCE, AND HOPE

DANIEL ELLSBERG
EDITED BY MICHAEL ELLSBERG AND JAN R. THOMAS

BLOOMSBURY PUBLISHING
NEW YORK · LONDON · OXFORD · NEW DELHI · SYDNEY

BLOOMSBURY PUBLISHING
Bloomsbury Publishing Inc.
1359 Broadway, New York, NY 10018, USA
50 Bedford Square, London, WC1B 3DP, UK
Bloomsbury Publishing Ireland Limited,
29 Earlsfort Terrace, Dublin 2, D02 AY28, Ireland

BLOOMSBURY, BLOOMSBURY PUBLISHING, and the Diana logo
are trademarks of Bloomsbury Publishing Plc

First published in the United States in 2026

Copyright © Daniel Ellsberg, 2026

All rights reserved. No part of this publication may be: i) reproduced or transmitted in any form, electronic or mechanical, including photocopying, recording, or by means of any information storage or retrieval system without prior permission in writing from the publishers; or ii) used or reproduced in any way for the training, development, or operation of artificial intelligence (AI) technologies, including generative AI technologies. The rights holders expressly reserve this publication from the text and data mining exception as per Article 4(3) of the Digital Single Market Directive (EU) 2019/790.

For high-quality outtakes and other material that we didn't have room to
include in the book, visit www.ellsberg.net.

Bloomsbury Publishing Plc does not have any control over, or responsibility for, any third-party websites referred to or in this book. All internet addresses given in this book were correct at the time of going to press. The author and publisher regret any inconvenience caused if addresses have changed or sites have ceased to exist, but can accept
no responsibility for any such changes.

ISBN: HB: 978-1-63973-551-8; eBook: 978-1-63973-552-5

Library of Congress Cataloging-in-Publication Data is available

2 4 6 8 10 9 7 5 3 1

Typesetting by Six Red Marbles India
Printed in the United States by Lakeside Book Company

To find out more about our authors and books visit www.bloomsbury.com
and sign up for our newsletters.

Bloomsbury books may be purchased for business or promotional use. For information on bulk purchases please contact Macmillan Corporate and Premium Sales Department at
specialmarkets@macmillan.com.
For product safety–related questions contact productsafety@bloomsbury.com.

CONTENTS

Foreword by Robert Ellsberg … vii
Introduction by Michael Ellsberg … xxi
Preface by Jan R. Thomas … xxxi

PART I: PERSONAL ESSAYS

The Piano (1997) … 3
Christian Jews (1997) … 21
The Accident (1997) … 29

PART II: SELECTIONS FROM THE ELLSBERG NOTEBOOKS, 1971–2021

Undated Selections … 45
1971–2021 … 53

PART III: ESSAYS ON MORALITY

Against Terrorism (2001) … 279
Massacre and Humanity (2001) … 283
Murder Mystery (1989) … 289
Nuclear Holocaust and Evil (2009) … 291
My Anguishing Secret (1984) … 297
The Implications of the Twentieth Century for Theology (2002) … 303
Dark Wisdom (2004) … 309
43 Seconds (2000) … 317

Acknowledgments	321
Notes	325
Index	349

FOREWORD

by Robert Ellsberg

> My chosen epitaph: "He helped to end the Vietnam War, and he struggled to prevent nuclear weapons from being exploded ever again."
>
> —Daniel Ellsberg

My father was a complicated man. On the one hand, he had an acute appreciation for beauty in all its forms: music, poetry, the sound of the ocean, the colors of the sunset visible from his dining room in California. After his death I found a closet piled high with packets of photographs—almost all of them close-up shots of flowers. He kept a frequently updated anthology consisting of photocopies of his favorite poems, many of which he had memorized and remained capable of reciting even in his last months.

All of this was in contrast with his long-standing preoccupation with the darkest moments of history, and the potential for greater tragedies to come. The bookshelves that surrounded his downstairs office were sorted according to labels such as Torture; Bombing Civilians; Nuclear First Strike; Terrorism; Lies; Genocide; and, finally, Catastrophe. As he noted in one of his last interviews in the *New York Times*, he spent so much of his life thinking about these things not because he found them fascinating, but because he wished to make them literally *unthinkable*. In his efforts to alert the world to the danger of nuclear annihilation, he engaged in action (including almost a hundred acts of civil disobedience), gave countless speeches and interviews, and wrote an extraordinary memoir, *The Doomsday Machine: Confessions of a Nuclear War Planner*. Yet by the end of his life, acknowledging the lack of progress in achieving his goals, he expressed regret that he hadn't done more.

All the while, it could be said that a major part of his life was spent *thinking*—trying to understand and unravel the mysteries of the human condition and to devise ways of thinking that might turn the tide of history. He could sit for hours, scribbling his almost illegible notes onto a yellow pad, otherwise staring into his own private abyss.

Many of his central concerns are reflected in the writings compiled in this volume. They show that he was not just concerned with the political or strategic aspects of war and nuclear planning—problems that could be fixed with a change in leadership or better policies. These threats to human survival were rooted in certain deep-seated problems with humanity itself. Some of these pertained to human nature in general: our willingness, almost unique in the animal world, to kill members of our own species. Then there was the tendency to derive our identity from our membership in a group, which set limits on our capacity for empathy with outsiders, those considered the "others."

> We are a very flawed species, dangerously so. We are dangerous to ourselves in the short and long run and we are the enemy that threatens the long-run survival of most other species. Seeing humanity's flaws, depression sets in. I am ashamed of my species, and I am sad for us and other species.

But other problems were more specific to the nature of rational, bureaucratized organizations in which individuals were encouraged to subordinate individual ethics ("which deal largely with obligations toward and concerns for others than oneself") to the ethics of the organization, defined in terms of obedience to authority, or loyalty to the boss or the "team." This tendency was compounded by the compartmentalization that made it easier for bureaucrats to deny their sense of personal responsibility for the outcome or consequences of official policy.

In the years following the end of his trial in 1973 for his part in copying and revealing the Pentagon Papers, he engaged in a wide-ranging study of these problems. He considered the example of Nazi Germany, examining the various forms of complicity, whether on the part of the masses, on the part of soldiers and officers who executed immoral policies, or on the part of officials. Among these was Hitler's architect, Albert Speer, who alone among the Nuremberg defendants pleaded guilty, even for things in which he had not been directly involved.

As Speer explained: "For being in a position to know and nevertheless shunning knowledge creates direct responsibility for the consequences—from the very beginning." This view resonated with my father's experience of what he called the "moral stupidity" shared by many organization men, motivated by the desire not only to keep one's job but also "to keep one's status, one's self-image (as a good person, as tough/manly, autonomous, obedient, loyal), and the good opinion of teammates, bosses, sponsors, constituents, and allies."

In a lecture in May 1971 titled "The Responsibility of Officials in a Criminal War," delivered only weeks before the Pentagon Papers were published, he had copied a quote from Speer in which he found a damning indictment of his own early culpability with regard to Vietnam War policy:

> If I was isolated, I determined the degree of my own isolation. If I was ignorant, I ensured my own ignorance. If I did not see, it was because I did not want to see ... It is surprisingly easy to blind your moral eyes. I was like a man following a trail of bloodstained footprints through the snow without realizing someone has been injured.

My father spent many years reflecting on the work of the psychologist Stanley Milgram, whose controversial experiments at Yale were recounted in his book *Obedience to Authority*. Milgram had devised an experiment in which unsuspecting subjects were assigned the role of conducting a test of memory. This test involved the testers' obligation to punish wrong answers by applying shocks of increasing voltage to a supposed "learner" (actually an actor in a separate room). The subjects were instructed by the "scientist" to continue with the test, even when, disturbed by the "learner's" protests and cries of pain, they wondered whether they should continue. They were told that it was necessary to complete the test and assured that while the shocks were "painful," they caused no "permanent tissue damage." Non-answers were to be treated as false answers, and many subjects continued to apply the shocks even when the "learner" fell silent. The disturbing revelation of the experiment was how compliant the subjects were in obeying authority, even when doing so caused them personal stress (the reason that such an experiment was later deemed unethical).

The mechanisms of this obedience, and what lessons it might offer about how to break the spell and induce disobedience or dissent, was for my father a topic of deep interest and importance. In his copy of *Obedience to Authority*, he heavily underlined one of the permutations in the experiment in which the "subject" was exposed to the example of a fellow "subject" (in fact, another actor) who said, "This is crazy! I refuse to continue." Milgram learned that in cases where subjects were exposed to an example of conscientious disobedience, they were able to awaken from their hypnotic captivity to authority.

He examined lessons from anthropology, history, and psychology. He studied the example of dissidents and those who acted on the basis of conscience, who took responsibility to act even at great personal risk. To understand these dynamics, he believed, was not just a matter of intellectual interest. The answers could make all the difference in ensuring a future for humanity.

And as his notes make clear, these reflections on averting catastrophe had deep personal roots. He noted, "When I was fifteen, I *experienced* a catastrophe." The story of "the Accident" that took the life of his mother and younger sister is described in detail in the opening section of this book. There he confined himself to recounting the story from various angles, without reflecting on the ways it may have affected his life—his own sense of survivor's guilt, his capacity for risk-taking, even his vocation as a whistleblower. But the ease, in his notes, with which he intersperses reflections on this story with his more wide-ranging reflections on authority, obedience, culpability in the face of disaster, and the responsibility to raise an alarm ("to tell truths that might save lives") shows that the connections were a matter of conscious reflection.

Over and over, he continued to deconstruct the events and their meaning. Was his father to blame for falling asleep at the wheel? Was his mother to blame for forcing him to keep an appointment she had made to attend a birthday party for her brother in Denver? Was he in part to blame on account of his impending decision to abandon his assigned destiny as a concert pianist?

He could draw the parallel between his own fear of losing a mother's love and the organizational or group conscience that made it unthinkable for so many officials to become whistleblowers: to be seen by their colleagues as disloyal, apostates, violators of trust, unworthy of being considered an insider. This parallel led him constantly to reflect on his own example. What had allowed him, in particular, to break free? To defect? To cease the desire to be the president's man? To raise the alarm that someone you trusted, a figure of authority, might be asleep at the wheel?

Many of the flaws in humanity have been evident throughout history, from biblical narratives of holy war to the *Iliad* to the mad destructiveness of World War I and the many examples of genocide, of which the Holocaust stood out not just by its scale but by the application of mechanized, industrial methods of execution. And yet with the splitting of the atom, humanity had entered a fantastically more perilous stage of history—conceivably the Final Solution to the human problem. Flawed humanity had suddenly become equipped with the technology and scientific knowledge to threaten its own survival.

Einstein observed, in a famous sentence, "The unleashed power of the atom has changed everything save our modes of thinking and we thus drift toward unparalleled catastrophe." To this my father notes: "What change was Einstein calling for? We need to use our human capacity for change on our own propensities—specifically, our readiness to gamble with catastrophe. *We need to change what it means to be human.*"

The extensive reflection on "what it means to be human" is one of the more surprising themes among these selected thoughts, or *pensées*, to borrow the title of Blaise Pascal's famous work. The allusion to Pascal is not casual. The seventeenth-century French scientist and Christian apologist left his most important work in the form of aphoristic notes and fragments for a grand project of Christian apologetics. This project began with his own characterization of the human condition: "Boredom, inconstancy, anxiety."

Yet for my father, the question of what it means to be human was not oriented, as it was for Pascal, toward the prospect of individual salvation, but toward the survival of all humans and other earthly creatures. What would save us, he believed, might require some wholesale evolution of human consciousness. Did we have time to achieve this? We were like the crew of the *Titanic*, steaming forward at full speed in fields of ice, racing toward a rendezvous with disaster. Was it already too late? Or was there still time for a mutiny?

Reflecting on his own experience, he pondered the factors that had prompted his own awakening to a sense of loyalty and responsibility to something higher than obedience to executive authority—or to a community larger than the organization, the administration, the brotherhood of insiders. What were the steps that tracked this journey?

My father began his career in the late 1950s as a defense analyst for the RAND Corporation, granted access to the most highly classified secrets of our nuclear war planning. His concern was never about fighting a nuclear war, but about preventing it—especially by means of deterrence and an effective system of command and control. He believed this work to be of the highest importance; he was trying to save the world. Yet what he came to recognize was that these plans were characterized, on the one hand, by a fantastic degree of murderousness, far exceeding anything ever imagined, and on the other, at the same time, by an incredible degree of make-believe and fantasy. Together, these two qualities represented a kind of madness, depicted accurately in the film *Dr. Strangelove*. It was a madness, he later realized, not inconsistent with extreme intelligence and rational capability.

An important turning point came in 1961 when he was presented by the Pentagon with a graph indicating the estimated casualties that would result from executing the existing plan for general nuclear war. This plan called for destroying every city in Russia and China with a population over a hundred thousand. The predicted loss of life from blast and radiation (the latter covering large portions of adjacent allied countries) was six hundred million. (In light of later calculations about the risk of nuclear winter, he realized that even this estimate was a vast understatement.) Of the piece of paper that contained this estimate, he said that it "depicted evil beyond any human project ever."

That the word "evil" came to his mind was perhaps evidence enough that he was not suited for this line of work. And yet it meant that the execution of evil plans did not require, as many people would suppose, monsters, highly aberrant or "clinically disturbed" people—"people not like us," as he put it. It could be carried out by intelligent, ordinary family men like his colleagues at RAND, who were neither better nor worse than anyone else. It spoke to Hannah Arendt's reference to the "banality of evil," or as he would say, "the banality of evildoing and most evildoers." From that point, he had one overriding life purpose: to prevent the execution of this plan. He continued to maintain his security clearances and insider status, believing he could best achieve his purpose from within.

His two years in Vietnam (1965–67) as part of an interagency task force to study and offer advice on the war launched the evolution of his own consciousness. The first stage was his exposure to the human reality of the war. The people of Vietnam, he would say, "came to be as real to me as my own hands." He returned from Vietnam committed to helping our country extricate itself from this futile and mistaken policy.

But then came the experience of reading the Pentagon Papers, a secret history going back to America's support for the French effort following World War II to recapture its colonies in Indochina. His new understanding of this history changed his entire perspective. Everything the United States had done in Vietnam was an extension of that initial effort by the French—to impose, by force, a regime of our liking on the people of Vietnam.

"Is this right?"—not "Is this mistaken or futile?"—became his predominant question. It was a question he had never heard from his colleagues. Nor was it documented in the Pentagon Papers, in which moral and ethical questions were never raised. "The only questions asked were: Will this work? Is it expedient? Is it worth the risk? Will we get away with it?"

To have continued this war, year after year, for reasons of state, against the wishes of the people we were supposedly defending, was not a mistake but a crime—a crime that had to be resisted. But how? That question was answered in August 1969 when he attended a gathering of war resisters in Haverford, Pennsylvania, where he encountered people who operated from a completely different set of values. Many of them were inspired by the principles of Mohandas Gandhi and Dr. Martin Luther King Jr.

One of them was a young man named Randy Kehler, who mentioned in his speech that he would soon be going to prison for refusing to cooperate with the draft. It is impossible to overstate the impact of this encounter on my father. After fleeing the conference room and sobbing for a long time, he asked himself, "What could I do to end this war if I were willing to go to prison?" That question, like the Accident, divided his life in two—a before, and an after.

The exposure to people who represented a different philosophy of life—based on the power of truth, the priority of life, compassion for others, and willingness to endure sacrifice and suffering in the service of what is right—brought him to a completely new understanding of his life and its purpose. And though he continued until his death to deal in political considerations, weighing strategy and tactics that might reduce the risk of nuclear war, his underlying preoccupations centered on moral, and, for want of a better word, "spiritual" considerations.

He realized that the fate of the earth, threatened by nuclear weapons, made it urgent that we recover our capacity to think in these terms:

> What is missing ... in the typical discussion and analysis of historical or current nuclear policies is the recognition that what is being discussed is dizzyingly insane and immoral: in its almost incalculable and inconceivable destructiveness and deliberate murderousness, its disproportionality of risked and planned destructiveness to either declared or unacknowledged objectives, the infeasibility of its secretly pursued aims ... its criminality (to a degree that explodes ordinary visions of law, justice, crime), its lack of wisdom or compassion, its sinfulness and evil. (*The Doomsday Machine*, 348)

He was aware that to speak this way entailed the risk of being dismissed as a fanatic, an extremist, lacking in "objectivity." And yet, if we are truly to step back from the brink of catastrophe, we must confront the true moral dimension of our problem. By what right—for what reasons of national security or "defense"—could one person or one country presume to gamble with the fate of the world?

He did find himself pondering his vocation, often referring to the mythical seer Cassandra ("a crier in the wilderness"), who was blessed by the gods with the power of seeing the future, yet cursed in that nobody would believe her. In releasing the Pentagon Papers, he had believed that he was perhaps "Cassandra with documents"—that is, armed with the receipts that would justify his warnings that past patterns of lies and escalation were being repeated by the Nixon administration. But his documents, which ended with the Johnson administration, couldn't prove it. They justified people's opposition to the war, but most people believed that Nixon was committed to getting the United States out of Vietnam. Seventeen months after the release of the Pentagon Papers, Nixon was reelected in a landslide.

Like Cassandra, my father characterized himself as a "'doomsayer' (not to be believed, to be thought mad, extreme)." This characterization applied even more to his warnings about nuclear doomsday. But "as for me," he added, "I want to *change* the future—not only foresee and warn." To do that, he sought to "protest, reveal, risk for others, seek understanding, prevent danger, evaluate risks, avert evil, and teach by word and example."

Perhaps, he said, the right word for this role was "prophet." Most people think of prophets as those who are able to foresee the future. Yet the biblical prophets were not fortune tellers. They were so attuned to the underlying spiritual and moral pathologies of their time that they could soundly anticipate the disaster that was sure to follow. They, too, wanted to "change the future." Through their warning they hoped to effect moral and spiritual conversion. They hoped that the people might "choose life," opt for justice, and restore right relations rather than drift blindly toward destruction.

In words that might have been uttered by Jeremiah, my father noted:

> I am living in a society that is preparing a catastrophe.
> I taste ashes in the wind.

Unlike the biblical prophets, he did not believe in a personal God. His parents were ardent converts to Christian Science, a faith he himself had been quick to abandon. This rejection extended to an aversion to organized religion in general. Yet at times he seemed to tap into a deeper spiritual spring:

> I am seeking wisdom, enlightenment. I am studying, meditating, seeking teachers, looking for explanations and examples of human societies.

And elsewhere:

> Can we divest mysticism from its ties to mainstream religion, especially religious beliefs and doctrines? I don't believe in a God that listens to us, responds to us or protects us (as in war). One can, however, for calm and reassurance, profitably consult with and attune to spiritual energies such as Love, Beauty, Consciousness, and Unity.

The word "conversion" (which in its root means turning around, going in a different direction) appears a number of times, sometimes in personal terms:

> What happened to me? I was at the height of my—and RAND's—influence and prestige. I had the equivalent of a religious conversion: I was "Born Again."

But in confronting the dangers of our time, he also suggested that what was needed was not just new policies or a revision of our war plans, but a social conversion in the form of moral "evolution." He did not despair of this possibility. One time, while participating in a protest, he found himself grouped with a cohort of "people of faith." One of them asked him, "Are you a person of faith?" "No," he answered, "but I am a person of hope."

I thought of that line during his last months, as I was writing the introduction to a twenty-fifth anniversary edition of a book I had written on saints, prophets, and witnesses for our time. In my introduction I credited his example with leading me to my own calling, remembering and sharing the stories of those throughout history who offered a heroic example of faith, hope, and love in action.

I cited his identity as a person of hope, and noted that in that spirit he had dedicated his life to preserving the planet from the perils of nuclear war. His hope was not an expectation that all would turn out well, but a form of action. I quoted him: "I choose to act as if we had a choice to change the world for the better and avoid catastrophe."

At the time, he was dying of pancreatic cancer, and I knew he wouldn't live to see my words in print. But I did have the opportunity to read my introduction aloud to him. He listened intently. I had hoped he would be pleased to hear how his example had played such a role in my own vocation. But he wasn't. He frowned and said, "I don't want you to say that." Was he disturbed by a reminder of my Catholic faith, which he tended to regard personally as a form of rebellion? Or was he made uncomfortable by the implication that he was some kind of saint?

In that light, it was interesting to me, in reading this collection of his notes, to find a surprising reference to my book, and a "lesson" he evidently drew from it:

> The lesson of Robert's book, *All Saints*, is that these people's life stories, their examples of sanctity, are healthy to contemplate now, in the late 20th century. These were whole lives of change, not just moments or isolated acts.
>
> Many of the saints were not perfect; they were not irreproachable in all aspects, all the time, all their lives. Doesn't that make their lives all the more exemplary and inspiring for us?

That was my dad. He knew that he was not irreproachable "in all aspects, all the time," all his life. But the survival of the world could not wait for irreproachable people. It would require many people of compassion and hope who could recognize the dangers facing our planet and were prepared, as Albert Camus put it, "to speak out clearly and pay up personally." It would require a kind of awakening to the moral and ethical dimensions of our crisis.

He had hope that such awakening could occur. This hope was not the same as naïve optimism. He reckoned realistically on the low odds. But low odds were not zero odds. He retained hope that catastrophe could be avoided. The basis for that hope came in part from the example of certain historical "miracles." Among these miracles, he noted the fall of the Berlin Wall without a shot being fired and the peaceful collapse of apartheid in South Africa—both seemingly impossible, until they happened. It was that sense of hope in the face of seemingly hopeless odds that kept him going.

> I fear there's not enough time and it's too late to achieve enough change in enough people. But I'm not going to give up.
>
> If we go down, we'll go down fighting, helping each other.

His own experience had shown that you should never discount the potential for unexpected consequences. He hoped his release of the Pentagon Papers might help end the war. And so it did—though not in a way he could have foreseen. The Nixon administration, in its obsession to silence him, was not satisfied with indicting him on charges carrying a penalty of 115 years in prison; it set up the illegal "Plumbers" unit to commit a range of crimes against him. When these same Plumbers were later arrested at the Watergate Hotel, Nixon resorted to paying them hush money and committing obstruction of justice to prevent them from revealing their crimes against my father. When this conspiracy was uncovered, not only did it result in the dismissal of the case against him, but also it ultimately forced Nixon's resignation. That, in turn, effectively ended the war.

You could never know. Nor could you underestimate the power of an act of conscience or truth telling. Randy Kehler, when giving his speech at the conference of the War Resisters' International, could not have imagined the impact his words would have on one person sitting in the audience.

As my father liked to say, "Courage is contagious." We can't know what we will accomplish, and we might not ever know the results of our actions. Yet in light of what was at stake, the chance of making a difference justified the risk, and at the end of the day, he believed, that was a good way to use your life.

He knew that he was not alone. In one of his last interviews, he said that many people don't really think or care much about the suffering of people far away, the "others," those not of their tribe. But there were those who do: the resisters, the peacemakers, the truth tellers. "Those," he said, "are my tribe."

What was his counsel for them? Perhaps it is in the last line of these notes:

What can we expect?
   Prepare to step into the moment when sudden surprise opportunities for change arise . . .

Knock on doors, many doors, not knowing which may open.
Be ready to drive through.

What was his hope for them? As he wrote in a final letter to his friends and fellow peacemakers: "My wish for you is that at the end of your days you will feel as much joy and gratitude as I do now."

INTRODUCTION

by Michael Ellsberg

What is evil?

How does evil get done?

Particularly: How does evil get done by "good" people—*our* people: our leaders, politicians, military, soldiers, countrymen? Ourselves?

What should you do if you find yourself participating in evil—if you find yourself part of a government or organization committing evil?

These are among the deepest questions my father spent more than fifty years pondering. In the realm of ideas, he was mostly known for his writing on the Vietnam War and his role in trying to help get us out of it (*Papers on the War*, 1972, and *Secrets: A Memoir of Vietnam and the Pentagon Papers*, 2002), as well as for his writing on averting nuclear holocaust (*The Doomsday Machine: Confessions of a Nuclear War Planner*, 2017).

The more Daniel examined these issues, the more he saw that they were both examples of a deeper dynamic: How could "good" people—*our* people in government, including *himself*—have participated in plans and organizations that deliberately targeted civilians? In a note from 1997, he says:

> My personal ethic is that Evil is never to be done and cannot be justified ... It is to be condemned, resisted, organized against, averted—even at the possible cost of self-sacrifice.

If "evil" is taken in a commonplace way, to mean simply a strong form of moral wrongness, this ethic might verge on banal. But my father often capitalizes the word, as "Evil." And when he writes about capital-*E* Evil, he means something very specific: terrorism, which he defines in the essay "Against Terrorism," as "the deliberate killing of noncombatants, war on civilians."

I consider this essay—written with moral urgency the month after 9/11—to be the moral core of the book. I quote it at length below, because, if you take away only one message from this book, I hope it will be this one. Its message is relevant to many violent conflicts today:

> I propose this as a moral/political absolute: to regard all such killing [i.e., war on civilians] and threats of all such killing as forbidden, to be absolutely and unconditionally condemned, to be regarded as something that under no matter what circumstances one must not participate in or conceal, to be exposed and denounced and obstructed and resisted, individually and through all formal structures . . .
>
> My proposal is to see all such killing as murder: mass murder. Whether done by the aggressor or the defender. Whether done by a revolutionary movement or state or a counterrevolutionary movement or state, First, Second, or Third World. It is not to be accepted as a Lesser Evil, whatever the alternatives. Just Evil: not to be done.

This "moral/political absolute" against mass noncombatant killing may seem easy for people to agree with. However, as my father points out in the essay, for most people it's easier to agree in theory than in practice. In practice, almost no one agrees with this principle absolutely. Instead, most parties of war carve out exceptions for their own side's war on the other side's civilians, or for what he described as "wantonly disproportionate" collateral damage.

One of my father's most pressing questions was: How do government officials so often participate in Evil *in good conscience?* What does it even say about the "conscience" of officials, for example, that it could be compatible with the creation of U.S. nuclear plans that targeted six hundred million civilians in the Sino-Soviet bloc?

These existential questions bedeviled my father starting in 1961, when he first saw the U.S. war plans. He learned that our government had a contingency plan that would have deliberately killed—*murdered*, my father would say—a hundred Holocausts' worth of innocent lives.

However, for my father, his need to understand how these plans came into existence led him deeper than policy and history. After the Pentagon Papers trial ended in 1973, my father entered into an intensive period of reading, reflecting, and note-taking. These intellectual explorations led him to ponder, urgently, what was it about humanity itself—and in particular, male humans organized in violence-prone groups—that allowed for such plans to be created? Most of the men involved in such planning—including himself, at one point—viewed their involvement as morally necessary. Few people, my father points out in these pages, ever believe they are actively committing *evil*. What, then, does that teach us about morality and conscience themselves?

My father thought about these questions desperately and constantly. The middle section of this book presents a fraction of the hundreds of notebooks he filled in his attempt to find answers.

***

My father, a decision theorist by training, taught me about a decision theory concept called "revealed preference." The basic idea is that the way people actually spend their time and other resources reveals more about their preferences in life than what they might say their preferences are.

Judging by how he chose to spend his time, my father's revealed preferences in life were reading, thinking, and writing notes to himself about what he read and wrote. In terms of how he spent his waking hours, there's not a close second. Even the phrase "waking hours" may be misleading, since he often processed what he was thinking about late at night in his dreams, and then woke up to write about his dreams, as they related to his ideas, in the morning.

I was born in 1977, well into the period covered by these previously unpublished writings. The archetypal image I have of my father during my childhood is this: He is sitting in his chair, hunched over a book, writing notes furiously in the margins, then writing more notes in his legal-size yellow pads and the mini steno pads he carried in his shirt pocket. I have never seen, and likely never will see again, such prolonged and intense concentration in a human.

I'm glad we never had occasion to test it, but I half-believe that if a fire had broken out in the house while my father was engaged in his reading and note-taking, he would not have noticed the growing heat, smoke, and roar around him, and he would have been saved only by our yanking him by the arm.

I must admit, there's a bittersweetness to this archetypal memory. The sweet part comes now, as Jan and I get to harvest the fruits of all this attention spent reading and writing, and share those fruits with the world. The bitter part of the bittersweet is that ... well ... all that attention spent on his notes—his obvious "revealed preference," time wise—was not spent on the little boy tugging at his legs to play. My father's parenting was, by the standards of a father and son living in the same home, not particularly involved. There's no other way to say it: to a large degree, writing these boxes and boxes of notes was what he was doing when he was not being a very active father to me.

My father and I shared a deep mutual love. I have many happy memories of us together from my boyhood and adulthood. He was there for me many times in many ways when I truly needed him. My love for him deepened, and our relationship enriched, as I learned—through time and life growth—to let go of and forgive this and certain other aspects of his parenting of me that were not ideal. Chief among them, ironically, was his constant lecturing to me, on all the political and moral topics of this book.

Yet during my father's final months, whatever I felt about his parenting in the past, I came to feel that he had ultimately been the perfect father for me. I told him this, in a letter I read to him, and he was heartened. I told him that one of the core things I most value about myself is that I'm a writer. And I simply cannot imagine myself as a writer without him. Thus, I cannot imagine a version of me that didn't have him as my father.

My father was often thought of as a truth teller, for telling the truth documented in the Pentagon Papers. But I wasn't around during that time. My lived experience of him was more as a truth seeker. He didn't stop reading and thinking about things until he thought he had found some truth. In fact, he was often blocked in his writing, or more accurately, in his publishing, precisely because he didn't feel he had found the bottom of the issue. In his reading and writing, he was rarely satisfied with the answers he had come to—there was always some unexplained aspect of the thing he was thinking about that animated him to keep going deeper into it.

I think, as a writer, that's my greatest inheritance from my father. That elemental wonder, equal parts bemused and outraged at the madness of the topic at hand, has kept me always searching for the core of whatever I'm writing and thinking about. It's also given me my sense of the absurdity of so much of human life in groups—a sense I treasure, and that forms the core of my own writing.

Since my early twenties, my intellectual interests diverged significantly from his at the level of topics. But at the core, our intellectual interests are the same: the madness within humanity. By my father's example, and by his nurturing of the intellectual and writer within me, he raised me, year after year, decade after decade, as the writer I have become. In addition to all the other things I loved about him, I will always be grateful to him for that.

***

The vast majority of the ideas in my father's notes—almost a hundred boxes' worth, now housed at the University of Massachusetts Amherst—went unpublished. This always caused me great consternation. From my vantage point, it seemed sad—like a loss to the world—that he would spend so much time coming up with all these brilliant ideas, most of which would never see the light of day. But he didn't see it that way. For him, reading, thinking, and writing his ideas down were ends in themselves. They were sources of intrinsic pleasure for him.

By any standard, my father successfully shared his ideas with the world through his writing, across four published books: *The Doomsday Machine* (2017), *Secrets* (2002), *Papers on the War* (1972), and *Risk, Ambiguity and Decision*, submitted for his economics PhD in 1962 and eventually published in 2001. In between these widely spaced books, he found time to publish countless articles and op-eds dealing with the issues of the day. Further, he constantly gave interviews across an even vaster array of print, radio, podcast, and television. My father felt it was his duty to speak out—loudly and often—to urge readers, listeners, and viewers to consider the moral implications behind the news cycle.

But hidden behind this large body of publicly available work is a secret that most people never knew: My father suffered from a lifelong block around his writing. Not a writer's block, but a publishing block.

My father could write up a storm, as his nearly one hundred boxes of unpublished notes attest, along with thousands of unpublished computer files, from which the material in this book was selected. Yet, as anyone close to his writing process knows, trying to get him to *publish* any of this writing was like pulling teeth. Jan Thomas and I were among those closest to his writing, along with my brother, Robert, my mother, Patricia, and Tom Reifer.[1]

My father was a masterful writer for the public when he was able to do it, but it was not a skill that came naturally to him. It was a great psychological burden for him to organize his thoughts in a way that would meet his own standards of analytical and historical rigor. You have not seen jaw-dropping levels of procrastination—you have not seen tortured struggle within a writer, self-recrimination, guilt—until you have witnessed my father with a publishing deadline ahead of him.

I recall a night at age nine, in 1986, when I was roused from my sleep and whisked off, with my parents and Jan Thomas—then my father's assistant—to a FedEx facility near the San Francisco Airport. It was the last place you could mail an overnight package from the Bay Area, with a midnight cutoff time. My father was sending off a grant proposal to the MacArthur Foundation for a prospective book on the nuclear era. I was happy about the whole affair, because my parents let me go to school late the next day on account of the unusually late night.

My father got the grant. But what the grant makers surely did not anticipate is that it would take him the next thirty years to produce the proposed book. The result was his masterwork, *The Doomsday Machine*, published in 2017 by Bloomsbury. His editor, Nancy Miller, knows a thing or two about his publishing block. For thirty years, he labored and agonized, holding himself to an impossibly high standard, trying to write a book worthy of what he felt was the life-and-death stakes of his subject matter. For the majority of my life, he was stuck on that book, finally publishing it just six years before his death in 2023.

Part of his block stemmed from simple perfectionism. In his constant reading and research, he was always discovering new insights and angles into his subject matter. He couldn't stand the idea of putting something out that didn't tell the "whole picture"—and he continually felt he didn't have anything close to the whole picture, even when he was a literal expert.

But there was a deeper and darker layer to his publishing block.

As you will read on these pages—in "The Piano" and throughout his notebooks—my father grew up in what amounted to an emotionally abusive household, in which his mother's love was conditioned almost entirely on his progress toward her dream that he become a concert pianist. Any wavering of his commitment to his destiny as a pianist could trigger his mother to rescind her affection for him until he proved his dedication again.

It does not take a trained psychoanalyst to see that for my father, publishing publicly—"getting it right"—seemed to take on the emotional resonance of the performance anxiety placed upon him by his mother. This bit of analysis came from Daniel himself after years of therapy and rumination.

After Nixon ordered the Plumbers to break into the office of Dr. Lewis Fielding, seeking blackmail information on my father, the phrase "Daniel Ellsberg's psychiatrist" became widely known and used throughout the history of the period. Interestingly, few people know *why* my father was seeing a psychiatrist, whose notes on my father the Plumbers hoped to find in what the Smithsonian Institution now calls "the world's most famous filing cabinet."[2]

He was not seeing the psychiatrist for medication. He was seeing Dr. Fielding for help in understanding a variety of his personal challenges, chief among them: his publishing block—which he felt was holding back his career as a researcher.

In contrast, the type of writing that came naturally to my father, and what he greatly enjoyed, was improvisational thinking through notes and rough sketches, with detailed examples and counterexamples and analogies, along with thickets of tangents springing from tangents. Without any pressure of "performance" for the public, the ideas spilled out. Ideas for ideas' sake.

As a writer myself, I never shared my father's feeling that writing was a valuable activity in and of itself, regardless of whether it got published. I always felt that the purpose of writing is to be read—to find an audience, however small or large, that appreciates it.

It is fair to say that my father did not care whether any of what's in the notebooks (part 2) and unpolished essays (part 3) in this book got published. (The essays in part 1 were originally intended for publication, and he always liked the idea of them being out. Now they are.) He never expected his notebook entries and other unpolished writings to see the light of day.

Of course, Jan and I disagreed. We believe—and we hope you will, too—that the ideas in my father's unpublished writing are not only fascinating and provocative, but also timely and relevant to the challenges of our time.

EDITORIAL PHILOSOPHY

My father's unpublished writing comes in three forms, corresponding to the three parts of this book.

Part 1 consists of three personal essays about his childhood, which he wrote in 1997, in the run-up to *Secrets*. At first, *Secrets* was intended to be a full autobiography. These autobiographical pieces were cut when he and his editor at Viking decided that *Secrets* should focus on his Vietnam and Pentagon Papers years. They are by far the most "polished" writing he ever produced that was left unpublished.

The vast majority of my father's unpublished writing consists of handwritten notes. Our favorite selections of these are presented in part 2. His handwriting was almost completely illegible. Fortunately, there is one person on the planet who can consistently decipher his handwriting, and that is Jan Thomas. (For me, finally being able to read those notes he was working on furiously for decades, and seeing the richness of his thinking within them, was poignant and meaningful, so I'm grateful to Jan for that as well.)

Even with Jan's miraculous rendering of his hieroglyphics, the notes themselves—while bursting with brilliant ideas—don't in their original form make for easy reading. They were, as I've mentioned, notes mostly for his own interest, not even remotely intended for anyone else to follow his chains of thought.

It fell to Jan to splice together my father's scattered ideas, spread across thousands of notebooks, into readable form. These are 100 percent my father's ideas. When necessary, Jan interpolated connective words into the notes to make them comprehensible. The writing would simply be inaccessible to anyone but the most motivated researcher without this level of editing.

Part 3 is drawn from a body of my father's unpublished writing and thinking that is smaller compared to his unpublished handwritten notes. This consists of what I might call "proto-drafts" toward published pieces. They were typed on a computer, starting in the 1980s. They read *almost* like drafts of essays intended for public consumption.

The key word is "almost." As mentioned, there was an enthusiasm gap between whether my father felt that a given piece of writing should or might get published, versus his feeling free to riff without any such pressure. Absent that pressure, he wrote—as you'll see—like a firehose.

When not burdened with expectations to write for the public, my father wrote in long, complex sentences, asides within asides within asides, stitched together with copious subclauses, em dashes, parentheses, and semicolons. As a writer, he never met an em dash, a parenthesis, or a semicolon he didn't like; he joined them together—like this; and this (and this)—as if hosting a big em dash (parenthesis) semicolon party, in sentences and paragraphs that often take two (or three—or four!) readings to tease apart.

My editorial philosophy in part 3 was to do only minimal editing where it was needed for clarity, to show the way my father thought and wrote to himself in these pieces. This minimal editing makes the pieces somewhat less readable than if they were polished, but it gives them the raw, unfiltered, private feeling of his actual thought process.

In the last few years of my father's life, Jan and I talked to him about collecting, curating, and arranging for the publication of his reams of unpublished work. It would be inaccurate to say that he was enthusiastic about this idea, but he did ultimately fully authorize our plan. In his characteristically blunt words: "What do I care? I'll be dead."

My father is dead now. But I for one care a great deal that he consented to allow us to compile this eclectic corpus of his important thoughts and musings.

I was blessed to have my father as a close example of what a life of the mind looks and feels like. Through the once-private writings published here for the first time, I hope my father inspires your own life of the mind as much as he inspired mine for over forty years.

PREFACE

by Jan R. Thomas

In my midtwenties, I left Knoxville, Tennessee, in my Volkswagen Beetle to cross the country, by way of Maine, on a solo journey. I had a strong sense that there was something else I was to be doing with my life, but I didn't know what or where. Four months later, I found myself in Oakland, California. Four months after that, in the spring of 1982, I became Daniel Ellsberg's assistant.

Early in my journey, while visiting Maine's Acadia National Park, I struck up a conversation with a local couple who invited me to stay overnight in their rustic cabin. By the dim light of flickering oil lamps, they told stirring tales of their antinuclear work with the Clamshell Alliance. I was riveted, and afterward I couldn't stop thinking about what they had shared. This first-ever conversation with peace activists opened my eyes to a broader world of concerns and responsibilities.

Once I reached Oakland, I knew right away that this was where I wanted to be. People were doing fascinating and creative things to improve the world; I was intrigued and wondered how I might fit into that picture. One thing led to another, and soon I found myself working with Dan. This was an improbable turn of events, as I had no background in foreign policy or activism, and no experience with media, research, logistics, or organizing an office. Yet given how things unfolded, I came to see it as meant to be.

My work assisting Dan was fascinating and challenging. I am confident that the word "genius" applies to him, and I'm far from the only one who has made this observation. As a rule, he was utterly absorbed in his labyrinthine intellectual processes, along with his vast-ranging reading and endless strategic conversations. He was not one to spell things out for me, so I had to think on my feet and figure things out on my own. I grew a great deal during my seven years in this role, which coincided with the Reagan presidency—a time when Dan was immersed in the global antinuclear movement.

After that, the arc of my career shifted from social work to social change work. I became a communications specialist, editor, environmental activist, and interfaith minister.

Thirty years later, in the spring of 2019, I returned to help Dan prepare more than five hundred boxes of his papers for his archive at the University of Massachusetts Amherst. Over the course of sixty years, reams of writings and other documents had accumulated in boxes, now piled high in his basement storage area. One option would have been simply to tape up the boxes and send them off to the archive. But this was Dan's lifework, in which he was still vitally engaged. We decided to take our time with the boxes and sort their contents carefully.

The seeds that grew into this book were contained in those boxes.

***

Peter Touchard—Dan's other assistant—and I spent countless hours in Dan's jam-packed office and his other storage areas, going through the paper remnants of his amazing life. As we organized the boxes' contents, we discovered many historically fascinating documents. We were able to reunite Dan with long-lost artifacts, some from more than half a century ago. It was particularly satisfying when items of special interest surfaced. "Where did you find this?" he would exclaim with delight. Dan and I were fortunate to share several years of this unusual method of life review.

For me, his own writings were by far the most interesting part of his many papers. I was particularly drawn to his handwritten notebooks, because I knew how significant they had been for him over the course of his life and career.

Dan wrote often on spiral steno notebooks and legal pads, which are collectively referred to here as "the notebooks." He always kept at least one notebook going. As he wrote, he became lost in his world of thought, remarkably oblivious to all else. He would become distressed and preoccupied when his current notebook was misplaced. This happened frequently, given the avalanche of paper he generated.

Over time, the collected notebooks filled dozens of boxes. I dived into these and was fascinated to discover a voice in them that was quite distinct from that of his typed writings. It was simpler, shorter, and more to the point, with many quotable turns of phrase and evocative observations.

All my life, I have gathered interesting quotations, so for me, the treasure hunt was on. As I reviewed thousands of pages of Dan's notebook entries, many passages leaped out at me. It became increasingly clear that this material was consequential and could be the foundation of a book. I was especially drawn to the morality-related themes that pervade Dan's writing, as well as to his autobiographical material. I found his contemporaneous reflections through the years to be original and compelling.

When I told Dan that I thought others would also be fascinated by the notebooks, he brushed me off. "No one will care about those," he objected. "I was just working out my own thoughts."

I laughed. "That's exactly what people will find interesting."

***

Six months after Dan passed away in 2023, his son Michael and I decided to put together a book featuring the best of his previously unpublished writing. Because Dan's papers were already organized, we were able to move fast. For eight months, I immersed myself in his handwritten notebooks, looking for gems to share. This was one of those special times in life when "what is mine to do" could not have been clearer.

Part 2 of the book is the product of my review of more than a thousand promising handwritten documents. From these files, I compiled a 2,500-page collection of the best handwritten passages. Then, using voice-to-text, I created digital content, which I edited into readable, coherent text.

The entries in part 2 span fifty years, from 1971—the year Dan released the Pentagon Papers—to 2021. They are organized by year to show the chronological progression of his thinking. Each year forms a chapter. Any undated writings appear in the first chapter of part 2, which introduces many of his important themes.

Although Dan's writing on morality has mostly remained unpublished until now, the topic was clearly front and center for him through the years. The question of evil alone was the subject of more than a hundred handwritten entries. Dan wrestled with many themes over the decades, including the ideas of "bureaucratic morality," conscience within hierarchical organizations, willful ignorance, and the ability of "good" people to do terrible things without losing sleep. These preoccupations appear repeatedly in his notes.

Dan's handwritten notebook writings are the sole contemporaneous direct account of what he was thinking during the era of the Pentagon Papers and the ensuing trial. They also shed light on the next five years—a period of deep inner inquiry after he became unmoored from his earlier life, work, identity, and friends.

Dan lived out his calling as few do, and at age ninety-two he continued to do so, even as he knew his time was short. What an extraordinary mind and committed heart he applied to the problems of our time. Yes, he was a nuclear analyst, and then an antinuclear scholar and peace activist. Yes, he helped bring about the end to the Vietnam War. And, he was so much more.

PART I

Personal Essays

The Piano
1997

In 1960, my first wife, Carol, and I were seeing a marriage counselor in Los Angeles. The counselor was a Baptist minister assigned to us at the Institute of Family Relations, which provided the case material for the column "Can This Marriage Be Saved?" in the *Ladies' Home Journal*, which is how I got the idea. Each of us saw him separately three times, then once together.

Toward the start of my second session, the counselor asked me what my childhood was like. I thought back to the playhouse, cherry trees in the backyard, kicking leaves, picnics, Barber Elementary School in Highland Park, Michigan, a suburb of Detroit. "I had a happy childhood," I said. "It was pretty ordinary. Normal."

"There wasn't anything unusual about it? No problems?" He had just seen my wife, who had briefed him.

"Problems? No, I can't think of any." I thought for a moment. Then I said, "Well, I guess there was one thing you could call unusual . . . I played the piano all the time."

"What do you mean 'all the time'?"

"Well, I only went to school half days, so I could practice in the afternoon. I practiced four to six hours a day when I was in grade school. And later in high school, I would practice eight hours on Saturdays."

He was grinning, and I started to laugh: "Okay, yeah."

It had been a long time since I had thought about it much. No one in college, except maybe Carol, had ever heard me play, and the same was true during my time in England, my time in the Marines, throughout graduate school, and now in married life in California.

All right, it was unusual. My practicing started when I was five, on a paper keyboard laid out on the dining room table, because my family didn't yet have a piano. Lessons were from a lady next door, who had confirmed my mother's growing suspicion that I had musical talent. She had noticed that I seemed to have a sense of rhythm, even when I was two or three, and that I would hum along with the radio. These were stories I often heard later, when there was talk about my vocation as a pianist.

From the time I was six or seven, in the late 1930s, I *was* a pianist. Piano was my life, my obsession, my calling. It was my fate, my good fortune. No one was making me be a pianist. My parents, especially my mother, recognizing my gift, my talent, were simply giving me every opportunity to develop it. That was how I understood it.

My aunt Clara and uncle Lou paid for lessons and a piano. Mother found me a teacher, the best-known in town. She arranged for my grade school to let me off school at midday so I could practice. She took it on herself to make sure I did my practicing, like a trainer, to help me conquer my own little-boy tendency to slack off. It was understood in our family that a talent for the piano that wasn't pursued every day from the age of five would dry up.

Every time I played in a recital, grown-ups from the audience, friends of my parents from church or Dad's office, would come up to me and say how lucky I was to have parents who were giving me this opportunity. They would say, "If only my mother had made me practice longer! How I wish I could play now! You will be so grateful to them later, for supporting you like this." I didn't have any reservations when I heard this, over and over, except that I didn't really need to be told; it went without saying. I had grown up knowing it. I never had any questions about it, as far as I could remember.

Mother was a pianist herself, which is how she was able to recognize my talent so early, and why she was willing to commit herself to nurturing it. But she hadn't started at five, which is when most serious pianists start. She had begun lessons in her late teens, and had managed to become quite good, which was very unusual with such a late start. She had even thought seriously about a career as a pianist; it had been her greatest ambition. But it just didn't seem practical. Still, she was in love with the piano. I always knew that, listening to her play in the rare moments when I wasn't at the keyboard myself, when she would take time off from housework and from studying *Science and Health* by Mary Baker Eddy—the foundational text of Christian Science.

And she played very well—I could tell as I got older and more skilled myself. She played, over and over, a Rachmaninov prelude, as well as several Chopin études and scherzos. The fact was, I realized many years later, long after I had quit at the age of fifteen, she was a better pianist than I ever became, and the pieces she was playing were more difficult than any I was capable of.

What kept me from realizing that at the time was that she had a romantic style, which I perceived as feminine, sentimental, even sloppy. It involved, among other things, playing chords slightly unevenly between the two hands, the left hand hitting the keys a little before the right, along with frequent changes in tempo. After she died, I heard old recordings from the twenties and earlier and realized that she had been replicating perfectly the traditional style of the best male pianists of her day.

I was learning, at our used upright, a much more rigid, hands-together, even-tempo, classical style from a disciplinarian. My teacher, Margaret Mannebach, was literally from Prussia. Short and plump, she had glasses and bright red dyed hair in a braid coiled on top of her head. When you made a mistake repeatedly or didn't follow her directions, she would clench her hand into a fist with the knuckle of the middle finger protruding and ram it furiously into the muscle of your forearm as you played, left or right depending on which side of you she was standing on. It was painful the first time and excruciating when she hit the same spot over and over.

Mother and I would be sitting, twice a week, in the dim hall outside her studio at the Detroit Institute of Musical Art, waiting for my lesson, and time after time one or another girl would emerge from the lesson ahead of me nursing purple bruises on her forearm, tears running down her cheeks. Then it was our turn to go in.

I don't think I got hit as often as the girls ahead of us; I was better than they were. But I can remember waiting for the first hit, trying not to flinch when I heard myself make or repeat a mistake. Mother would sit in a chair behind the piano during the lesson and she would often cry silently as she saw me grimace with pain. But she never protested. Miss Mannebach was the teacher, and I was on scholarship.

I was auditioned by Miss Mannebach, who was the best-known teacher in Detroit, when I was about seven. She was the accompanist for the Detroit Symphony. She told my mother I had promise, and she took me at half price: $3.50 a lesson, I think. Even that was more than my father could afford twice a week, and Mother got the money for years from her older sister, who had a jewelry store in Denver.

As a scholarship student I had my lessons at odd times, usually at Miss Mannebach's lunch hour. Twice a week my mother would pick me up outside school just before classes broke for lunch and drive me downtown to the Detroit Institute of Musical Art, an old red brick building at the edge of the Art Center where the huge marble Detroit Library and Art Museum were located. I would eat my lunch, a sandwich in wax paper and a carton of milk, in the back seat of the Plymouth while we drove.

Miss Mannebach would make her lunch on a hotplate in the closet of the studio and eat it during the lesson, usually a disgusting-smelling (not Campbell's) tomato soup. She would often be in a rayon bathrobe, for some reason, during these sessions, perhaps relaxing during her lunch hour. She stood by the piano, keeping time with gestures of one hand and sipping her soup, the sharp smell of which made me slightly sick, from a metal mug.

For all that, she was a pretty good teacher, except that all her students were oriented entirely toward recitals. We didn't learn to sight-read or to cover a wide repertoire; we practiced over and over the limited number of pieces we were going to perform in the next recital. Each of these we learned note by note, slowly, trying to get each note right from the start. As a professional later explained to me, as he was aborting my career; this was not the right training for a concert pianist. And in fact, almost none of her students went on to real success. But my family didn't realize that for the decade I took lessons from her.

Another problem was the sheer amount of practice she demanded. When I was eight or nine I practiced three hours a day, which soon went up to four. In the fourth grade, Mother talked to the principal of my local grade school and a woman was sent to our house to give me an IQ test. I remember it lasted for several hours, arranging blocks and weights and answering questions. We never learned my score, but after that the school permitted me to attend only in the morning, so that I could practice piano in the afternoon.

Sports and activities were mostly in the afternoon, so I missed all that, and I couldn't play with the other kids after school because I was still practicing. By the time I left elementary school at the age of twelve, I was practicing six hours a day.

All this time was spent on only a handful of pieces, for the next recital. Plus exercises. Note by note, measure by measure, over and over, a metronome measuring out the beat, gradually, very gradually, getting faster. Keyboard exercises to strengthen the fingers and wrists, repeated till they ached with pain, then repeated some more. The hard parts, hands separately, hands together, over and over and over.

Some of it was fun. Listening to the sound of the beautiful parts filling the room, there were so many choices to be made: where to put the accent in a phrase, how to finger it, how much pressure to put on a key, shading, what voice to bring out in a chord progression, subtle pauses and delays.

But there wasn't time for anything but practicing. I loved to read, but didn't have time for it. Almost any moment that I wasn't on the piano bench, whatever else I did except eating meals or going to the bathroom had a faintly guilty tinge to it, a feeling that I should be in front of the keyboard instead of wherever else I might be. Time for reading was stolen. Sometimes I read in bed at night under the covers, with a flashlight. I have a feeling every child does that sometimes, once they get into reading, but not every child has books disappear on them if they seem too absorbed.

I remember very clearly going into the living room where the rest of the family was gathered to ask, "Has anyone seen my copy of *Little Women*? I can't find it anywhere." I searched all over the house, but it had vanished before I'd even finished. I was infatuated with Jo. It must have been summer, or I wouldn't have been reading it during the day anyway. A month or so later, after I had given up on finding it, I was poking in the laundry hamper for some reason, and astonishingly, *Little Women* appeared at the bottom under the dirty clothes. I remember the moment well. I raised it high and raced through the house, waving it and yelling, "I found it! I found *Little Women*! How did it get into the clothes hamper?"

And I tore into it right that afternoon from where I had left off. It had to be summer, still. I must have practiced all that morning, or I couldn't have read a page. But within a few hours, a few chapters later, I put it down for a moment to get something from the kitchen, and when I came back it had dematerialized, never to be found again. I kept looking for a long time, but it never turned up. I don't think I ever fully suspected what had happened to it. I know I never accused anyone.

Much the same happened with other books I can remember: *Pearl Diver* and Lowell Thomas's *Count Luckner, the Sea Devil*. For a long time in my childhood, I could remember nearly every word of each of those—at least up to the point when they disappeared.

***

Piano recitals were held in June, in a red brick building owned by the Detroit Federation of Women's Clubs. June in Detroit was hot and humid. There was no air conditioning in those days, and though the windows were open in the afternoons when we rehearsed, the air, both outside and in, felt like steam heating set to the highest level, and the piano keys were slippery with sweat.

Sometimes, while waiting for my turn, I went down to the basement, where it was damp and cool. Under the staircase was a table covered with piles and piles of slightly mildewed *Reader's Digest*s, twenty or thirty years' worth—complete sets bound with twine. I would slip the string off a year's collection and begin to compare issues quietly, to see which would be the most rewarding to smuggle home.

I could take only three at most, one or two under my shirt and belt in front and one in back. So I had to choose carefully. I would look to see what books had been condensed, and I glanced through the joke pages and the articles, especially the feature "The Most Unforgettable Character I've Ever Met." I would get the choice down to five or six, usually from different years, then down to two or three, which I put aside before I bound the pile up again.

When the rehearsal was over and we were ready to leave, I would slip down to the basement again and stuff the *Digest*s under my clothes, pull my belt tight, and walk carefully out to the car. The magazines were cool against my stomach and back, and stiffened my posture. When I got home I hid them away. In the summer there were hours of daylight when I wasn't practicing and I read the magazines cover to cover.

Acquiring and reading those *Reader's Digest*s are among the best memories of my piano career. I never got caught. It was the only theft I can remember committing in my life, other than palming a few corks from a tray at Woolworth's when I was about ten to see if it could be done.[3]

When the day of the recital finally came, I kept a strict ritual. Half an hour or so before it was my turn to play, I would go down to the men's room and soak my hands in a washbasin filled with water as hot as I could stand. If it was too hot at first, I would pull my hands out and run cold water over them and into the basin, then put my hands back in. When I got used to the temperature, I would make it hotter again.

I rubbed my hands together under water, clenched them, grasped each finger in turn and massaged it, pressed the upper knuckles and the insides of the palms. When my hands were red and completely flexible, I took them out and dried them. Then I knelt in one of the stalls with my head over the toilet, thrust one finger down my throat, and made myself vomit. That made my body and my head feel light when I stood up. It made me more confident, loose and ready, when I walked out on the stage to the piano.

***

My first clue that I had not spent my childhood acting on my own inner voice came in my late twenties, after my mother died. An old friend of my mother's, someone whose name I had often heard her mention but I had never met, visited my wife Carol and me at our home in Belmont, Massachusetts. Carol was pregnant with Mary, our second child, so it must have been 1958. The visitor mentioned that my mother had been pregnant with me when her friend visited her in Chicago in 1930. She said, "I was so struck that your mother was certain that you were a boy. And that you would be a pianist."

I had grown up hearing that my ear for music, my talent, had manifested itself early in life. And that it was only after recognizing my gift that my parents had dutifully supported my inner destiny, my vocation. I had never doubted that story before, even after I had come to suspect they had overestimated my childhood talent.

But according to our visitor, Mother had known that her son would be a pianist when I was still in the *womb*? That put a startlingly different light on things. The implications were so out of line with the family narrative I'd grown up with that I just couldn't absorb the information. For several years I didn't think much about this story, until the session with the marriage counselor made me recall it.

Three years after that session, I remember standing outside the front door of our house in Brentwood, under a canopy of purple bougainvillea, calling my son Robert to come into the house to do something. I was at home in the afternoon, so it must have been a weekend. He was seven years old. He wanted to stay out and play with a friend across the street.

I said to him jokingly, like a stereotypical father pontificating about his own hard childhood, "You know, when *I* was your age, I couldn't be out playing with my friends in the afternoon. I was practicing piano all the time." And it struck me, for the first time, that what I'd just said wasn't a joke. How could that have happened? A child unable to play with friends in the afternoon. How could my own father have let that happen?

I asked myself, what if Carol—Robert's mother—had insisted that Robert spend hours every afternoon playing the piano, instead of playing outside? Was there a chance in the world that I would have allowed that? Out of the question! Even if I hadn't had that experience myself, it was unthinkable.

From that moment on I had some questions to ask of my father, who was now living in Huntington Woods, a suburb of Detroit. On my next trip cross-country to Washington, D.C., I scheduled a stop in Detroit, and my father met me at the airport. In the taxi on the way home I put questions to him I had never asked before. For once in our lives he gave me straight answers, as if he had been waiting to be asked.

"What was all that about, all that piano and that practicing?" I asked him. "Why was I doing that?"

"Your mother wanted a pianist," he said. "She was determined you would be a great pianist."

That was it. Nothing about talent, about vocation, about opportunity or destiny, or their duty as parents. Nothing of what I had been told from age five to fifteen, or till this moment, age thirty-two. Nothing but two sentences I had never heard spoken till now.

"Well, what was your impression of why I was doing it, of what *I* wanted? Didn't you think I was doing it because *I* wanted to?"

"You were a normal kid. You didn't want to spend all your time inside playing a piano. You would rather have been outside, or with your nose in a book. But you were a good boy, and you loved your mother. You wanted to do what she wanted."

Simple as that. I could only keep asking the questions that had come to me in Brentwood.

"How could you have let this happen? Why did you go along? How could you let her make me practice all the time?"

He told me: "Your mother hadn't wanted to have any children at all. That was our agreement when we got married. I had two children already, and she was going to help me raise them. But I thought she ought to have children of her own. I thought it would be good for her. Every woman ought to have a child. I made her do it. I persuaded her. So when she had you, I thought I had to let her raise you the way she wanted. She wanted a pianist."

We sat for a while in the taxi in silence. Then he added something. "There was more to it than that. I thought that if I interfered, she might leave me. Your piano was all she cared about, in the marriage."

I said, "So I was working for you, too."

"You could say that."

***

After that conversation, I had lunch with Mother's older sister Clara, who had paid for my piano lessons. I asked her, "Clara, if Mother had lived, how do you think she would really have reacted if I had quit the piano?"

She thought for a while, eating her food. Then she said, "You couldn't have quit."

I said, "I don't mean when I was a little boy. If she hadn't been killed and I was older, say I went off to college, and I was on my own, maybe twenty. And I decided to quit."

She shook her head and said decisively, "You couldn't have quit."

There was something so final about her tone, and it was such a strange answer to my question, that I didn't pursue it. But the next day I was having lunch with her brother, my uncle Lou, and I told him that I had had a strange exchange with Clara the day before. I repeated it to him and asked him what he thought. He thought for a while before answering. Then he said, "Well, I think Clara is right. You couldn't quit."

"But that's not what I'm asking! I'm asking, if I *had* quit, what would have been her reaction? What if I'd just decided to do it?"

"Well, you could have quit, of course. But it would have been at the price of your relationship with your mother. It would have meant totally cutting yourself off from your mother. And you wouldn't have been willing to do that."

According to my half-brother Harry, I did quit, twice that he knew about. He was still living with the family then, and he remembered it well. He said that on two separate occasions, when I was nine or ten, I got fed up with practicing, I got angry, I said, "That's it. It's over. I'm not going to do this anymore."

I asked him what happened.

"You became a nonperson as far as your mother was concerned. You just didn't exist. She didn't look at you, or notice you, or answer you if you said anything to her. You would be sitting at the table and ask her to pass something and she wouldn't hear you."

"So what happened?"

"Oh, after a day of this, or a day and a half, you went back to the piano."

I have no memory of any of this, or of ever trying to quit the piano, or wanting to. Which perhaps isn't so hard to understand.

***

Later in that session with the marriage counselor, I had the kind of breakthrough insight that occurs in Hollywood scenes about psychoanalysis, yet, in my experience, rarely in real life. It was accompanied by a breakdown into unstoppable crying, the first of several in my life, though never again in therapy.[4]

For the first time, at age twenty-nine, I understood that I had been continuously afraid of losing my mother's love throughout my childhood. I had lived with the fear—or the knowledge—that I would lose her interest in me and, consequently, her love, if I quit the piano or if I failed as a concert pianist.

I suddenly realized that I had been working for my mother. All those long hours of practicing, child labor beyond the reach of any protective laws, working to maintain her interest in me and her love. In constant fear of death—death of her love and of our relationship. The death of a meaningful life for me.

But that labor was the least of it. I knew how to practice, how to work hard at it, how to take apart and polish and repeat, how never to be satisfied, how to experiment; I could be sure of being good enough at practicing. But for Miss Mannebach the practicing was all aimed at public performances or at recitals whose goal was simple: execute high musical standards for the ears and minds of oneself and one's teacher, mother, audience. That was her advertising, how she got new students.

Every time you stepped out on that stage before the public, you could fail decisively, irrevocably. Oh, a mistake, even a bad performance, could be recovered from, could be redeemed later, if you were sufficiently self-reproachful and redoubled your efforts to do it right.

But there was always a risk that you would reveal yourself in a performance to be *not a promising pianist after all*, not really a talent worth investing a teacher's efforts or a mother's attention and hopes and love in. To inspire that conclusion in my mother would mean a certain and immediate emotional death.

Those were the stakes in every major recital. That danger couldn't be avoided just by willpower and diligence and effort, which were enough to keep hopes alive indefinitely in the course of practicing. In a recital, you could fail definitively, and by doing so, lose everything. You had to take the chance, the gamble with death. It was a forced game of Russian roulette.[5]

In that session, I became conscious that I had worked very hard for a decade to earn Mother's love, at frequent peril of losing it. I don't think I felt sorry for myself, then or later. Or maybe I'm wrong. Maybe what I felt was sorrow for the boy I had been.[6] My mind returned to the idea of how much worse it could have been for me, even without moving my upbringing to the ghetto or Calcutta. I could have been one of the many children for whom a mother's love wasn't available on any terms. Or I could have failed to earn it.

I could have lacked the minimum talent needed to arouse her hopes. That was the situation I perceived in my sister, Gloria. She was given some lessons, but she was a rotten pianist, so she was let off with no questions asked. She wasn't unloved, but I took it for granted that she didn't have a chance at capturing a fraction of the attention I got from Mother. But maybe my feeling of having the inside track, being the favored one, was largely a way of not noticing that I was working an awful lot harder than Gloria for what I was getting. I have no idea what she did with all the time I was practicing and she wasn't.

I *had* earned the love; I had been loved, and I knew it. So why was I suddenly crying so hard?

Fatigue and relief and painful awareness. Belated awareness of a long, long strain and suppressed fear. Relief from no longer carrying a very heavy burden, and relief from the fear that it might break me. Horror at a sudden awareness of the dangers I had survived, the risks I had run so often for so long.

It was as if mists cleared and I found that I had been walking near a precipice. A letting into awareness of a long-endured and long-repressed sense of danger and dread, and of strain and fatigue. And finally, the sense that I should have known this all before, that in some way I did know it but had allowed myself to be fooled and blinded. And with these feelings, also shame.

It was a lot to cry about. The crying was like panting at the end of a marathon. I cried for the rest of the hour, hardly able to gasp out the thoughts that were coming to me. When I left the counselor at the end of the hour, I went outside and walked around and around the block for another hour, still sobbing.

***

The high point, and the end, of my training with Miss Mannebach came with my performance of the Beethoven Third Piano Concerto with a hired orchestra made up of most of the members of the Detroit Symphony. It was in the spring of 1945; I was fifteen. During the recital, my nightmare occurred. There came a moment when my mind went blank as to what notes came next, I stopped, couldn't continue, then went back to an earlier break and started again, hoping but not knowing that my fingers and my memory would carry me through this time. They did. In all, the concert went very well.

After that, my mother took me to be auditioned by a new teacher, Mischa Kottler. He was the musical director of a major radio station in

Detroit and he frequently concertized. Mother thought we had gone as far with Miss Mannebach as she was likely to take me, and it was time for me to prepare more professionally for a music school and a concert career.

Mother didn't tell me where the money was to come from for these lessons, which would be much more expensive than Miss Mannebach's. But it was 1946, after the war, and Dad was earning a big salary for the first time in his life, as the chief structural engineer of a major energy installation.[7] Lessons wouldn't depend on Aunt Clara and Uncle Lou anymore.

Kottler lived and taught in a large house with beautiful rugs, art objects, and bookshelves filled with art books and scores. His piano was a concert grand, set in the middle of a large living room. The ambience was very different from Miss Mannebach's little studio. Kottler himself was bulbous, with a warm smile and sparse hair on his round head. His hands looked soft and slightly pudgy, somewhat feminine. But as I learned later, when he demonstrated different touches on my forearm, there was iron strength under the fleshy exterior.

Kottler used a very different hand position from what I had learned under Miss Mannebach, more relaxed and curved, close to the keyboard. One could hardly see his fingers move separately as his hands, like paws, glided back and forth across the keys, spilling silken runs and arpeggios.

At this first meeting, he was to decide whether he would take me on as a student. Money wasn't enough; he had to judge my ability. I had brought much of my music with me, volumes of Chopin waltzes and preludes, Beethoven sonatas, Bach, Schumann, all so I could show him the pieces I knew. He questioned me on my training and my repertoire. He listened closely as I played pieces he picked out, nodded appreciatively. I thought it had gone well.

At the end he said, "You're a talented pianist. Your technique is very good. You have a good tone, very good feeling, your playing is very musical. But I won't take you on the understanding that you are preparing for a concert career. You don't have the right preparation for that, and it's too late to acquire it."

It was a matter of repertoire, he said. Mine was entirely too limited. "You know half a dozen Beethoven sonatas," he said. "You should know all of them, or at least have read through them. You should know half a dozen concertos, not just two."

Pointing to the volumes I had brought, he said, "You should be able to sight-read all of this. But you haven't learned to sight-read." He told me I could never catch up, not even in college.

This was staggering news. It came out of nowhere, after ten years of total commitment apparently misdirected. He was saying that my decade spent practicing, each year, a handful of pieces for a recital, learning each note by note, perfectly, no mistakes, for eventual performance, had been entirely misplaced. "You shouldn't have been preparing for recitals at all. To prepare you for a serious career, you should have been learning to sight-read, learning harmony, expanding your range, reading through a whole library of music . . ."

Kottler spoke with total authority, firmly and confidently. He didn't want to leave me with any false hope. He was talking about an aspect of the profession that Mother and I had heard nothing about, never considered or discussed, speaking with a finality that seemed to leave no room for argument. We had, it seemed, been conned up until this moment. It was as if I were being informed as an actor that I was the wrong gender or race to play the roles I had trained for and rehearsed with an earlier teacher.

"You're already a good pianist," Kottler said. "I would be happy to take you on as a student, to learn to play better for your own enjoyment. But only on that understanding. You have no prospect for a concert career, and I wouldn't be training you for that."

Mother looked glum but said nothing. My own enjoyment? That was not my calling, and certainly not what I had been preparing for. I had just heard, in the space of two or three minutes, that the single goal I had been pursuing for two-thirds of my life was closed off to me. It had been an illusion for years, the hours of practicing each day had been misspent. I couldn't be what I had understood from my earliest years I was destined to be, the only thing on earth it mattered I become.

I said I thought I would still like to study with him, with that understanding. I was looking at Mother, who was not giving much sign of reaction. He told us to think it over and let him know. We shook hands and left. In the car on the way home Mother and I agreed that he seemed very professional and would be a good teacher for me. It was settled; I would make an appointment to begin lessons with him.

It is astonishing for me to look back on this. I was leaving a concert career behind, a week or two after I had performed a concerto with a symphony orchestra. Actually, Kottler's judgment on repertoire and sight-reading, from a perspective of many decades later, looks quirky, peculiar. Why couldn't I have learned sight-reading starting at fifteen? Why was it too late to read through a broad repertoire?

So said a teacher, a first-rate professional, whom I took a few months of lessons from—just for enjoyment—forty years later. My technique *was* very good, he said, and my musical sense. "You could play anything you wanted," he said. A concert career had not been out of my reach at all, if I'd wanted it enough. Not, presumably, at the very top ranks. I didn't press him on this—on just how good I might have become. I was no virtuoso. However, he contradicted the impression that I'd had since childhood, that you had to be in the top rank to make a living as a performer, and that only a half dozen or so pianists could do it.

What is amazing is that neither Mother nor I challenged Kottler's judgment, either during that session or later between ourselves. We didn't argue, we didn't look for a second opinion. There was enough plausibility in what he had said about my training to make it unlikely that we would have gone back to Miss Mannebach. But nothing could have been more natural than for me to say, "That's absurd! Of course I can learn to sight-read, if that's what's required! If you're not willing to take me on, then we'll find someone who will."

"Come on, Mother," I can imagine myself saying, taking her arm, "let's get out of here! Thank you, Mr. Kottler."

Of course, it's fantasy that I would have said that to his face, at fifteen. But I could have said it to her in the car as soon as we had left. I could have said it forcefully, confidently, because she could be expected to be crestfallen, uncertain about my reaction and the future. I had just been humiliated in front of her—though in effect we had both been, by Kottler's simple judgment. He had washed away a decade of lessons into which she had poured her dreams for me and for herself.

I didn't say anything, but what's even more astonishing is that she didn't either.

Maybe my silence was the confirmation, after so many years, that I really wasn't a pianist after all. But Mother couldn't have accepted that conclusion so quickly, out of the blue. No, looking back over half a century, the suspicion comes to me that Kottler was confirming for her a feeling that might have been growing within her for months or years: her judgment as a pianist—one who was better than I—that for all my hard work, I wasn't really going to make it as a concert pianist. It was only a confirmation.

There had been little hints of this in the past year, suggestions so odd and out of key with my life up till then that I'd ignored them. She had mentioned a couple of times that I might, after all, in my studies in the music schools to which I was headed, become a conductor or a composer.

Conduct? Compose? What was she talking about? That wasn't what she cared about. That wasn't what I had been practicing for since I was five! I'd paid no attention. Those were different courses altogether. I couldn't dream that they would satisfy her. Or me.

It was over. What I had, perhaps unconsciously, imagined could end only with the death of one of us, or of our relationship, had ended quite suddenly, nonviolently, at the simple words of this stranger.

Two months later, Mother was dead.

Christian Jews
1997

We were Jews, whatever that meant. We were descended from the Jews in the Bible, which seemed like a good thing. But my parents, my sister, and I didn't follow the Jewish religion. My grandparents hadn't either. My mother's parents weren't very religious, I was told, and my father's parents were militant atheists.

We were Christians. We were Jews, and in religion we were Christians. I never heard the two words put together—Christian Jews or Jewish Christians—but if anyone had ever suggested that that's what we were, my parents would have agreed without hesitation. There was never any doubt in our family that both of those terms applied to us.

My mother had become a Christian Scientist before she married, and she converted my father. This conversion came about, my father told me, from seeing two "demonstrations," or Christian Science faith healings. He also told me that one of her incentives to marry him—in fact, a condition she made for marrying him—was that he would take her away from Denver so she could practice Christian Science without creating tension in her family. They weren't very religious—her family went to temple only a few times a year on special occasions—but it upset them that my mother had become a Christian.

Later my father experienced healings personally: the eczema on his hands disappeared. Thus, he became a Scientist himself. In fact, he became obsessed with it. He gave up drinking Scotch and smoking cigars and memorized long passages of *Science and Health* and the Bible.

It would be fair to call my parents fanatical Christian Scientists. They read *Science and Health* every day for an hour or more, and we all went to church every Sunday and almost every Wednesday night, long services at which people gave testimonials to healings and other "demonstrations" of the truth of Christian Science.

I was excused from medical examinations in grade school, and I never saw a doctor till I went to boarding school at the age of twelve.[8] Up until that time, when I stopped going to Sunday school because of piano, I was a pretty good Scientist myself. I believed in most of the teachings and testimonials, up to a point. Yet I grew up maintaining a private view that if I was ever in really serious health trouble, I would find my way to a doctor on my own—though it wasn't obvious to me at the time just how I would do that. I knew my father would let me die rather than let me see a doctor.

My main health problem was headaches. We would often go to movies, to see Shirley Temple or Greer Garson (whom I was in love with) at the big theater in Detroit's Fisher Building. We would go to matinees. For some reason, there was never time for lunch on those occasions, and I would end up with a headache. Even outside the movies, I would get a bad headache every week or two, not a migraine but a strong, dull pain in my temples that wouldn't go away, along with some nausea. I wasn't even allowed to take aspirin.

The only thing that made me feel better was a cold washcloth on my forehead, especially with some ice in it. I would lie down on my bed in the dark with the shades drawn with my head on the washcloth on the pillow, or on my back with the washrag filled with ice on my eyes and temples.

But all this had to be hidden from my mother. (It usually took place in the late afternoon, when my father wasn't home yet.) If I heard her coming up the stairs, I had to whip the washcloth off the pillow and hide it under the bed, because it was too much like a medical treatment for pain. My icing was giving reality to my belief in a headache.

It was all right for me to be lying on my bed, though it would have been better if I had been reading *Science and Health*. But sometimes she felt the wet pillow and caught me. I had to be secretive in getting the ice out of the freezer in the kitchen and smuggling it up the stairs. This went on regularly, for years.

Sometimes the headaches would cause me to throw up, which I had to hide from my father. Once or twice he caught me kneeling on the floor of the bathroom with my head resting on the toilet seat and he was enraged and contemptuous. In his words, I was "on my knees to mortal mind."

To Christian Scientists, sickness was an illusion, a false belief, because it contradicted the truths that only what was permanent and eternal was real, only those states of being that manifested the goodness and the will of God had reality. All else, including sin, sickness, and pain, presented only an illusion of permanence and reality that could be dispelled by better understanding. Their grip on our mind and feelings could be loosened by "knowing the truth" of their unreality in the light of God's goodness and ever-presence.

Scientists rejected the notion of "faith healing." Their watchwords were "knowledge" and "understanding," not "faith." "Healing" implied there had been something real to be healed, rather than simply a false belief to be seen through and discarded. "Mortal mind" was the source and sum of false beliefs about reality: the false belief that there was substance and intelligence in matter, which was inert and impermanent and had no true reality.

I have a great resistance to reconstructing these doctrines that I spent so much time learning from my father in my youth, though I find that the terms do come back to me after fifty years of not thinking about them. The point is that there was a coherence to the teachings, which needs illustrating to anyone who has never heard them (that is, most people) in order to make the practices that followed from them seem anything other than bizarre. To take medical steps to treat a supposed illness or injury, even to name it, was to "give it reality," in other words, to act toward it as something other than an "error," a false manifestation of mortal mind. By acting on it, one would reinforce the false belief in its reality, prolonging the illusion and the experience of pain.

The practical merit of these attitudes and practices is to turn one's attention away from pain or painful emotions and to bring one to focus instead on thoughts of goodness and wholeness, which does have a calming and pain-relieving effect.

I remember the time I was chasing a soccer ball in second-grade homeroom in Detroit and ran my forehead into the flange of an iron radiator next to the wall. I was knocked on my back and blood began to stream down my face from a gash in my left forehead—the injury left a white mark for the next thirty years. The scar stayed visible because my mother, who was called immediately, wouldn't give permission for it to be sewn up, or even bandaged.

After a couple of days the teachers complained that the appearance of the wound was bothering the other children, and my parents permitted them not to "bandage" it but to cover it till it healed with a flat piece of gauze that would hide it from sight.

Twice in playing with my chemistry set, making low-level explosives with sulfur, potassium, and magnesium, I created explosions that burned one of my hands badly. My hand, my pianist's hand! Why had I been using a flame so near magnesium powder?

Anyway, I remember the flash, my scream, and my brother rushing to the kitchen to get some butter to put on the burn, which my father, who had been reading the paper in the living room, forbade him to apply. Instead, he had me sit in a chair across from him and repeat after him, over and over, "the scientific statement of being" from *Science and Health*, one of the core doctrines of the religion:

"There is no life, truth, intelligence nor substance in matter. All is Infinite Mind, and its infinite manifestation, for God is All-in-all. Spirit is immortal Truth; matter is mortal error. Spirit is the real and eternal; matter is the unreal and temporal. Spirit is God, and man is His image and likeness. Therefore man is not material; he is spiritual."[9]

I wasn't allowed to look at my hand while we were saying this, and I wasn't permitted to whine about the pain. Before long an impressive blister began to form. It was huge, like a balloon. It was too big to put a bandage on, and again the children at school complained about having to look at it.

Mother herself had red, oozing sores on her ankles that I would have been glad to have her cover up so I didn't have to look at them. She would put her legs up on a chair while she read *Science and Health*, and I couldn't keep from staring at them with horror and fascination. I hated to think she was in pain, and I wished I could do something for her.

She claimed that the condition arose from bumping her ankles together, though years later my brother told me she had varicose veins, which could have been operated on. She put gauze pads on them so she could wear stockings, but blood continually seeped through. She often thought they were getting better, that she was finally experiencing a demonstration, but it was never permanent. The absence of reprieve for her began to spur doubt in me, though to my father it simply meant she wasn't a good enough Scientist.

***

I didn't know what it meant to be a Jew in religious terms. I didn't know anyone my age who practiced Judaism when I was growing up and I didn't really know what it involved, beyond reading and believing the Old Testament, like Christians, but still following dietary restrictions and some other rules that Christians had dropped. I knew it entailed not believing in the New Testament or Jesus. And having different holidays.

My parents were raised as secular Jews. They didn't seem to know any more about the Jewish religion than I did. I don't think my mother had ever been to a synagogue, though she said her older brothers and sisters went perfunctorily on a few occasions each year. My father's parents were both atheists, along with being political radicals, anarchists, or, as my brother characterized them recently, "nihilists."

They had left Russia in part to escape both the ghetto and the tsar's military draft, which had just begun to be applied to Jews. My father told me that his mother had grown up largely on big estates on the border of Poland and Russia, which her father had managed for Russian aristocrats. When she and her family moved to Moscow, she experienced a shock in her first week there. She didn't understand the idea of curfew, and as she returned from visiting a friend in the ghetto after dark, she was arrested and spent a night in jail. That was it, as far as she was concerned.

She had already met my grandfather, who was a year older—about seventeen. She showed him a picture of a steamship to America in the window of a travel office. She refused to marry him unless he found a way to get them over there. He was about to be subject to the draft, which entailed a seven-year enlistment, and she felt stronger about that, too, than he did. So she pushed him to leave for America. Once there, he made enough money to send for her to join him the next year, in New Haven, Connecticut. My father was born there less than a year afterward, in 1889.

In his young life, he had come to believe in the truth of the teachings of Jesus and especially of the teachings of Mary Baker Eddy, and it was natural for him to hope that other Jews, and everybody else, should do the same. "The Jews should all convert," my father said to me toward the end of his life.

He was always preaching at every opportunity. Christian Science doesn't have preachers as such—they instead employ readers at their Sunday services, who read assigned passages from the Bible and *Science and Health*—but they allow certain members of the church, called lecturers, to give public speeches about Christian Science. I used to think that Dad had missed his real calling, to be a lecturer. He was good at evangelizing, but above all it was his obsession.

Metaphysical argument was his passion. He would spring it on anyone, picking up on something they had said, or that he had overheard in a streetcar or an elevator or even just standing in a line. It would start with an innocent question, the opening to a Socratic dialogue, but it quickly became a monologue. Dad would begin to lecture on the nature of reality, the practical implications for sickness and health, the goodness of God and the eternality of truth.

He was unstoppable. He really could go on for hours, without eating or drinking, if you let him, and there was no way not to let him, except to leave, which his family couldn't do. If you asked a question, he always had an answer and would weave it into his narrative.

But if you tried to interrupt with anything other than a question—such as an objection or an attempt to change the subject—he would just ignore your intrusion and carry on. He was in a kind of trance—just as his listeners were after a few minutes.[10]

Fairly late in life I realized how much like my father I had been for years, on different subjects—the nuclear arms race or Vietnam or something I had just been reading and thinking about. An old man of the sea, an ancient mariner. That is hard on a wife—especially my second wife, whose father had had the same habit—as well as on children, colleagues, or anyone subject to it.

"It was interesting," people would say to me afterward to explain why they had listened longer than they wanted to a monologue of mine, till they became aware they were feeling trapped and oppressed. It was interesting but not, finally, what they really wanted to hear about at that moment, at such length.

What people described as the later, prolonged, trapped stage of a conversation with me was the same feeling I had when talking to my father—that is, of being talked at by my father—about Christian Science.

The Accident
1997

On the Fourth of July 1946, a hot afternoon on a flat straight road through the cornfields of Iowa, my father fell asleep at the wheel. He drove off the road long enough to hit a sidewall over a culvert that sheared off the right side of the car, killing my mother and sister.

My father's nose was broken and his forehead was cut. When a Highway Patrol cruiser arrived, he was wandering nearby the wreckage, bleeding and dazed. I was inside, in a coma from a concussion, with a gash on the left side of my forehead. I had been sitting on the floor of the back seat, on a suitcase covered with a blanket, my head just behind the driver's seat.

When the car crashed, my head was thrown against a metal fixture on the back of the seat, knocking me out and opening up a large triangular flap of skin on my forehead. My legs had been stretched out in front of me across the car and my right leg was broken just above the knee.

We were on a stretch of road between Davenport and Des Moines, Iowa, on our way from Detroit to Denver for a vacation with my mother's relatives. An ambulance took my father and me to a hospital in Davenport, where I stayed in a coma for thirty-six hours.

My half-brother Harry read about the accident the next morning on the front page of the *Detroit Free Press*. He took a plane to Chicago that afternoon and then a bus to Davenport. He said later that when he saw what was left of the car in a junkyard, the right side looked like steel wool. It was amazing that anyone had survived.

As a Christian Scientist, my father didn't want any medical attention for either of us. He didn't have anything done to his broken nose, and he wouldn't let the doctors set my broken knee or stitch up my forehead. He had a gash on his own cheek that he didn't want touched, but at one point when he drifted out of consciousness my brother told the doctors to go ahead and stitch him up. Harry says that Dad never forgave him for that.

When my mother's brother and sister arrived from Denver, they insisted that my leg be set, but by then it was somewhat crooked and had to be broken again to be set properly when I was moved to a hospital in Denver. The surgeon there, a knee specialist, told me that if it had never been set correctly my right leg would have been about an inch and a half shorter than my left. After I got off crutches, I didn't have trouble walking, but I could never again bend my right knee all the way.

Because my head wasn't stitched up till my uncle and aunt arrived, I was left with a large jagged U-shaped scar on my left forehead. I thought it looked interesting, so I didn't mind it.

Until recently, whenever anyone asked me how old I was when the accident happened, I would say "Fourteen." But I knew that there must be something wrong with that answer, so I eventually did a mental calculation. I knew that the accident happened a year after the war, and I was born in 1931. So I would correct my answer to fifteen.

Fourteen was the age of my sister, Gloria, at the time of the accident.

My father told the story of that day a number of times throughout the years. He recounted the fact that all that morning Gloria had been sitting up front in the passenger seat next to him. Both of us wanted to sit there, because you could look out the window and it was more comfortable than sitting on the suitcases on the floor in back. It was supposed to be my turn to take the passenger seat in the afternoon, after lunch.

Mother had packed a picnic lunch and we ate it in a little park in the middle of a small town on our way from Davenport to Des Moines. It was very hot and dry, there were white walls and a statue looking out on a little square surrounded by stores. The park was just an enclosed stretch of grass between two intersecting streets at the center of town.

We ate sandwiches, sitting on a patch of grass next to a stone bench. There were no other people there, or in the square. It was midday on the Fourth of July; the stores were closed and it's likely that everyone was at a celebration somewhere else.

In my dad's telling, after lunch we were packing up to go and Gloria ran back to the car first and got in the front seat. She refused to move, although it was my turn to sit there. She was determined to be there again. As Dad told it, she insisted, "I'm going to sit here if it kills me."

Dad's voice always started to break when he told that part. He would begin to cry, tears running down the sides of his nose and down his cheeks as he said, with his voice in a thin, cracking falsetto: "*And it did kill her, too.*" Then he would break into sobs, gulping and choking, as he repeated, "It did kill her. She died, poor little girl . . ."

This last detail about Gloria was the end of Dad's account of what led up to the accident. I heard it a number of times over the years, always the same way, so I remember it word for word:

"Adele was determined that we had to be in Denver by the sixth of July, because her brother Lou was giving a party on the seventh. A cocktail party, for Christ's sake! [After becoming Christian Scientists my father and mother never touched alcohol.] She wanted to meet all of Lou's friends. So we would have to be driving on the Fourth of July, and we'd have to leave the night before.

"I was chief structural engineer on the new *Philadelphia Inquirer* building. I was designing floors that would bear the weight of the heaviest rotogravure presses in the world, on an upper story. They called me at the last minute before I was going on vacation and said I had to get out there. I got hardly any sleep and I spent all my time at the site. When I got back from Philadelphia on the afternoon of the third, I was exhausted. I knew I couldn't go that night. We would just have to leave the next day. I needed to rest.

"But Adele said we had to go. There was no way we could get there in time for the party unless we got started that night. Then she asked me to help load the car. She was supposed to have had the car all loaded when I got back. But now she said I had to do it. July in Detroit, it was hotter than hell, I was exhausted from my trip, and I was lugging her sewing machine out to the car, trying to squeeze it in the trunk, laying suitcases down on the floor of the back seat so you kids would have a place to sit while she stretched out her legs on the back seat."

(I realize, as I write this, why she had to have her legs up on the seat: her varicose veins, which she never had treated by a doctor because she was a Christian Scientist. She needed the suppurating sores on her ankles elevated. That's why I was sitting on the floor, with my back to the left side of the car, instead of sitting beside her facing forward. Who knows, maybe that saved my life.)

"And there was another thing that was bothering me [he told me once, telling this story; he didn't always mention this part]. I called your mother on the phone from Philadelphia the night I got there, and she mentioned an old beau of hers who had called her from out of town, out of the blue. He wanted to have dinner with her sometime. Now, when your mother and I were going to get married, we made an agreement. I knew she'd had boyfriends, she was thirty years old, and I said I would never ask her about anyone before me and I didn't want to hear about any of them. We agreed that neither of us would ever bring up the past, or torment the other about our past private lives. So when she said this bozo's name, I thought to myself: 'Dolly, Dolly, you are breaking your promise. You swore you would never do this. You're doing this to get under my skin.' So on the way back from Philadelphia I had had this on my mind, too. I was pretty blue.

"Well, it was worse than that. For some reason Adele had lost all her spirit that spring. She didn't seem to have any interest in life, all of a sudden. She didn't even have as much interest in your piano playing.

"She turned her attention more to the PTA at Gloria's high school. She had just become president of that. But she didn't have much energy for anything. And she certainly didn't have any time or attention for me. As far as I could see, she had lost all interest in our marriage, in being married.

"Driving that night, and when I was on the road the next day, I was thinking she was going to leave me. I was driving her to Denver, and she was going to stay there, with her brother. Why was she taking her sewing machine with her? Going for a month in Denver, what did she need her sewing machine for? She was going to stay there. That's why she was so anxious to meet all Lou's friends, and why she had to make a good impression on them. She wanted Lou to want her to live there, to be his sister in charge of his socializing, just like her sister Bertha was Lou's secretary.

"So I was thinking to myself, I'm driving my family to Denver and they're all going to leave me. Okay, maybe I'll just drop them off at Lou's and turn around and drive right back myself. I didn't tell her what I was thinking.

"So finally that night we got going. Adele had it figured out. We were going to drive from Detroit to the shores of Lake Michigan, where we were going to sleep out on the beach. Some friend of hers had told her you could do that, camp on the sand. That was another wonderful thing. Your mother was supposed to have made motel reservations for us, but she forgot till too late, and it was impossible to find a motel vacancy the night before the Fourth of July. So she got this idea that we could sleep on the sand. We brought blankets for that.

"That night I didn't sleep a wink. I wasn't asleep for a minute. It got too cold, and the sand was cold under the blankets. After a while your mother and Gloria got into the car, and they were able to sleep. But I couldn't sleep at all."

I remember that night clearly. I was lying outside next to my father, on top of a blanket and under another one, looking up at the stars. It was a clear night and we were on the shore of Lake Michigan, far from any lights or smog. The sky was filled with stars. I had never seen so many stars in my life. And every few minutes, one of them would streak across the sky. It was a night of falling stars, all night. I would drift to sleep, my eyes would blur and close, and then they would open again later and see another bright star fall.

"When we got going the next morning after breakfast—your mother had at least remembered to pack some food for breakfast and lunch—I was worried that I wouldn't be able to keep going. It was hotter than hell by the middle of the morning, and the road got flat and straight. We were going through cornfields, endless fields, all the same. It would have been hard to keep my eyes focused even if I had had some sleep, and I hadn't.

"So I said to Adele, 'We're just going to have to look for a motel and stop. They'll have vacancies during the day, even if it is the Fourth of July. I have to get some sleep.' She said no, that was impossible. We had a tight schedule, if we were going to get to Denver on time, and we had to keep it.

"We weren't running into any motels anyway. But I was getting more and more tired. It was getting hard to keep my eyes open. Finally I said, 'Okay, I'll just have to pull over and nap for a while.'

"And she said, 'We don't have time for that. We won't get there in time for the party if we stop.'

"I said, 'Then you'll have to take over the driving, while I sleep in the car.' She said no, she wouldn't do that. She had said from the beginning that she wasn't going to do any driving, I would have to do it all. She had to be fresh when she got to Denver, for the party."

He drove on. Just after our picnic lunch, his eyes closed on the road to Des Moines, and the right wheels went off the pavement onto gravel. That woke him up, and he remembers seeing Gloria looking up at him with a puzzled look on her face, as if to ask what was wrong. He tried to get the car back on the highway, but the rough edge of the pavement tore out the inside of the right rear tire, as the highway patrol concluded afterward. The wheels couldn't get back onto the asphalt before the right side of the car plowed into a concrete sidewall that was flush with the highway, above a culvert.[11]

***

A day and a half after the accident, I woke up in a white hospital room. Everything was white, the bed I was on, the bandages on my legs, the walls, the light. It must have been the middle of the night; I had been in a coma for thirty-six hours, but there were doctors and nurses in white around my bed. It was like an operating room. Perhaps they were putting my leg in traction.

Someone said, "You've been in an accident. You're lucky to be alive. Your father is okay." I asked about my mother and sister. Someone told me they were dead.

An untoward thought came into my mind—I will explain it below—but I said nothing. A nurse said, "You're a brave boy." Then I lost consciousness again.

My aunt visited me in the hospital a month after the accident, and I asked her if she had just arrived. She was astonished and said she had been talking to me nearly every day for the past month. That turned out to be true for other visitors, none of whom I could remember at all. The memories of those first weeks in the hospital didn't come back over the course of the rest of the summer. In fact, they never have.

My memory is continuous from that time on, and for the years and hours up to the crash, but there is a thirty-day gap of near-total amnesia.[12]

Life commenced again, in the hospital and later in school and college and the rest of my life. Yet, for reasons I could not explain, I had no particular thoughts about my mother or sister. No tears about the accident, then or ever, no sadness, no anguish, no sorrow either for them or for myself, for what I had lost. My mother, who had been the polestar of my life for fifteen years, vanished from my thoughts from one day (with a memory gap of a month) to the next.

For several decades I felt, from time to time, slightly uneasy about my total lack of conscious sorrow about the accident and absence of longing memories for the dead. My lack of feeling seemed odd, puzzling, not to be admitted. Whenever I thought of it, which was not often, I felt slightly ashamed, before I would push the thought away.

I didn't want others to be aware of my lack of sadness. I knew they might react to it much more strongly than I did, and I couldn't explain and justify it. I was sure that people—especially those who knew about my piano training—would interpret my absence of mourning as a memory of bitterness toward my mother, hostility, as if I hadn't loved her, and she hadn't loved me. I knew that that was the opposite of the truth.

But I never regretted the lack of suffering, I was grateful for it. I enjoyed the feeling I did have, which, even in the hospital and all the more when I was released, was . . . free.

I was free to do whatever I wanted, every hour, every day. ("It was air / And playing," writes Dylan Thomas, "lovely and watery / And fire green as grass.") It was wonderful. Everything, nearly everything, was fun. Interesting, pleasurable. Oh, there were the demands of schoolwork, but I liked the courses and loved the reading, it was easy to excel, I wanted to do what I was doing, nearly all of it. It was all play.

It was uncomfortable in the hospital lying in bed all the time in a cast up to my waist, but nothing was demanded of me, I could read, practice magic tricks, learn scores, joke with visitors. But when I went back to school in the fall it was really no different, it was even better. I was on vacation, all the time.

At the same time I continued for years to have brief feelings of unease, of guilt, when I was doing something I liked at times when, in earlier years, I would have been practicing. As before, pleasures taken in time not spent practicing were guilty pleasures, though not less pleasurable for that. But at last the guilt wore away, along with the feeling that this freedom was something special, forbidden, self-indulgent, and all that was left was the wonderful freedom, the sense I was in command of my time and my life.

It seemed for a long while that this feeling of endless vacation, this happiness, might last for the rest of my life. It lasted a long time, most of the next eighteen years I would say, till about the time my first wife asked for a divorce.

***

In 1982, at a seminar in Wellfleet, Massachusetts, under the direction of Robert Lifton and Erik Erikson, I was introduced to the work of Lifton and others on "survivor syndrome." This is a set of characteristics generally shared by those who have lost loved ones in a traumatic way, like those who lost relatives in the bombing of Hiroshima, or a major accident or natural disaster, especially when the survivors came close to dying in the same incident.

At the top of the list of these symptoms, I learned, is aborted grieving, an "inability to mourn," usually accompanied by some guilt or reticence about this very inability. Another is "paradoxical guilt," over surviving when others did not, an exaggerated or unfounded sense of responsibility for the tragedy. It's also called "survivor's guilt," and it often results in a determination to warn others against a similar fate. A lot of the specific descriptions sounded familiar to me; they put into a wholly new light some of the puzzles of my own experience.

This new understanding was highly relevant to a particular aspect of the story leading up to the accident. As I mentioned, sometimes when my father told the story, he would describe the ways my mother seemed depressed before the trip. She had lost interest in my piano, and just about everything else. He confessed to feeling afraid that she was planning to leave him in Denver. This is why, he surmised, she was in such a rush to get to her brother's cocktail party—to make inroads with his social circle there.

Was he right about her intentions? Who knows. But whether she was planning that or not, he thought she was. This perception must have made him either anguished or depressed—or perhaps both—along with being totally exhausted. This was a dangerous state to be driving in.

And why was Mother acting so depressed, as he described her? Why was she so indifferent to her marriage, to her children, to my piano, to everything except getting to Denver in time to launch a new life with her brother?

It's impossible to know for sure. But this is what I thought when I heard Dad tell this part of the story: *me*, that's what caused her depression. I did it: by giving up, by not resisting Kottler's verdict and pressing onward with my piano career.

My half-brother Harry would go on to recount to me his memory of the silent treatment I received from my mother the few times I tried to quit the piano, none of which I recall myself. Nonetheless, given these episodes, I must have grown up fearing—at least on a subconscious level—that if I told the truth about who I was and what I really wanted, Mother would have lost interest in me. Our relationship would be over, along with my piano career. And that would be like death.

And I wasn't wrong, it seems. When I finally did hear Kottler's judgment that I wasn't a pianist and I chose to accept it, one of us died inside. And it wasn't me. I was alive, alive and free at last from the pressures of the piano. But not for long. It came at a price: Mother's life. I began to draw a direct line between my failure as a pianist and the events that led to the accident. That was a debt that would have to be paid.

As I learned at Wellfleet, psychologists say all children who lose parents early feel survivor's guilt. They feel responsible for the tragedy, feeling that if they had acted better or been more worthy of love, they could have kept their parent around.

But not all children have such valid grounds for their feeling of guilt as I did. So it still seems reasonable to me, despite all the arguments I've heard that there's no real basis for it.

It occurred to me recently that Dad's frequent story—about Gloria's insistence about sitting in the front seat—may have a more complicated subtext, especially for me as a young man.

As I mentioned, Dad always quoted Gloria as saying, "I'm going to sit in this seat even if it kills me!" And then Dad would always say, in a high-pitched voice through his tears, "And it *did* kill her, too. She died, poor little girl."

On the one hand, it was a dramatic and horrifying story, and it was easy to see why it would break him up. On the other hand, Dad was a good storyteller, and he may have just made up her saying that. He always invented dialogue that improved the drama, and he came to believe his own creations. Of course, it was a fact that she was sitting up front that afternoon in the "death seat" next to the driver, and that I would have wanted a turn to sit there.

I had no memory of it one way or the other. But in repeatedly telling me that it had been my turn after lunch, it seems to me now, he was describing another "accident"—that Gloria was sitting there instead of me when the car crashed. He was pretty close to saying, "You were supposed to die, not Gloria. It was your turn. She took it."

Was that what he was crying about? Would he have cared as much if I had died instead of her? Would he have broken up the same way if he was telling the story to Gloria instead, in the wake of my death? Probably. I guess I would like to think so.

I do know that from the time of the accident onward, a thought that used to recur to me at odd times was "*I owe a life.*" Just that: a thought in my head, not a voice. No context, no *why*. I didn't know where it came from, and I don't even remember connecting it with the accident. It wasn't clear what it meant to owe a life. But it was a kind of free-floating command, an obligation. It told me: at some point, I must pay my debt. But how did you do that? As I'd later learn at the Wellfleet retreat, this type of logic is consistent with, and characteristic of, survivor's syndrome.

I know that after the accident I never expected to live long. I had the feeling that I was on borrowed time. I figured I had a few good years ahead, free years, and I should enjoy them.

***

This brings us to the untoward thought I had when I woke up from the coma in the hospital, thirty-six hours after the accident. This is my only memory between the accident and the end of my amnesia a month later.

When a hospital staff member told me that my mother and sister were dead, the thought that came into my mind was:

"Now I won't have to be a pianist."

The fact is that I was already no longer fated to be a pianist at the time of the accident; that life sentence had been lifted two months earlier, by Mischa Kottler. What *was* this thought doing in my head, then, at that moment?

After Kottler delivered the bad news to me and Mother, I still kept practicing, more or less at the same rate, though not eight full hours on Saturdays. I did end up taking some lessons with Kottler, with the understanding that they were for my pleasure, not for a serious career. But absent any chance of my becoming a concert pianist, my mother was indifferent to these lessons. I think I chose to take them so as not to embarrass Mother by quitting piano abruptly. In the back of my mind, I fully expected to quit when I went off to college in a few years.

It turned out that I quit sooner than that. Starting right after the accident—except for an intense music theory class my freshman year at

Harvard, which I almost failed—I never touched the piano again for the next twenty-five years. And even after that, I played only sporadically.

Once I quoted my strange, sole thought upon learning of my mother's death—"Now I won't have to be a pianist"—to a close friend. She later told it to the *Time* journalists writing their cover story on me while Patricia and I were putting out the Pentagon Papers. Readers understandably reacted to the quotation, especially when it was repeated in the *New York Times Magazine* in a hyped and horribly garbled context, with shivers.[13]

***

Now, as I write this, I'm listening to a CD of David Helfgott playing the Rachmaninov Third Piano Concerto. In the next track, I know from the program notes, Helfgott will play a piece I have not heard for fifty years, Rachmaninov's "Prelude in C Sharp Minor, Op. 3, No. 2." "The Bells of Moscow," people call it.[14]

I used to hear it all the time in my childhood; it was the most played piece in our household. It was my mother's favorite piece, and she always played it sooner or later when she sat down at the piano, in those rare moments when I wasn't practicing. Sometimes she would perform it for company. She did it wonderfully, with strength and bravura. We never got tired of it.

I never learned it. I tried once, but it was too hard, and I didn't try long. It was her piece anyway.

Now Helfgott is playing the prelude. I'm hearing it for the first time since she died, fifty-four years ago. It sounds familiar. It sounds like home. Tears come to my eyes and my face contorts as I listen.

But the triad of descending chords that starts it and is repeated over and over doesn't sound to me like bells, it never has. It sounds like what it always did to me: the footsteps of Death. Or of God. The last chord especially, the descending fifth, rings on the floor like the commanding knock of a staff, a long scepter, in the grip of a God of Death.

I'm about to write what has stopped me from writing for most of a year. I realized this as I was in the shower a few moments ago, having started the new CD and left it on as I got into the shower. As I stood, hearing the music faintly and knowing what I was going to write, a line from Pablo Neruda came into my head. "Tonight I can write the saddest lines." Tears come, in the shower. Can I be crying at last, for my mother? "Tonight I can write the saddest lines. / I loved her, and sometimes she loved me too."

Sometimes? No, no, not just sometimes.

A psychoanalyst sat down to dinner with me in the early eighties at my request to talk about my life and help me understand it—not professionally, but as someone who believed in my work and wanted to help it. We had just met at a seminar on psychohistory that was still in progress. Her first question, as she was settling herself at the table, was "Tell me about your parents. What was your relation with your mother?"

"We were lovers."

She jumped. She was experienced, a dozen years older than me, but she wasn't expecting that. I was fifty-one at the time. I had never said it before.

I went on, "Not physically, of course, at all, but in every other way."

I don't think I had ever thought it before, certainly not at the time. When my mother was alive I hadn't had any other lovers, I didn't really know what the word meant. In two bouts of psychoanalysis I had never used these words, or anything like them. But in answering this question at this moment in my life it seemed the obvious way to put it.

What I had wanted most in the world was to make her smile, to make her laugh. I wanted her to hug me and say she was proud of me. I'm not sure whether she ever said that; she was very sparing with praise. She tended after a performance to tell me what parts needed more work, what I could do better next time. But she did hug me a lot, and tell me I was her darling boy and she loved me. I adored her, I cared only for her, and it seemed to me that she cared only about me, and my playing.

We were totally absorbed in each other, I told my analyst friend. She was preoccupied with my piano, but with me, too. She was interested in my thoughts and ideas, and she laughed at my jokes, though she was never one for saying anything funny herself.

My father would tell jokes often, which I have passed on to my sons. (When I do that, I warn them that they are fated to remember jokes their father told them and to tell them to their sons someday even though they don't think they are very funny.) But it was for my mother that I wanted to be funny, not my father. When I learned something interesting or had ideas, it was her I wanted to tell.

She often had headaches, her forehead would be furrowed as she read *Science and Health* or sewed, and I would go behind her and reach down with my thumbs and smooth out the two deep frown lines between her eyes, and have her close her eyelids while I did it. Or I would do it from in front, smooth her forehead with my thumbs.

"And where was your father in all this?" the analyst asked.

"Nowhere. He was out of it." We were the real partners, she and I, there wasn't room for my father, or, it seemed to me, my sister either. He was off to the side, a little wistfully it seemed sometimes, but on the whole absorbed in his job. My sister was behind him, an afterthought, as I recalled. She wasn't a pianist. Mother and I were the pair.

My life revolved around her, and hers around me. Even when I went off to boarding school, hers was the only opinion of me that mattered; she was the one I wanted to achieve for.

This is who died, the person I lost, on the Fourth of July when I was fifteen. And—here is a mystery, this is what I couldn't bring myself to write over the past year, along with what I have just told—this is the woman for whom, along with her daughter, my sister, I never grieved, not an hour or a tear, from the day they were killed.

When the Rachmaninov piece ends, I search on my shelves for a book of Neruda's poetry to check the line that came to me from "Tonight I Can Write."

Oh, now I'm crying for sure. Over these words, in which I find my feelings for Mother, my lost love. For the first time in more than fifty years, the first time in my life, it feels to me that I am crying over my mother's death, grieving. I'm crying for me, for the loss of my mother.[15]

PART II

Selections from the Ellsberg Notebooks, 1971–2021

Undated Selections

First, I saw the war as a challenge and a problem, then as a stalemate, then as a moral disaster and a crime.[1]

For 10 years I had seen myself as working for the President, not questioning his predominance. From 1964 to 1969, the first five years of my involvement in South Vietnam, I saw the President as the solution to the problem—through escaping, winning, or ending the war.

Then in 1969, seeing a continuing crime, I understood that the President alone could not end it. Seeing Congress as a possible solution, I gave them information that could challenge them to stop it.

A year and a half and two invasions later, clearly Congress was part of the problem. The public is the only possible solution.

Now the public has information. Will they use it?

***

Is it an error, an aberration, an abuse or misuse of power when we end up on the wrong side—or when we end up *being* the wrong side?

It turns out that war is not more easily ended than won. "This year" is always a bad year to lose Vietnam to Communism.

At one point, a proposed title [for the Pentagon Papers] was *The Existence of Stalemate in Vietnam*. The study showed that stalemate was much older than I thought in South Vietnam, so the remedies were even less likely to make any difference than I had imagined.

Going back to Washington, I discovered that efforts to get out were as frustrating as the efforts to modify strategies, to win. It was the other side of a stalemate.

I was outraged at the low body counts given for the 25th Division.

Even now, the press is more concerned over whether the reported body count is exaggerated than whether the real body statistics are too high, or even justified.

The media asks "Are we killing as many as we say we are? Are we killing enough to win?" rather than asking "Are we killing too many, and for the wrong reasons?"

The stakes [in Vietnam] were different from what was said publicly. Presidents regarded the stakes as more important than others supposed, and they accepted risks with a low promise of success. Great emphasis was put on the short run, especially on events before the election, to protect the President's prestige.

Psychologist Maria Piers said that with respect to the decisions to escalate the war, "The dread of shame connected with losing the war was certainly of overwhelming importance for all five men in the White House. Conversely, it was the guilt over killing that motivated Ellsberg, and indeed all opponents of the war. The 'shameful' defeat that would accompany withdrawal from the war seemed to them a small price to pay."

Piers concludes, "Those in command can usually deal with guilt, but shame of being a loser seems to be unbearable . . . It seems that in all wars the avoidance of shame plays an enormous role. It has sent whole armies to their deaths."

The issue is not only that mistakes were made, but that we learned so little from them.

***

I am changing. When did this begin?

I am the "possessor of secret knowledge": SIOP,[2] the Missile Gap, the Cuban Missile Crisis, Vietnam escalation and realities, the Pentagon Papers, and Nixon's aims and plans.

It seems that, like Ishmael in *Moby-Dick*, "I alone survive to tell the tale."

My mission: "prophet," perhaps?

Am I Cassandra, a crier in the wilderness?

I seek to *warn, protest, reveal, risk for others, seek understanding, prevent danger, evaluate risks, avert evil,* and *teach by word and example.*

To teach that violence has unforeseen bad consequences—and that alternatives exist—is to introduce the possibility of great change.

***

My longtime preoccupations include power, bargaining, coercion, crisis, risk, threats, and decision-making under uncertainty.

Also among my current preoccupations: secrecy, lying, ambiguity, evil, guilt, shame, truth, and nonviolence.

***

How does the unthinkable become thinkable? How does the unspeakable become doable?

Important things not sufficiently recognized or conceptualized:

—risk-taking, gambles, and threats
—avoidance of humiliation, failure, blame, and reproach
—obedience, conformity, membership, and group identity
—hidden or unrecognized conflicts of values, aims, and interests.

Humans don't need to see others as non-human in order to deceive them, neglect them, kill them, wound them, enslave them, or ignore them and their plight. It is sufficient to see them as "inferior" humans, or less deserving, or dangerous, such that they are not "us." Their deaths may even be seen as exemplary, necessary, or to the benefit of one's own group.

The "others" are said to be undeserving of rights by virtue of:

—a lack of merit, effort, membership, or lineage
—what they have done or might do
—what others of their group have done.

War and violence are the prime causes of war and violence. Violence leads to resentment, suspicion, fear, and counterviolence—all of which are kept down by the threat of further violence.

The economic development that results from preparing for war has been the Engine of History.

***

Most people have the ability to live with quite contradictory notions. For example, we were fighting for democracy in South Vietnam, *and* the government we were supporting was a corrupt dictatorship, itself torturing and imprisoning thousands of people.

It was an essential quality in an official to be able to hold two such contradictory views at the same time, to believe both, and to draw no logical conclusion from this contradiction.

I had this quality. My boss had it. We *all* had it.

My sense is that something is wrong with the existing ethical system both of leaders and followers.

Bureaucrats and leaders do not act in ways that they believe are evil. They believe that what they are doing is *not* evil, but is "right"—even *obligatory* under the circumstances.

Power corrupts. When in power, a politician has opportunities available to him that he could not even imagine earlier.

Power experienced while in office is addicting. It undermines objectivity such that the politician comes to believe that his tenure is indispensable to the country and to national security, and that anything is justified to preserve it.

Compartmentalization is required by bureaucracies and organizations.

"It is not your business to monitor or control."

"Don't worry about consequences."

"Stay in your lane."

***

If you want peace, *understand* war.

"There is no way to peace—peace is the way." —A. J. Muste

Act as if peace were possible.

"Peace" cannot include threatening and preparing mass annihilation.

I cannot imagine any regional conflict whose resolution would be made easier by the possession of nuclear weapons.

Oppenheimer said in 1949, "The least we can conclude is that our twenty thousandth bomb will not in any deep strategic sense affect their two thousandth."[3]

[On the possibility of accidental nuclear war]: "This is the way the world ends: with a 'glitch.'"

The approaching end of the story [i.e., the end of civilization as we know it] redefines our sense of the planetary narrative, including our past and our future.

How will survivors of World War III, long after, understand the planning and preparation for it? What will they infer about us?

***

Hypothesis: Humans do not, as a species, have the equivalent of an individual's (or an organization's) instinct of self-preservation.

In the past, underlying the massive failures to prepare has been the belief that certain conceivable events were, in practice, *impossible*. Our experience supports what we would like to believe: that *Mankind Cannot Destroy Itself*, that *History Cannot Stop*.

To make a prediction is to run the risk of being found wrong.

With weather or stock market predictions, notice the use of carefully obscured hedges. These are unobtrusive before the event, and unequivocal after the event. This is the way to protect against the charge that "you were wrong" or "you didn't warn me."

We must imagine the future, even with the likelihood that the coming changes will elude our predictions.

As we are on a rapidly changing trajectory, time spent studying the distant past is borrowed from time available for studying the recent past and its implications for our immediate future.

***

Most people conform and accept. A minority protest, withdraw. A tiny minority resist, take risks.

We have come to make a citizens' arrest of the nuclear arms race. We are willing to go to jail to say, "No business as usual."

Protesters are willing to violate traffic laws to end violence in Vietnam, while the Government is willing to violate the Constitution to keep the war going—to keep people from disturbing the war.

My old associates cannot comprehend a moral act of responsibility; witness their need for descriptions like "guilt-ridden." They also can't make sense of any public statement from me, except as "publicity-seeking."

My former colleagues' perspective: Why give up access to the powerful in order to speak to powerless, ignorant mortals . . . the masses . . . people who don't count and never will?

"Nobody wants to be the last guy shot in a war. But nobody wants to be the last guy put in prison for resisting." —Bob Eaton, war resister

***

I am proud to be one American among millions who learned a different way of being a patriotic, good American during a bad war.

I learned that I could love my country and love peace and justice at the same time: by saying no to my country's officials, no to war—and yes to truth, to democracy, to peace.

Should we not recapture the definition of our own responsibilities as citizens, as humans, from the hands of officials and their allied protectors?

If you believe that "when you die, you are dead," it is all the more horrific not to use your life well.

***

Janaki Tschannerl[4] says that we need prophets, not just forecasters. We need to imagine new relationships, new ways of acting—not just "alternatives," but whole new kinds of relationships and systems, new ways of feeling and becoming.

[Rep.] Barbara Lee told the story of her birth. The hospital wouldn't admit her mother for a C-section and left her on a cot to die. Barbara had to be removed with forceps. "It was a struggle to be born," she said, "and I've been struggling and fighting ever since."

Joanna Macy asked her, "Why are you not embittered?" Barbara replied, "Because if you dwell on those feelings, you end up in a place where you don't want to be."

In 1967, I was with the March on the Pentagon when a group of people came charging up the steps. It was the Yippies.

In their meetings, the Yippies had defined their aim for the March this way: "We're gonna sit in all the halls and we're gonna raise the Pentagon 300 feet in the air."

In short, they were looking to "levitate" the Pentagon.

When I heard that Abbie Hoffman had died, what came to my mind is:
"Abbie was born with the gift of laughter."
Also: "All Power to the Imagination."

***

Is Earth a "failed experiment"?

How is humanity to live its *transient, finite* life?

***

Martin Buber says we each have in us something precious which is in no one else. It is revealed to us only if we perceive our strongest desire of our inmost being.

What is your immortality project?
    Are you wasting your life?
    Are you writing what you know?
    What do you want to accomplish before you die?

What I will do when the war is over: be with Pat; read and write; and renew and perfect the American Revolution.

1971

"Truth is the first prisoner of war."

Truth doesn't just die; it merely fades away . . . into safes.

***

I was responsible for the release of the Pentagon Papers to the Congress, the newspapers, and through them to the American public. I don't know all of the technical and legal arguments, but I am not concerned about the issues that relate to me. This was a moral judgment, not a legal judgment.

This was an act of hope. I have acted in the hope that the American people, having access to the realities that successive Administrations have tried to hide from them, will inform themselves and will then act to free us and the people of Indochina from this war.

As an official and researcher who was one of very few granted access to this study, I increasingly realized on studying it that the very secrecy and concealment of its information over 20 years had been crucial to the expansion of the war, and would support further expansion.

I felt confident that no harm could be done to this country by releasing these papers that was remotely comparable to the harm that had been done by concealing them, and that would be done by concealing them further.

The facts are now out of the safes and into the newspapers. Now get them into your heads and guts—and act on them.

It was not my purpose to go to jail. It was my purpose to help end this war, and to do so by telling the truth.

It happens that the Executive, in reacting to me, revealed to the public that telling the truth had become dangerous and that I had been willing to confront the danger.

In 1971, these truths came to seem more important to many than the truths in the Papers themselves.

Use of a radical, novel, powerful, and possibly illegal tactic of nonviolence is a form of useful work that is perfectly suited to illustrate the evil being combated.

I have never before shrunk from violence—from imagining it, planning it, preparing for it.

I have wanted, and I have gained, the respect of violent men. Now I want the respect of gentle women, gentle men, and children.

***

Is there such a thing as being "born for jail?"

My father has learned from me, just as I have learned from my son—a chain of resistance, of refusal to collaborate.

Do we have the courage and the self-confidence to face the realities of what we are doing, and what is wrong with our society?

Can we get out of the war without citizens taking risks?

To guard liberty for all, it may be necessary to risk one's own liberty by combating tyrannous authorities and executives who act outside the law.

***

Nearly everyone, *en masse* or as individuals, is capable of great unconcern about the killing, dying, pain, or deprivation of others. This fact can be exploited by rulers—just as can the potential for envy, ambition, patriotic fervor, and violence. There is a "need not to know"—a need to be deceived.[5]

The temptation is strong to obey powerful men passively and unquestioningly. Such unqualified obedience is dangerous.

Viewing ourselves as powerless, as "not responsible," is a way to escape feeling guilty about what we are collaborating in.

"The President knows more than we do. He knows best. He knows what he's doing."

The truth is that we *all* share Speer's responsibility.[6]

***

There came a time when the Vietnamese people came to be as real to me as my own hands . . . moments when the war became real.

What country in the non-Communist world looks as much like a colony as South Vietnam? In what country is there, by any standard, so much intervention?

Stalemate policy is wrong, illegitimate, outrageous, murderous, illegal, criminal, intolerable. Yet this policy is very strong and can't be changed from within the Executive branch.

Why is there such entrenched resistance? It is because stalemate policy reflects perceived interests.

To oppose this war is to oppose something our government has been engaged in for a quarter of a century. It is one of our more enduring national purposes.

***

When I was ignorant about the war, I was willing to risk my life, or give it, to help my country understand the war—in order to win it.

Now I know that it is far more important for us to leave the war than it ever was to win it.

Just as much understanding is needed to leave the war as to win it. Yet we are as far from understanding ourselves and our role in the war as we are from winning it.

How could I now find an excuse for *not* risking prison (and anger, hatred, reproach) to help provide this understanding, while millions of people are dying in Vietnam for want of that understanding?

***

My life had been organized around enemies (conflict and strategy) and secrets.[7]

Bureaucrats don't get in trouble for classifying. They might get in trouble for *not* classifying.

A CBS Special Report said there are 6 million cubic feet of classified documents in the Pentagon. According to Rep. William Moorhead, there are 20 million classified documents.[8]

The choice before me was *not* how to design a security system, but rather, what to do about *these pages*?

For me, the challenges to secrecy and the right to know were secondary to challenging the war itself—to stopping the lying, killing, and dying.

Q: "How could you take it on yourself to give out these Top Secrets?"

Essentially, I was being asked, "*Who authorized you to stop lying and killing?*" The answer seems obvious: I was giving out facts about our history, secrets that had been concealed from the public by wrongly stamping them Top Secret. These facts were urgently needed by our citizens to stop more lying and dying.

Q: "Are you saying that no secrets should be kept? Should anyone be free to release secrets anytime?"

I was not "opening a safe drawer at random and scattering the papers." In other words, it did not "just happen" that the 7,000 pages I released turned out to be wrongly classified and highly relevant. I didn't "luck out" in this.

I had the Papers because I had become one of the leading experts (such as we have) on this war. Far from stealing them, I had been asked to help produce them, and then to analyze them, because of my background on the subject.

I was not attacking the security system or proposing a new design for one (although that is urgently needed, as these Papers show).

Ultimately, I was exercising the kind of judgment that the public has a right to expect of its servants, and should demand.

***

After I released the papers, some people were afraid to write to me . . . to shake hands with me . . . to receive a phone call from me.

Isolation from my friends, from those I respected, is huge but unavoidable. Any involvement with me could lead to very heavy penalties for them, and I am not willing to let others share these risks unnecessarily.

After 15 years of serving the State, perhaps it was a reflection of the mystery and power that the State held for me that I found it difficult to conceive of challenging it without spending the rest of my life in prison or exile.

I had seen them destroy reputations, isolate people, and ruin careers. Surely they would "get" me.

***

To teach has its own power. A central aim of my life is to affect people's lives by changing their understanding. This was the power I hoped to experience.

Change your life. Change your part of the world and its contribution to evil and oppression. Learn from women, children, blacks, and other oppressed peoples who have grown up to resist.

The Quakers say:
    Cast off fear.
    Face and tell the truth.
    Be willing to risk.
    Embody courage, self-confidence, and self-respect.

What are we to do with our lives?
    What could you do if you were prepared to change your life in a big way?
    Look at what you are doing. Is this work fit for a free man or woman?

Someone told me recently, "I wish I had your guts."
    My reply: "What makes you think that you don't?"

I will accept the label of hero if it is recognized as a way of acting that is within the reach of everyone, not as a special quality that distances me from others. It must not deny the example of the multitude of people who have influenced me, whom I think of as heroes.

1972

I don't think there has been a waking hour in my life in the last six years when I have had no thought of the war. It is an ache.

I've believed some strange things in my life. In the years when I was risking my life to support our policy, I believed most of the things that were said in support of the war.

I, like Kissinger, have spent most of my professional life advising on the uses of violence in support of authority and order.

With all the complexities and uncertainty of South Vietnam's politics, as well as the limits on legitimacy of the DRV's [North Vietnam's] cause (as in most revolutions and independence struggles), one simplifying principle emerges: there is *no legitimate basis* for the U.S. to be killing *any* Vietnamese, or to pay any Vietnamese to kill other Vietnamese. Nor are the interests of Americans served in doing so, except those of the ruling classes. All apparent justifications are lies and misconceptions.

I had read the entire Pentagon Papers, including about the war's origins, and I was the only one on the team who had actually been in Vietnam.

The Papers showed that the Vietnam War was a 25-year war, initially undertaken by the French as a colonial re-conquest. Eventually it became an American war. It was never a civil war; it was a war against self-determination.

This war violated the UN Charter and the Geneva Conventions. It was a crime against peace.

**

The lies were loose and running wild, and part of the truth was in my safe, where I kept the copied documents.

Like some recent White House officials, I discovered that I had evidence in my authorized possession of Executive crimes and an Executive cover-up. Both were still going on.

Now that I knew, I would be participating in a cover-up if I concealed this evidence.

My act, to release the Papers, was but one of thousands of actions aimed at ending the war by focusing the attention of our fellow citizens and asking them to face the truth about the war, then share that truth with their loved ones.

Never once did I argue that my act should be excused or go unpunished, if it were a violation of law. Nor did I complain that the legality of my act was being tested in a court—although, as I came to know the law, it became doubtful that my prosecution was executed in good faith.

**

We are responsible for the effects of our actions. We are also responsible for becoming as aware as we can of these effects.

Underneath someone's "innocence" may be the desire to avoid the awareness of power, or of being able to affect others, or of *having* effects on others. In this way, one avoids responsibility and guilt, as well as anxiety, shame, reproach, loss of self-esteem, and threat to one's job.

Fear, like happiness, comes and goes.

(Have I lately become *unresigned* to prison?)

"You look like Daniel Ellsberg. Have you ever been told that before?"

**

Why didn't I change sooner?

In part, it was because false history blinded me.

Pat helped me see the human side. Yet I still saw the war as being *conducted for* the Vietnamese, and as existing apart from our involvement.

I didn't see the victims of the war as our responsibility. But in fact, they were victims to our own Presidents' purposes.

I didn't confuse my power to end the war with the President's. No other individual had the power to end the war—not those who risked or gave their lives in Vietnam, nor those who went to prison to oppose it.

I ask my questioner, "Do you think the President has an unlimited right to keep secrets from the American people? To lie? To order officials to lie or conceal evidence from Congress and the people? To send U.S. troops into combat? To use nuclear weapons?"

What are the limits? And who monitors those limits?

***

Once again the question comes: "What does it feel like to be called a traitor?"

I think to myself, Who needs this?

Is this part of the price I must pay for trying to warn the country?

Is this part of my "sentence"?

[On my being accused of Treason]:

Treason to whom? Treason to democracy? To an open society? To my countrymen?

Is it to be "my country, right or wrong"? Or worse: "my President, right or wrong"?

I don't think that people who raise the question of treason realize how lucky they are to live in a country in which telling the truth, criticizing the President, and exposing deception by the Government are *not* treason.

What I did was not a routine act in my life. Nor was it a casual one, undertaken without awareness of possible harm.

I would hope that *any* employee with roughly my background and responsibilities, if confronted with material such as the contents of the Pentagon Papers in the current circumstances of Vietnam, would consult his broadest sense of responsibilities and loyalties.

***

We need to de-sanctify secrets and *sanctify human life*.

***

Some of the sanest people I know happen to be in an organization called the War Resisters' International. This is a community of resistance, a community committed to nonviolent change.

I first met a number of members at the Triennial Conference in August 1969. I had face-to-face contact with several people who were on their way to prison as draft-resisting witnesses to the evil of our longest war.

Just a month later, their sacrifice helped me to take the step of freeing the history of that war from my official safe to deliver it to Senator Fulbright.[9]

***

To resist is to provide a mirror, to show the "coercer" in the role of coercion, controlling, forcing, opposing. It is to reveal to him his values and his assumptions of authority, right, and hierarchy.

When obedience becomes lying, then truth-telling becomes the best form of civil disobedience, resistance, and patriotism.

Just as you have only one life, you have only one conscience. And just as you cannot recover a lost life, you cannot recover a wrecked conscience.

Take responsibility for your beliefs, your actions, your lives.
    Free your own power and use it.
    End complicity and silence.
    Join a community of risk, of concern, of change.

***

I want to reread the books that formed me: Dumas, Hugo, Beau Geste, Sartre. Also Tolstoy, Dostoevsky, Stendhal, Proust, and Flaubert.

Then, think of writing "the truth" of what we see, feel, and do today.

Is a great rewriting of the past, a shredding of related documents, to be a result of the Pentagon Papers? Will shredders turn out to be more effective than Xerox machines?

As I travel across the country in Autumn 1972, Orwell's description (in *1984*) of "controlled insanity" as a prevailing mental condition does not seem a dozen years away.

At the end of a talk I gave recently on a college campus, a student came up to me to say, "You make us realize that we're not crazy."

I had quoted earlier from Orwell's *1984*, whose protagonist, Winston Smith, wondered whether he himself was a lunatic. "Perhaps," Smith said, "a lunatic was simply a minority of one."

Smith also said, "It is by staying sane that you carry on the human heritage."

1973

Implicit in the term "national defense" is the notion of defending those values and ideals that set this Nation apart. For almost two centuries, our country has taken singular pride in the democratic ideals enshrined in its Constitution, and the most cherished of those ideals have found expression in the First Amendment. It would indeed be ironic if, in the name of national defense, we would sanction the subversion of one of those liberties—the freedom of association—that makes the defense of the Nation worthwhile.

***

At Harvard, you learn good general-purpose attitudes that make you acceptable, trustable, and likable by a variety of large organizations—including the government.

I've always had a calling—pride, respect, interest, challenge—in my work. And always: great freedom, which I used to choose projects I liked and thought important, rather than for power, money, or advancement.

Issues I focused on: the failure to learn from failures and improve performance; recurrence of crises; failure to avoid crises; anti-learning mechanisms; failure to report upward; and failure to recognize uncertainty and act appropriately to hedge, maintain flexibility, and investigate.

(See Studs Terkel in today's edition of the *New York Times*, about work vs. vocation, calling, pride, creativity, recognition, identity, and purpose.)

Until 1969, under the pressure of trying to understand and act appropriately toward recurrent failure in Vietnam, I did not question the almost exclusive authority of the President or the appropriateness of this concentration of control in his hands.

I was burdened with special knowledge from my time in Vietnam, by the information in the Pentagon Papers, and by the inside knowledge I had heard from Mort Halperin about Nixon's secret escalation plans.[10]

My attitude was similar to that of Presidents and presidential advisors who discount all other opinions because "they don't know what I know." One is left with the feeling that one "has to" rely on one's own judgment.

There was no way anyone could blackmail me into betraying or damaging this country.

I risked my freedom, and would have given my life, to stop the kind of damage our war in Vietnam was doing to this country and its institutions. I would certainly sacrifice my reputation to do that. Threats of slander couldn't stop me, any more than threats of prosecution and lifelong imprisonment had.

The basic judgment I acted on was moral and political, not legal: that the power and policies of the Executive branch had to be exposed and resisted. Everything that happened during our trial and Watergate has vindicated that judgment.

***

It is said that one has no right or obligation to learn what one has "no need to know."

Decisions affecting many individuals and groups should not be made by representatives of one group or interest only; no matter the integrity or sincerity of the person. That person's views will be affected greatly (and more than he knows) when he has a large material or career interest in the judgment or decision—or the group that selected him for the position does.

The temptation to evil, and toward judgments that lead to evil, is not usually a *conscious* preference for one's own narrow self-interest, materially or in career or power. More commonly, it is a bias reflecting the intent of a group much smaller than one's own society: an agency, administration, party, corporation.

To rely on reporting that is entirely from the chain of command is to be kept ignorant of uncertainty and controversy—and of warnings, evidence, risks, failures, errors, and the reality of major obstacles. Leaders need to be aware of problems, which subordinates act to conceal, before they can act to change them.

***

Concern for consequences is related to whether one feels personally responsible for them, and thus at risk of judgment. When one is clearly not responsible, not at fault, then there is less anxiety and concern if things "go badly."

To be "responsible" is to face the possibility of loss of respect, dignity, opportunity, and role. Anxiety disappears as responsibility is relinquished.

In the last 3 years, I have met many in the antiwar movement who, like me, think first about—or have among their first considerations—the contribution they can make to others, or to consequences other than money, career, status, or approval.

When weighing whether to carry out a lesser evil: if it is *not* the case that you *must* do it, then *you must not do it*.

***

On Trustworthiness:

I disagree with much of the Executive branch on the trustworthiness of the Congress, the press, and the public.

Our Executive leaders have abused our trust. At the same time, they have refused to trust the public's judgment and values.

***

Question questions, and question answers.

Think slowly.

Don't stop.

***

Planetary misadministration has led to overpopulation, pollution, and climate change.[11]

Is this the final stage of "human evolution"?

A jump to the next level will require courage.

Put yourself on the side of the *next* epoch.

Axiom: Humanity is only one spirit.

Just as each individual cell in a body comprises the unity of that body, every man, woman, and child on the Earth is part of a single body, which is called "humanity."

Hegel says that Spirit is in the process of realizing itself, and Divine Spirit cannot be fully manifested until it has been awakened in the whole body of humanity.

Love is the recognition of the same consciousness in others as in oneself.

Love finds itself in all things.

***

I loved Mother. For me, her loss meant the annihilation of meaning, purpose, value, and love.

Robert Jay Lifton says that with the death of a close relative, the survivor is left with unattached ambivalence. This is due to the loss of a relationship in which feelings of hostility—as well as of dependence and love—had been expressed, resolved, projected, and denied.

In all of this, the subject has strong feelings of anger and frustration that he must suppress, hide, or redirect.

I had wondered if Mother didn't love me. But I came to understand it wasn't that simple: She loved me, even if conditionally. She wanted *the best* for me—which, to her, was what she had wanted for herself.

NOTES ON THE PENTAGON PAPERS TRIAL, 1973

We really did try to dance—to "Zen-sword-fight"—through the prosecution.

Our focus was on the war and the public's understanding of it, as well as on secrecy, awareness, tyranny, and legal precedent.

We accepted the possibility of loss, defeat, imprisonment, and shame.

I knew from October '69 on that among my risks was facing false testimony from former friends.[12] The actual occasion of it is one of the least pleasant aspects of this experience.

[On McGeorge Bundy's testimony]: I agree with what he has said on the stand, and I'm glad that he came here to say it.

It does not harm national security to state that a study shows him and his Administration in an extremely harsh light.

[Out of approximately 100 prospective jurors]:

—Exactly *one* has admitted reading the contents of the Pentagon Papers.
—Almost none of them read the *Los Angeles Times*.
—Almost *all* of them want out of Vietnam.
—Nearly all of them *have changed* their views on Vietnam.

—Nearly all who had a view associated the case with when it first came into the news, when the Papers were given to the newspapers.

—Most of them who have a view accepted—or still accept—the premise that we need to "Win or Get Out."

COMMENTS BY PROSPECTIVE JURY MEMBERS:

Q: "What do you know about the Pentagon Papers?"
A: "Someone had gotten into the Pentagon and taken some papers."

"Some people say we should never have sent the boys over there. But we did."

"At first, as a soldier my involvement was being obedient, just doing what I was told. I thought I was doing the right thing. Now, I've come home, and I've changed my thinking; I don't think we should be there. I don't condemn our government's actions, but I don't condone them either. The war should have ended a long time ago. We either should have ended it or gotten out. Now I think we should get out."

"It seems to me that sometimes, if our economy is bad and there is a war going on, we seem to get involved in order to help our economy. But after the economy got better, I expected our soldiers to leave. When they didn't, I thought, 'Maybe there is another purpose involved. Maybe it is for the purpose *stated* at the outset: that they are there to defend the freedom of the people over there.'"

"Casualty reports didn't tell the real story. They would pick a specific time period or unit, so as to minimize the reported casualty rate. I thought it was unfair that the people didn't know what was really happening with casualties."

A comment about my having worked at RAND, a "think tank"[13]:
"They just put men in their rooms and they think about how to improve the country. I would go stir-crazy myself."

"Could it be true that they are keeping us *that* much in the dark?"

1974

How could you go wrong, obeying a President?

There is danger in linking great power to authority. People perceive "obeying authority" as a *moral imperative*, once they have accepted a given authority. By that view, one cannot have a "clear moral imperative" that calls for disobedience!

U.S. imperialism was born in the World War II phase, in a mood of extremely ambitious objectives. It was an opportunity to own most of the world, with all the "skin" associated with being the general banker and policeman, along with the gratifying, economically beneficial "obligations."

Rulers convince themselves that their interest *is* the public's interest—and that the public simply doesn't realize that "What is good for Rockefeller and Nixon is good for the country."

The costs of war rest lightly on elites. Yet they have far greater influence on our foreign policy and practices than the broader public does.

Can self-determination be denied indefinitely by the U.S. to a small foreign country, while preserving self-determination in this country? Can this occur in the face of significant resistance, and in the absence of any compelling argument of vital U.S. national security needs?

It seems that the notion of "weak dominoes" is not enough to convince the public of the need for this costly, challenging effort.

***

In 1969, the time had come to disobey an obviously illegal order, an unconstitutional order. I had wrongly obeyed it too long.

It took 7,000 pages to show that there was never:

—a good reason for our war
—a good reason for the lies or secrecy
—anyone saying "But that would be wrong."

Nothing in the Pentagon Papers, the history or current realities, remotely justifies the wrong we are doing in Vietnam—or the lies and subversion of democracy at home.

I had to decide what I should do with these historical analyses. I acted after significant reflection, spurred by my experience of the problem and the effects of secrecy.

Far too many secrets are kept. Secrecy is endemic in nearly all bureaucratic institutions. It is maintained almost entirely (especially in the U.S.) by practices, attitudes, and sanctions outside of criminal prosecution.

Those *without* access can't judge the scale of the problem, while those *with* access can't act on it—or even discuss it—without those actions changing their whole careers.

***

Should there be any secrets? Yes, if guarded by a system with safeguards against abuse.

Safeguards are needed to prevent:

—too many secrets
—the wrong kind of secrets for the wrong motives
—secrets from the wrong people

—secrets kept too long
—secrets determined by one branch
—secrets determined by one person, with no monitoring, review, appeal, or declassification.

(The exception: confidential advice that is given to the President by an individual personal advisor with direct access to the President. This cannot be demanded by Congress.)

It would be better to have no formal secrecy system, no administrative or criminal sanctions or rules, than to preserve the present set of practices and understandings.

No embarrassment to any nation in the world is more dangerous to that nation, and to all nations, including ours, than the U.S. public's ignorance of how and why and in whose interests our government acts.

He who controls the past controls the future, and he who controls the present controls the past.[14]

Those who keep our past secrets condemn us to repeat them.

You cannot spend a generation overthrowing popular governments and suppressing self-determination abroad without endangering self-determination at home.

From Will Durant, *The Story of Philosophy*:

"It has been the one song of those who thirst after absolute power that the interest of the state requires that its affairs should be conducted in secret . . .

"They who can treat secretly the affairs of a nation have it absolutely under their authority; and as they plot against the enemy in time of war, so do they against the citizens in time of peace."

***

I was the only full-time student of "Lessons." It was my goal, my aim, my dream to get the Executive to improve its intelligence operations by learning, studying past errors, and looking at track records.

See, for example, my Crisis Study.[15]

Elements of my background that lend authority to my expert witness testimony:

- —I am a former hawk, a U.S. Marine Corps lieutenant, and rifle company commander.
- —I have a PhD in Economics from Harvard.
- —As a specialist in decision-making under uncertainty, I was an analyst for the Departments of Defense and State, focusing initially on U.S. nuclear policies and risks before switching to a focus on Vietnam.
- —I worked at the RAND Corporation and was viewed as a "whiz kid."
- —I was a consultant to Henry Kissinger and a researcher on the Pentagon Papers.
- —I worked on NSSM-1 [a 1969 memo about Vietnam options], and I was the sole researcher on an interagency study of the lessons of past foreign policy crises.

In short, I had seen the evidence. I had the "inside dope."

***

I felt guilt over not being sentenced—and I felt guilt about feeling relieved about that.

***

"Don't trust any *war* over 30."

Our war against Vietnamese independence is entering its 29th year. FDR and Truman supported French sovereignty, tolerated "misuse" of U.S. aid, and ignored Vietnamese appeals for support for independence.[16]

When 1976 comes, "by the rockets' red glare, our bombs bursting in air," will our flag *still* be there?

The problem of this war is hard. A war that has gone on for 29 years has not been generated by a system that is easy to change.

Yet a difference *can* be made—even by efforts of small scale or risk.

Note that the risks won't remain small if we don't undertake those efforts *now*.

By a historical accident and a unique configuration of 1971's politics, a spotlight was put onto me and onto the larger efforts to demonstrate just how "wrong" our nation's policy was. It revealed how frightened the Government was of truth, honesty, disobedience, and freedom.

The Administration's response to my action was part of a larger chain of events that brought it down.

What would have happened in Vietnam if there had been no antiwar activists?

No effort was "too much," and nothing that was done was less than essential. Thousands of lives were saved.

As Tran Ngoc Chau said, "We lived useful lives."

***

The media plays a role in its coverage of civil disobedience by generally denigrating it.

In response to my civil disobedience, I am accused of believing that "the means justifies the ends." In fact, I acted *because* I took Means seriously.[17]

For me, breaking the law was not a Means; it was a *consequence* of my Means, which were: telling the truth, ceasing to conceal, and sharing what I knew with Congress and the public.

At the time I thought that letters, lobbying, vigils, and rallies brought little concern to Nixon and had little effect. The Watergate tapes—and what we now know of what Nixon's plans would have been otherwise—show that I was wrong.

***

How to live one's life? With whom? For what?

What to do? And why try?

Because:

Things can get much worse—but this *can* be averted.

Small successes are possible and are worth great effort.

The stakes are moral, human, and ecological.

Sometimes people say admiringly to me, "If I had your guts . . . ," then they go on to tell me stories of their own lives of truth-telling, risk-taking, and system-bucking.

What they admire in me is what they respect in themselves, privately, without being able to boast. Perhaps they doubt that it is even respectable. But they tell me about it, knowing that I will want to know—as I do.

What they are most grateful for is the confirmation that *they are not alone,* and *they are not crazy.* (See Orwell, *1984.*)

Exercise freedom and responsibility for your whole life.

Throw in your whole weight, not occasional involvement.

Accept the risks of freedom and commitment, instead of the risks of obedience and conformity.

And if you feel locked in: Are you helping your children to escape?

1975

I grew up with a certain "given" set of answers imposed by Authority, learning false answers to questions such as:

- —"Why was I born?" (*to become a concert pianist*)
- —"Why am I doing what I'm doing?" (*ditto*)
- —"Who am I working for?" (*Mother*)
- —"What are, and are not, my viable alternatives?" (*this question was not permitted to be asked*)
- —"Do my mother and father care for my independent desires and concerns as distinct from their own?" (*ditto*)

Consider the manipulative processes that prevented such questions from coming to awareness earlier: tacit threats, lies, concealments, the imposition and acceptance of subordination, the protective suppression of anger and resentment. At its heart was the conditionality of supposed "Mother-love," with the looming potential sanction of its total withdrawal at any time.

If, as Mrs. Leonard said, my piano was keeping my parents' marriage together: Was my exploration of my selfhood the *cause* of the imminent breakup of the family? With my increasing independence, the family fell apart, and my rival (my sister) and my deceiver/manipulator (my mother) died.

It was my father's hostility to my mother, his despair, and his fatal, homicidal subordination to her hateful haste and unloving demands that led to her death.

***

During my time in the Marines, I was a platoon leader who protected his troops by arguing against the overeager company commander.

Company Commander: "The only thing that will work is to send all these taxis together up the road."

Me: "That is absurd. Can you imagine what would happen under artillery?"

It concerned me that if/when I left the platoon, the troops would no longer have a protector.

Some of my peak experiences:

- —The exercise choreographing tanks in OCS [Officer Candidate School].
- —Earlier: lying on the ground under helmet and pack, looking at ants close up.
- —That night: in my tent, in the rain.
- —Total absorption in finishing my draft of BNSP[18] on 4/7/61, just before the Bay of Pigs.

***

There have been times in my life when total despair for humanity would not have depressed me or caused me to resign from effort and life. But I am not sure this is one of them.

To live without illusion? If reality is, obviously, conclusively, what it seems likely to be, then I think I prefer some degree of illusion or doubt.

***

At Concord Bridge: "They came 3,000 miles and died."[19]

They died because they had come to impose a foreign rule from a capital 3,000 miles away. In the end, they were no match for people who were determined to govern themselves.

Now the Capitol and White House are distanced from most towns in the U.S.—indeed, from the ghetto in Washington, D.C.—by more than miles. They are distanced by a concentration of power that inoculates its holders from knowledge of, let alone human empathy and concern for, the needs and desires of most of those who share the same language and history and traditions.

Actually, they do *not* share the same history, because the history that is most relevant to policymakers is *secret*.

***

By 1968, there were few believers in the war. It was widely expected that it would be over by 1969 no matter which candidate won, as both had pledged to end it. That is how democracy is supposed to work.

But the war did not end. By 1974, four and a half megatons of bombs had been dropped.

The bureaucrats "did their jobs." Those who could no longer do so with a good conscience did them with a bad conscience.

They were like the French torturer in Algeria, described in Frantz Fanon's *The Wretched of the Earth*, who had insomnia, nightmares, and anxiety about his terrible job. He went to a psychiatrist so that he could do his job without these symptoms.

***

Can one find any segment of U.S. society that had an interest in continuing the war, an ideology to justify doing so, or power to achieve it?

Yes: those whose economic interests are worldwide, who are threatened by economic nationalism anywhere. Their interests would be endangered by the example and precedent set for nationalists everywhere, if forces fighting for independence won a victory in Vietnam.

The threat of falling dominoes is not primarily of Communist regimes, but of actions by regimes (whether left or right) to control the benefits of their own resources, such as nationalizing industries, raising prices, or establishing import restrictions.

Kissinger said, "Let's, for God's sake, see this as a serious matter on which reasonable men can disagree, and where all morality and human concern is not on our side. When there is a matter of U.S. influence and credibility, it is a moral commitment."

***

The loss of awareness of evil, of the meaning of what one does, is the evil of our time.

What does it take to get evil done? What does it take to get someone to do something he would normally regard as evil—or to do right, to stop, to disobey?

What sort of personality is required to carry out torture?

Milgram's answer: an order from an authority, which leads the person to see himself as an agent, an instrument—i.e., not responsible.[20]

(Note the difficulty of inducing autonomous, spontaneous human decision-making, once the subject starts to obey such an order.)

Hypothesis: lesser evils lead to greater evils.

***

In late 1963 and 1964, after the Cuban Missile Crisis, I set out to examine crises as a form of "communicating to an enemy."

Instead, I became aware of crisis behavior as a form of communicating to, concealing from, or misleading a *domestic* audience.

"Necessity is the mother of deception." In a crisis, urgent necessity facilitates the exercise of imagination in inventing a "suitable, plausible, convincing, useful lie."

Why did I *never* hear anyone raise the question "Is this right?"

Why were ethical or moral principles never mentioned?

The only questions raised were:

—Will this work?

—Is it expedient?
—Is it worth the risk?
—Will we get away with it?

Corruption is easiest and strongest when it is non-conscious. Hence the role and function of self-deception as to one's working goals and actions—sources of one's identity and values, autonomy, and cues for action and opinions.

Hypothesis: the very concept of "conscience" simply doesn't apply to organizational behavior.

Bureaucracies provide a way to unhook from a sense of personal responsibility—and hence, from the critique or inhibition of conscience—through the agentic mode of obeying legitimate authority.

In 1961, Gary Snyder presented me with "an alternative way of being." The memory stuck, and in 1970, I set out to see him again.[21]

By then I was in a "different line of work" from the bureaucrats: telling the truth about the war—not "the" truth, but truths compared to the usual reporting. I was resisting Authority and the war, taking risks of my career and reputation—and later, my freedom.

My committed, risk-taking behavior was the same as, or inspired by the same values as, a large class of critics of the war, consisting of many young people, along with a relatively few Radical Outsiders my age or older.

A much larger class of insiders disliked the war without resisting it. However, I had a peculiar, unique background and character traits not shared by other insiders: guilt over my role in Vietnam, and a big secret to impart.

Young people have more intense consciences (especially social conscience) and feeling of responsibility for the plight of others. They decry society's failure to live up to their ideals, many of which they share.

***

What is actualization within a very sick society, or a highly repressive one?

Is it healthy to be in a state of constant resistance, perhaps without much immediate apparent effect—or perhaps without any effect?

Is it healthy to feel constantly guilty, powerless, cowardly, and compliant for *not* doing so?

If I am willing to "kill for my country," am I also willing to torture? lie? starve other people? subvert democracy?

Learn to be angry about the right things.

***

We are in a stage of overt struggle to expand or contract our Democracy.

I suspect the current system is not viable. I choose to work for human freedom to enlarge, in hopes of having a free and humane future—indefinite or not.

***

After a Conversation with Dave Dellinger[22]:

Dave says we need to combine personal humanity and politics and create oases of practical love and trust. We need to join the political and the personal, the spiritual and the material—to defend against despair and sustain a sense of continuity and meaning.

Individual enlightenment and individual example are no longer adequate to create the changes in consciousness that could prevent species-suicide (which may prove to be humans' karma, whatever "we" do).

We must work to change values, as well as the structures and conditioning of society—from loyalty, not to tribe, but across nationality to humanity, life, Earth; from bureaucratization to humanism; awakening from hypnotic, patriotic, bureaucratic slumber to open our own eyes and say "no" to power.

***

How am I to live my life? What is the future of humanity and all life, and how may my life relate to that?

Is there a way out? Is there another way to live together with neighbors, countrymen, humanity, nature, and our whole selves?

I am seeking wisdom, enlightenment. I am studying, meditating, seeking teachers, looking for explanations and examples of humans and societies.

Pat notes that meditation is *a* way, not *the* way.

Mystical experience, feeling, insight come not only or mainly from meditation. Awakening can hit at unpredictable moments of daily living, often in nature.

Do separate waves in the ocean exist? Yes, for some purposes, such as when we are riding a wave and trying to stay on top.

It is also true that waves are continuously undergoing a change of form.

Moral: kinship, even "oneness," does not annihilate meaningful, creative, beautiful (or not) differentiation!

Our society has effectively secularized most activities—except for a sanctification of the State, National Security, obedience to the rules, and individual acquisitive success. This secularization is based in individualization, isolation, and selfishness, alongside the loss of community and the impulse toward mutual obligation.

This does not seem a sufficient basis for values, goals, and actions that satisfy *all* our innate instincts and desires, that permit us to achieve fulfillment, satisfaction, and serenity.

On the national level, it leads to behavior that can increasingly be seen to be suicidal, as well as homicidal and oppressive.

In the artificial environment of cities, people are removed from participating in natural cycles of plant and animal creation and growth cycles. They are also sheltered from the vicissitudes of the natural world.

The total consumption of oil 50 years ago was 5% of present day, and the total transport of oil across oceans 50 years ago was less than the amount of spillage now.

We need a return to self-sufficiency, with trade the exception. California could have five or six largely self-sufficient regions.

What if humanity was a fatal error for Earth?

The dangers to species and Earth began to appear in the last 5,000 years, especially the last 100 to 300 years.

Even if glimmers of a wrong turn can be seen in pre-Socratic Greek scientific theorizing, objectifying things—that's only 2500 years ago. It's hard to conclude that it was inevitably in human genes for us to become a threat to the Earth itself.

Does history have direction? Is it good (for humans)?

The period of written history has had, for its subject, the last, decaying phase of the human species. What may await us: extinction by pollution, totalitarianism, or one or more cataclysms.

Yet, a basis for joy still exists. Humanity may transcend its present direction and survive longer, in which case there will probably be some return to Neolithic-like smallness, community, being-in-Nature, and sacredness of Life and Reality.

***

We evaluate the world as if we had chosen it or constructed it—as if we had discovered a continent, or chosen a distant vacation site, or planned and constructed a model city.

But *this Earth evolved us*. To say that it chose us, planned and constructed us, or found us might be somewhat misleading—but less so than the reverse statements, or any assertion of totally independent evolution of Earth and us.

Act on the hypothesis that it is the will, purpose, aim of the Cosmos that the human species should survive a while longer—and that its creative, evolutionary, aesthetic usefulness is not at an end.

Act as if the Cosmos *wanted* humans and spiritual virtues to flourish—at least, in our lifetimes, and well into mid-term posterity.

Reality is the simultaneity of great horrors and great beauty.

***

My alternative to sharing the truth was to live outside jail as a knowing accomplice of war. Small as the chance seemed of influencing the war's course, releasing the Papers was by far the most effective nonviolent act available to me.

My isolation after the trial was immediate, stressful, and very prolonged. There was a feeling of being unable to cope, fighting hopelessness.

I was an ordinary, smart, somewhat bold and original intellectual—a minor, subordinate official—who happened to notice that history demanded and allowed me to take a dangerous, but perhaps significant, act. The effectiveness of my action was magnified in unexpected ways by certain other players and events.

Now I am returning to my former area of interest: the nuclear problem. I have known this to be my fate, my task, since 1960.

1976

I wanted to be loved by my parents for something other than piano. It had to be some form of excellence, wit, intelligence. In fact, I demanded this desperately.

Demands made on me for eventual achievement in piano were unattainable. Each test brought the eventual catastrophe and disillusionment nearer, sparking despair, shame, and guilt as I anticipated my future failure.

When I delayed practicing a piece for a piano recital, was I using my lateness to exercise power over my otherwise omnipotent mother?

What should my father have done, when he realized "who I was" and saw that Mother's wishes were not right for me?

I was systematically misunderstood in my motives and feelings. I longed to be understood, and to be seen for who I was.

***

I preferred relatively isolated, independent work within organizations. I rejected executive responsibilities, except for *The Advocate* and the U.S. Marine Corps.

I was good in the U.S. Marine Corps chain of command. I used the confidence of my bosses to win a sphere of autonomy.

For me, the authority-power figure that I was confronting was the entire Establishment, not a single individual. These dynamics mirrored my relation to my parents in that I felt used, coerced, let down, and betrayed by those who should have been allies.

Also relevant: the dynamics of passive complicity, relating to my father.

***

The function of an education at an elite university is to learn inattention and passivity, to learn to disconnect your daily work from the moral values of your family upbringing—sharing, love, trust, mutual dependence—and be part of maintaining a system of inequality, privilege, unnecessary suffering, war, and risk of extinction.

After talking with Robert about Harvard:[23]

At Harvard, you learn that the rules that apply to less intelligent people don't apply to you. You don't flunk out. You don't get expelled. In fact, being able to break rules or fail to fulfill course requirements and lie your way out of things is rewarded as much as really knowing and caring about a subject.

Graduates of elite universities understand things, explain things, manage things, and produce things—but they don't change things. Their knowledge is technical, not practical; it is not shaped to be acted on.

You can study anything, as long as you don't act on it.

You can study history, as long as you don't learn from it.

***

One should look again, and harder, at the supposed non-wrongfulness of the cause one has earlier believed to be just and good. Vietnam is a warning of how far, and how easily, such justification can be distorted, stretched, abused—a warning that became clearer as the war went on.

It *does* have effects elsewhere to demonstrate that a nationalist or revolutionary movement can frustrate and, with the help of U.S. dissenters, defeat U.S. efforts to dominate their country. However, we do not have the right to kill Vietnamese in order to avoid those efforts, to negate that awareness, or for any other reason.

***

When faced with a hopeless situation, the System is capable of staying out of overt involvement. But once overt involvement is reached—or, in cases of significant local interest and/or immediate risk of the Domino Effect—the System has no "Get Out" switch. Nor does it have a "Lose" switch. It does have a "Cool It, Slow Down, Go No Higher" switch.

If the costs of war become high, the objective is to win quickly—if possible, before the next election. Once costs are high, *expect* election promises of restraint. These promises will likely be broken right after the election.

***

Death, *per se*, appears to me to be neither evil nor bad; and birth, growth, and life appear neither necessarily good nor obligatorily to be brought about or prolonged.

However, the *imposition* of death, pain, or radical unfreedom on others in pursuit of one's selfish advantage—or in support of an order one understands to be wrong, unjust, or evil—is clearly wrong.

"Bravery" is based on the belief that one is fated to die young—say, between 25 and 45. Moreover, one believes he will probably die shamefully, in failure and rejection, "if death is left until the last moment." Therefore, one's death is one's own, to choose to use. One can shape its circumstances and pick the purposes it may serve.

Something is lost by dying sooner than is inevitable, but not so much as for others. Something is also gained: the dignity of being the master of one's life and death, of cheating fate—and meanwhile, the excitement and satisfaction of living boldly, of fearing death less than others, of serving causes fearlessly.

The difference that age makes is not about "closeness to death" or "shortness of life." I've always lived with those, having failed every time to "die on schedule."

***

Certain kinds of revelations of one's own values have a change-producing effect on others' values—and even on oneself, by clarifying one's own consciousness and conscience.

Any policy can be justified by some hypothetical "info."

***

Observance of certain limits, putting them above "subsidiary" goals and values, defined the social identities of my former comrades in government.

In releasing the Pentagon Papers, I was not merely acting on an expanded notion of freedom of choice; I was *changing who I was* socially—redefining it, exposing it in a new light.

One's values can never be lived out as if they were supreme and absolute. It is not just *what* you do. There is also the question of *how* you do something, and in what spirit, aim, and expectation you do it.

I am—emotionally, physically, spiritually—a very *ordinary* person. I am not worse and not better than most. I am stronger in verbal and intellectual skills, but that does not seem critical, any more than my relative weaknesses and lacks.

What I did, what I risked was *not* unique, or even close to it. Nor was it ordinary.

That such useful, desirable action is accessible to *ordinary* people may be a more encouraging demonstration than the performance of an evidently extraordinary saint or hero.

***

There's a great contrast between my TV interview/lecturer personality and the "Lenny Bruce," "Whiz Kid" adventurer.

I read a piece on me based on an interview, and I see a 45% misunderstanding of what I said. The article has turned it into bland near-gibberish.

I wonder: Why do I keep hoping *someone else* will write down my views?

***

Note the length of my concern with ethics: nuclear weapons, since August 6th, 1945; strategic bombing, since 1942; and truth vs. lies since childhood (the piano and Christian Science).

***

I retired, or "was retired," in April 1970 at age 40.

It was like a military officer retiring after 20 years of habituation to a way of life.

When one is depressed, everything bad becomes linked to one's responsibility and guilt.

I fear depressing and discouraging my friends. I feel shame at confessing my weakness and depression, after having become admired and successful. I fear losing this newly acquired respect.

Someone described a deep depression as "It is as if one had lost his ego." *Yes*.

See, for example, my indecision, procrastination, despair, apathy, lack of plans for the future, and feeling a lack of value in the world and in myself.

Jean-Nicolas Bouilly said, "Depression arises as a result of the disorganization of behavior patterns which is consequent on the loss of a significant object or goal in the external world... It is when active interchange between ourselves and the external world has ceased that depression occurs."

Hypothesis: The end of the war will produce widespread depression and disorientation among activists. This would be hard to admit to oneself, since one *should* be happy.

***

Did I have an "obsessive" concern with Vietnam?

Do I have a "compulsion" to read *everything* on a given subject?

I have a desire not to be understood *wrongly*—hence, too quickly.

Looking ahead, what do I want to be? How do I want to be seen?

How can we improve humans' lives *in this lifetime*?

Gandhi brought love, compassion, nonviolence, and Satyagraha to the suffering caused by human social institutions and practices.[24]

***

When, and under what conditions, was war and preparation for war *not* the principal activity or central stabilizer of states, economies, and social systems?

The threat of nuclear destruction runs counter to every moral value.

If nuclear weapons are defined as "permitted," "moral," or "necessary," then what *can* be forbidden? What is wrong ... evil; what is to be resisted, exposed, and denounced, if not preparing the means of nuclear annihilation?

The idea that Human = Humane is either a worthy aspiration or a species-self-serving denial. "Inhuman" does not equal "unhuman" or "non-human." Nothing is more characteristic of humans than, in certain not-unusual circumstances, to be inhumane.

My concern is to turn the values of our society toward survival—toward moderation, nonviolence, and nurture—so that both men and women exhibit more of these values.

Such values are not compatible, or at least not likely, within the present, mainly-male power structure and its orientation toward power-seeking.

Nor is such a change likely if women simply join male power-seeking.

Where does one look for hope that humans *can* be different?

***

Is it too late for humanity?

Will a future catastrophe be what lowers our population? Nuclear war? Climate? A new ice age?

Is humanity doomed, whatever it does, to a fairly quick extinction that will be shameful, frustrating, and agonizing?

Lecture title: "Is There Any Reason to Hope?"

The short answer is: *yes*.

1977

I recall a teacher running in the hall at school on April 12th, gleefully saying, "Roosevelt's dead." It was five days after my 14th birthday.

My social studies teacher brought a Nisei [a U.S.-born citizen whose parents immigrated from Japan] to our class to discuss U.S. concentration camps for Japanese people as well as the problem of cultural lag. This had prepared me for unease on August 6, 1945.

Soon after, August 6th told me that my country *had* gotten the bomb and had used it—"just like other weapons."

That class in high school changed my life. It taught me that technology might have outrun human compassion.

Robert said to Berrigan[25] and me, "Our technological capability has at last caught up with our moral vacuity."

From age 10 to 14 and after, I fantasized about fighting an anti-life, anti-freedom enemy like the Nazis—thus, Stalin's Russians, or what they might become if tempted.

But from August 6th, 1945, on, I secretly watched my own country as well, to monitor—and to resist—any signs of evildoing. I never told anyone this, but I had guidelines in my own mind of what I must not do, what must be resisted.

Looking out the window, I began to sob, putting my head in my hands.

***

The Accident that killed my mother and sister happened the year after the Bomb was dropped. This "killing" by my father . . . (by me?!) was, secretly, my "liberation." This secret was not to be discussed with my father or anyone else.

I thought of another secret, "a thought racing behind me," for 32 years:

My country had done something very, very wrong that could end human life.

How could we?

***

Humans' capacity for empathy is low-to-none with certain humans whom they have come to perceive as "the other." This is especially the case if pain, deprivation, or death has been inflicted on those identified "others"—especially from a distance, and especially "on command."

After the bomb was dropped on the Japanese people, I was told that this action by the U.S. was "necessary" and "justified" by the great evil we were fighting and the threat that it posed.

"If you can contemplate killing 100 million people, you can contemplate anything—and you do." —Sidney Lens

***

DE as:

—Someone with inside knowledge and a feeling of obligation, on the basis of past role

—Someone who "switched teams," broke a promise, "exposed dirty linen," betrayed a President and a Presidency, and sacrificed career, government role, and membership in the Elite

—Someone over 35 who learned, changed, took risks, and told the truth

No war is to be explained solely or predominantly in economic terms.

Don't look for exclusive alternative explanations.

Consider over-determination and harmonies of interest—look there.

I felt calm about copying the Pentagon Papers and wrecking RAND.

I was going to be punished worse than they were.

It was as if I had prepared a fatal car accident, knowing that I would suffer the agonies of a broken knee, which would prevent me from being stricken by guilt.

Hence, I felt unease when it turned out that I was not punished at all.

Prior to 1977 I did not feel guilt, although Pat said I should have.

I opposed the bombing and psyops, I rejected targets, etc. (Yet—*I knew!*)

What I *didn't* know about: Indonesia, Cuba, Brazil, Chile.

Now, today, after the Church Report,[26] I feel like Speer, reasonably or not: *shame* at the government and the whole counter-revolutionary crusade with which I was associated and identified.

The U.S. government acted *much* worse than I suspected. Its aims were bad, not just its means.

All, not just part, of my motives for ignorance were suspect. I *could* have known, and I *should* have known (although I was subject to expert manipulation, as well as risk and prohibition).

I am depressed at my loss of identity, self, and self-esteem.

The crisis of one's 40s is discovering the limits of one's own identity up until then—and the belief that it is now too late, or too much trouble, to create a new identity at 45. Indeed, the very need to do so implies a crushing individual failure.

I was not a hawk in the sense of a believer in violence and threats and U.S. domination, but in the sense of a passionate lover of my country, of certain of its ideals and notions of itself and its aspirations and potentials.

I believed in the basic goodness of the intention and practice of the Presidency.

I remain separated, by emotion and identification, from those of a later generation who, by political influence (Left or Pacifist) or historical perspective (born after World War II) are free of emotional, deferential love of country, of flag, of the idea of America as well as trust in the State.

I have fallen out of love with the State and its Establishment, and I have regained a hopeful affection in the democratic ideal, process, and people who are untouched by power—those outside the base of the existing pyramid of obstruction, power, and privilege.

***

Responsibility: In denying that a situation is within our control—that we are mainly responsible—we hope that we will be spared regret, shame, guilt, reproach, humiliation, rage, frustration, and penalties in other spheres.

Individuals within organizations may be freer in certain respects, in that they feel protected from personal responsibility through their unquestioning obedience.

Yet in another sense, they are *less* free: to be disobedient, to apply separate moral or other judgment, or to speak, initiate, or question.

Katherine White says to accept the evil in yourself, rather than projecting it onto others. Accept it as part of life, of the Cosmos, of humanity, of yourself. Know that evil is born of energies that can be creatively directed otherwise.

Imagine living—even briefly!—without guilt, shame, bitterness, anxiety, or resentment.

Choosing "what to die for" or what to sacrifice for is a form of autonomy.

***

If I am willing to die for my country, shouldn't I also be willing to go to jail for my country? To lose my reputation and my career? To risk my relationships with my neighbors?

A common characteristic of evil is the use of another as "other"—or, as Milgram demonstrated, the acceptance of oneself as a "mere agent," an "instrument."

The dictionary definition of "sin" is "a condition of estrangement from God as a result of having broken one of His laws." That is, it is a condition of shame, the result of a guilt-producing act.

Evidently God's love, closeness, and concern are conditional.

Perhaps most of what people experience as "Christian guilt" is really *shame*—fear not of punishment, retaliation but of being *cast out*, estranged, rejected, abandoned, exiled.

Most human-caused destruction, suffering, death, and enslavement (i.e., "evil") is performed by men, at the direction of men. These are typically "normal," competent, personally agreeable, and compassionate men who perform their acts in obedience to lawful orders—or, less often, in obedience to *unlawful* orders.

These acts are performed in good conscience, with neither guilt nor shame. Indeed, guilt and shame deter *disobedience* of orders to do evil.

Obedience is impelled in large part by nationalism, patriotism, group loyalty, and respect for authority. It is encouraged and supported, by the Establishment and most teachers, politicians, intellectuals, dramatists, and priests.

***

The U.S. is built on slavery, genocide, and continental expansion. This is hard for me to say in public.

We and our leaders use many devices to shield us from learning certain historic lessons. One such device is the notion that the Germans were uniquely evil. "Morally, the Germans are fundamentally different. Evil is defined as what the Germans did."

If the term "evil" is only allowed to describe what "they," our "enemies," have done, then it is useless. Actually, it is worse than useless, because it prevents us from facing important, relevant realities and keeps us from learning the lessons of past events.

To oppose the destruction of the human family and our Home, it may be helpful to evoke the concept of Evil—not in its current usage referring to a "foreign enemy" or a "dissident," but to reinforce individual conscience and a stronger identification with other humans and the living, interdependent ecosystem.

What created this threat to us, to posterity, to the species, was a process of Evil.

***

In this era of the potentially imminent extinction of most of life on Earth, there is now a moral dimension to every aspect of how one spends one's life. The foundation of all morality is that we must now live with awareness of the mortality of our species and the vulnerability of the Earth and all life.

Q: What is your aspiration?
A: To postpone human extinction, give pause to the process, to slow it down, to encourage reflection and resistance—to "un-tape the safety switches."

***

So what's new? For me, a new member of my karass,[27] named Michael Gabriel Ellsberg.

What will the U.S. be doing 18 years from now?

We are called to change our country—starting with ourselves, our lives—to help assure that, in important ways, the next 25 years will be nothing like the last 25 years . . . for Michael, and for all the world's children.

Every aspect of coming-to-life, passing-on-life, living and growing, is miraculous, mysterious, wonderful.

1978

I was shaped to believe that the standards that I must meet were my own internal standards of excellence, artistry, dedication, self-evaluation, and effort—none of which were satisfied by the acclaim of audience or critics. There was an obligation not to perform in public, but to *practice*—long, right, and well. That was the pianist's test that I could and did meet.

Practicing right (no great penalty for mistakes; do it again, better) was adequate for day-to-day relations with Mother, as well as for my own guilt maintenance. To "practice right" included feeling guilty when not practicing, valuing nothing higher (such as reading or sports), cramming for recitals, and feeling at best unsatisfied by my performance.

Performance, however, was a test that threatened total failure of Mother's hopes, hence of the relationship. Thus, a recital was to be risked only when it couldn't be avoided, or when poor performance could be explained in ways that didn't conclusively destroy someone's [Mother's] hopes.

"Promise," or "talent," was my cross, my destiny, my sentence. It was used to trick and enslave me into accepting a particular definition of myself and my desires and capabilities.

"You have unlimited talent. Therefore, you have a responsibility, and obligation, to develop your gifts. Otherwise, you are denying others and your own higher self, and you are being a bad person."

In all of this, I was unaware that I was paying a burdensome price, and that there were other things I preferred to do or be.

I looked at those who had "left the piano" with the same disdain that members of the Estate look at me.

The Accident taught me that a father was capable of doing great harm to a mother or sister by being "out of control." This was analogous to my reaction to the bombing of Hiroshima, 11 months earlier.

I had a notion that I "owed a death."

(Note my boldness in Vietnam in driving the roads!)[28]

What I had bought, what I had been given, was only a respite—borrowed time.

***

I have been possessed by a "need to know," by questions that didn't bother others.

Looking at my need to control (or to abstain from) dialogue, with either lecturing or silence:

—Do I feel a need to conceal? What, if so?
—Do I fear questions? being found out? finding out about myself?
—What am I afraid to find out about myself?

***

One of my central puzzlements in the analysis of power and coercion was *how to make a decision under uncertainty.*

How does one recognize and express uncertainty, yet act in spite of it—and act appropriately and reasonably?

Howard Zinn said that if violence is ever to be justified, the evidence must be overwhelming and clear. The greater the proposed violence, the greater must be both the magnitude of the social good and the certainty that it will be achieved by the violent methods—*and would not be achieved without them.*

***

After talking to Allen Ginsberg: I feel guilt and shame at what I have left undone over the years, and what I managed to be ignorant of. My anguish at the thought that we will destroy all the cities reflects my residual identification with the people, institutions, and class that will be mainly responsible for this.

I need, now, to undertake a change of identity—to discover how we have been lied to and manipulated, and how we have complied and remained ignorant.

***

At Rocky Flats: Before, Rockwell said they didn't want to arrest us after all—they decided to let the rain, snow, and hail evict us. They said we could stay as long as we liked, since "they didn't need the track."[29]

Now they say, after asking for our arrest, that [by sitting on the tracks], we did indeed obstruct a vital access route and impede their normal operations. We were "on the right track."

What could be more useful work than "sitting"?

We have a very "conservative" aim: to save the world and all that lives in it, to preserve it for our children—for all children.

An impending catastrophe looms ahead that can and must be avoided. Action is needed to avert both the catastrophe itself and the crisis actions that would be taken by authoritarians either in the face of the immediate threat or after the event.

At Rocky Flats, Forrest Williams said, "Live as if you had hope, as if you made a difference. Live an exemplary life. Do what is right in front of you."

1979

On my writing block and the piano:
    Practice: yes. *Perform*: at peril, with a risk of possible disaster.
    The "rewards" were not worth it. The audience was uncontrolled and unpredictable. There was no assurance of any feedback or reward.

"What counts are your own standards."
    Me: "Why perform, then? Why publish?"
"You owe it to yourself."
    Me: "Says who?"
"You know you really want to do it."
    Me: "Oh yeah?"
"You owe it to humanity."
    Me: "Oh? Why?"

By not writing, I pay the cost of forgoing the insights that are part of the writing process.

***

Why do I feel deep despair when I am late, despite my prior planning and my intention to prevent it? Or when I look for a missing paper and am confronted with my unfinished notes, tasks, and disorganization?

I have a problem with deadlines: being late to meetings, rushing to catch planes. As the appointed time approaches, I think of *other* unmet obligations, errands, tasks to be done. I calculate the time needed too narrowly, with no time for error or unfavorable conditions. Then when I phone ahead to ask for a later time, I underestimate the time needed for the delay.

I dawdle over the paper in the morning, lie in bed, dream more, while neglecting exercise, meditation, or time with Michael.

I formulate certain "needs" (people to call, materials to get) but never seem to attend to them.

I answer the phone, read for hours, then make last-minute lunch dates—to which I typically arrive late.

***

En route to Rocky Flats: Large, hierarchical organizations bring out certain potentialities and traits in leaders and in followers. The leader sees himself as a tough, patriarchal warrior-hero. The follower sees himself as part of the whole, as "self-respecting," obedient, loyal, disciplined, and patriotic.

In both leader and follower, there is an identification with grandiose, infantile, archaic fantasies of absolute power with no limits.

Absolute destructive power brings the belief that one is entitled to absolute authority, absolute compliance, absolute obedience, and absolute control—with no law or conscience holding the leader back.

One may follow, feeling that they have no choice because:

—no alternative course exists.
—if I do otherwise, they will kill me or hunt me or imprison me or my family.
—if I do otherwise, they will withhold trust, respect, promotions, job, membership.
—it is wrong to refuse to obey, and I will feel shame and guilt if I do.

***

"My Country, right or wrong."

For me this means, "My Country—when right, to be kept right; and when wrong, to be set right."

I became sickened with government lies to which I had been party. I decided not to lie any more for the U.S. government, or for anyone else. This posed the obligation to tell the truth, which I had the opportunity to do—at the cost of risking prison, but with the hope of freeing the public to influence a move toward peace and against escalation.

An example of "cheerful jail-going" may make it more possible for others to conceive of choosing to disobey wrongful orders.

In Denver court for arraignment for a Rocky Flats arrest:
Boot camp, prison, etc., have procedures designed to remove Shame for acts of unquestioning obedience ... from efforts to please and to conform to the wishes of the Superior.

Civil Disobedience does the reverse: it helps remove the Shame of having *disobeyed*.

We need to rediscover the individualistic morality and distrust of authority that are at the root of the American quest, character, and experience.

At my 5th arrest, on the tracks at Rocky Flats:
For love and democracy, for my love of all life, and for the sake of all living things: *I plead innocent.*

***

Stabilizing command and control systems for nuclear weapons is like "stabilizing" the *Titanic* on its course.

Given the U.S. and Soviet arms buildup, the proliferation of plutonium, regional conflicts, and economic and resource pressures, it is possible that the arms race has now reached a new point of "takeoff" into sustained growth.

Is time running out? Are we approaching—or have we already passed—a crossroads for stabilizing deterrence, averting instability, and reversing or averting a further arms race?

Our human species is newly mortal. But civilizations, administrations, nations, cultures, empires, families, and religions have all faced mortality.

Earth's ecology has survived long enough to support human life, but messing around half blindly with enormously complex systems is a dangerous game.

Murphy's Law: whatever can go wrong *will* go wrong.

1980

I loved my parents. But I had reason to be skeptical, watchful, cautious about them—and by extension, the whole adult world.

***

I am haunted by the possibility that my countrymen will become and behave like the Germans, who accepted and participated in the Holocaust.

See my earlier concern with the behavior, views, and morals of the U.S. government and its supporters and participants—of which I was one!

You must not do evil; you must resist it.

If the concept of lesser evil is admitted, then you must not do evil unless it could be better than a non-evil action, with respect to an overriding goal. In such a case: reconsider, postpone, search, consult, re-weigh, and examine values, models, and inferences.

If you do carry out such an action: do not celebrate it or exaggerate its benefits. Minimize irreversibility, long-term commitment, and psychological and political mobilization. Continue to search and strive unceasingly to recast the problem and seek possible alternatives, with high priority on being able to cease to do evil.

Why do I talk about the sins and flaws of the U.S. government? It is for the same reason that Abbie Hoffman focuses on the faults of the peace movement and Noam Chomsky on intellectuals.

It is not because we "like" others better, or because we identify with them or find them better or more helpful.

It is *the reverse*! We are more concerned and anxious about, and we are more committed to, "us," to good change, and to preventing "worse"—not just in material outcomes, but in *character*.

***

You, too, can be part of a tripwire, a trigger to nuclear war.

Alternatively, you can serve your country by *withdrawing your consent* to the nuclear threats that undergird our foreign policy.

1981

My father fell asleep and lost control at the wheel while in a mood of resentment, humiliation, fatigue, and a desire to be free—a "Monkey's Paw" wish.[30]

The moral of the Monkey's Paw fable is, "Don't tempt fate—and be careful what you wish for."

***

What to do when a prior oath of loyalty comes up against a totally unforeseen, extreme situation involving other loyalties, identifications, and deep concerns—such as God, humanity, nature, truth, individual human lives, or the future?

A commitment to absolute secrecy—especially within an institution with the power of the State, the military/police, or a nuclear physics laboratory—is likely to confront you with such a dilemma: *a previously unimagined conflict of loyalties*. In this situation, one must review, weigh, and re-examine one's loyalties, with serious consideration of self-sacrifice as an alternative to the total sacrifice or disregard of other humans, or principles.

There is no greater wrong that a government can do than to commit a nation to an illegal, illegitimate war.

***

It is worth one's effort, even one's life, to deal with the problem of nuclear weapons and the risk of nuclear war.

Nuclear reactors cause death, not by design, but through accidents, mistakes, ignorance, lack of foresight, and inattention to future life.

In contrast, nuclear weapons are not only designed to explode, but *will* explode, not by being triggered by lightning strike or being dropped, although this is possible.

Nuclear weapons will *kill by human plan and decision*, drawing on a different set of human characteristics and vulnerabilities—including the availability to do evil, a willingness to obey evil orders, and the desire to be a loyal team member.

Given the growth in the number and explosive power of nuclear weapons, the wars that occasion their explosion will be like lightning bolts that catalyze or detonate the larger event. As with a core meltdown of a nuclear reactor, ignorance—coupled with humans' lack of ability to foresee and conceptualize these phenomena—will have played a major part.

***

Michael Nagler[31] says that to moralize, especially absolutely, is to be dualistic, not holistic and dialectical. It is not the immoral "you" versus the moral "me" or "us." It is not evil versus non-evil acts, people, thoughts, motives, or effects.

Risks/downsides to moralizing: alienating others; making oneself unrelatable; provoking feelings of guilt, anger, or aggression; distancing or casting out; and provoking defensive rigidity and denial.

***

Massive injustice, and wars to preserve or extend unjust regimes, are as old as cities.

Military officials often say they abhor war and regard it as evil—"we know what it is really like," they tell us. Yet we would be well advised to read the fine print before delegating them the authority to represent "our" interests and values on matters of war, peace, and nuclear weapons.

Beware of what they may regard as evils greater even than a significant risk of nuclear war or the certainty of non-nuclear war. These may include losing office, prestige, or control of a political party.

(*Quoting Matthew 24:39 in the Bible*): "In those days before the flood people were eating, drinking, taking wives, taking husbands, right up to the day Noah went into the ark. They suspected nothing until the flood came and swept all away."

We live in "those days"—before the war.

We don't live in Egypt as Jews; *we are the Egyptians*.

***

Pat says that civil disobedience is my religion, and that nonviolent direct actions are my rituals, ceremonies, and celebrations of community.

Heard while in San Francisco Jail:
"You can't forbid me everything
you can't forbid me to think
you can't forbid my tears to flow
and you can't stop my voice when I sing."
(German peace activists)

Also heard while in San Francisco Jail:
"What's our dignity worth? You can't buy it.
What's our dignity worth? It's not for sale.
If you put it on a scale, our dignity will prevail.
It's not for sale."
(John Froemer)

1982

I am not ashamed of my time with the Marines, compared to my time at Harvard, RAND, the White House, and the Vietnamese Embassy.

This is because the Marines did not lie. They did not train, plan, celebrate, feint, or intend to massacre innocent people (although this intention was betrayed in Vietnam). They did not participate in, or advise on, decisions to intervene. They did not hate, nor did they generate contempt for the enemy. They were ready to take the risks. They despised nuclear weapons and they despised torture.

***

One of my great self-hatreds is my compulsiveness that usually keeps me from being on time.

It seems that I am unable to do anything other than dawdle and find diverting activities to occupy 10 minutes or so, at the *very moment* I should be departing—that is, a 20-minute distraction starting 10 minutes before the final departure warning. At that point it is too late to make up the time by dropping something else.

Note that this "symptom" is not "habitual lateness" in itself; it is the compulsive, inescapable, out-of-control nature of it.

My compelled lateness reminds me of my furious resentment of the coercion and expectations I dealt with in my piano practice. This resentment underlies and requires the compulsion—which in turn awakens the underlying guilt, hopelessness, self-destructiveness, and loss of relish or desire to live that are associated with my anger toward Mother.

One may need to act out this type of rebellion to avoid a feeling of total enslavement, extinction, and incorporation into the other person's autonomy, being, and identity—of which one becomes no more than an expression. Thus, one's compulsion becomes an alternative to Total Rebellion: to asserting full autonomy in a way that might lead to a severing of the relationship by the crucial person.

This feeling of the badness at my core probably goes back at least to age 2, after I could walk around and express my autonomy from a controlling mother.

I carry self-anger and guilt over my general passivity about Mother and her demands. I was complicit in my own enslavement.

[In releasing the Pentagon Papers], in part I was accepting the prospect of punishment, although for the *wrong* action—that is, as a punishment for my earlier complicity.

***

A long time ago, when I was in college a quarter century ago—when the world was young and right—I wrote a senior honors thesis called "Risk, Ambiguity and Decision."[32]

From my late teens, I grew up in the Church of Decision Theory and Systems Analysis, which had no notion of "good" and "evil"—only "better" or "worse."

***

I feel the urgent need to redeem death and complicity/passivity by facing the truth and discovering secrets, in order to learn lessons, do better, avoid mistakes, and avert catastrophe.

I discovered, with respect to Hiroshima, Vietnam in 1961, and Vietnam as far back as 1946 (which I read about in the Pentagon Papers) that massacre had *not* been a "mistake," unforeseen, or even undesired.

And I discovered that the President ("Father" figure) was culpable.

Massacre is made doable by a chain of command that continually invokes habit, obedience, and career, as well as by leaders' geographical and bureaucratic distance from the killing.

***

I have feared to uncover my own complicity in nuclear war planning from 1958 to 1961.

Even in the Cuban Missile Crisis, I was a hawk. I favored threats, I did not oppose the bombing of missiles, and I was against an oil blockade.

Upon discovering the President's culpability, I acted fast to "prevent more murders." I accepted the probability of punishment for this.

"History is a bath of blood." —William James[33]

1983

On July 4, 1946, my father fell asleep at the wheel and went off the road, killing a woman and child.

Does this underlie my need for vigilance against loved authority?

Should I have been in Gloria's place, saving her and perhaps Mother?

Do I *actually* recall fighting with her for the front seat?

Perhaps my memories are colored by the story Dad told many times about Gloria saying, "I'll sit here if it kills me!"

All survivors think, "Why them—why not me?"

"Am I not responsible?"

"Couldn't I have . . . (fill in the blank)?"

"Did I survive at their expense?"

When an opportunity arises to protect women and children by "just sitting," I feel a strong desire and obligation to do it. I feel similarly when it is time to "wake up the driver"—the Authority, the President.

Dad showed by his example that it is also possible to *kill* by "just sitting"—by falling asleep at the wheel during the ordinary, everyday process of driving.

I wonder what Dad's understanding is of the personal/religious meanings of the Accident.

Even before the Accident, my father refused to protect me at the cost of his own interests in his relationship to Mother. He used my piano-playing and my loyalty. He collaborated in my coercion and the lies about my identity.

On July 4, 1946, I was free to be a man, but I rejected being one like my father. I was critical of, and vigilant toward, my only model of Male Authority.

I did, however, have a model of Male-as-Rebel: my half-brother Harry.

***

My early exposure to the bomb in 1943–45 prepared me to perceive Hiroshima as a danger, an error, and a crime. This dovetailed with the critical lesson I learned in 1946 about the need for vigilance toward Authorities who could kill women and children—including Mother, my sister Gloria, and almost me.

I felt somewhat betrayed in 1969 by the passivity of those I admired. Yet as late as 1973, I saw them as having been deceived themselves—for example, about the "Missile Gap" and our war plans.

Had they actually turned out to be—like my father—passive, depressed, resigned *killers* of women and children?

***

We have created a genocidal option—the Doomsday Machine—in order to prevent "not having it when you 'need it.'"

Awareness of this enters like a splinter into the heart.

Will the violence of an actual nuclear explosion—accident, terrorist, or a "small" nuclear war—awaken humanity to its peril and to the need for action to change history?

***

Our policy is based not only on greed and exploitation and a lack of concern for hungry and poor people, but also—secretly and unaccountably—on lies, deception, murder, support of torture, massacre, extreme oppression, and preparation for hemispheric omnicide.

There is a sense of diminished personal responsibility, that one has no choice in the matter, that one has an obligation, that there are requirements that must be fulfilled "for the greater good" and "to avert greater evil."

All of this is a consequence of bureaucratic compartmentalization, precedent, and consensus.

An organization may be made up of decent, rational humans. However, empathy can be misleading as a basis of predicting or understanding organizational behavior and the prospects for modifying it.

The same is true when one tries to influence or predict the behavior, values, beliefs, or intentions of an individual who is a leader (or a cog) of an organization—even including a state!

Thomas Paine said, "To reason with governments is to argue with brutes."

Power addicts; then it corrupts.

The power-holder seeks to maintain his power, identifying his own power-holding with the health and goals of his organization. In this he differs, often secretly, from nearly everyone else except those directly dependent on him: the "Presidents' Men." His perceptions are corrupted by this identification, as well as by his position.

He will take greater risks—even to organization, country, and humanity—to preserve his power than to preserve his own life. This is the arrogance of power.

To join a larger group may require one, or one's sub-group, to acquire the enemies of the larger group—that is, to develop feelings of enmity to some other group, with this hostility being part of the identity or basis of cohesion of the larger group.

To define one's group in terms of fundamental opposition to identified "enemies" is to take a "fighting stance," reproducing in one's own group many of the very tendencies that are being opposed in the name of a new way.

Organizations do not act with empathy, compassion, or sympathy. They are like machines with non-organic natural processes. Humans within them are ordered, encouraged, permitted, induced to act like machines or parts of machines—without empathy, compassion, or sympathy.

More generally, these people are expected to exercise only a selective, prescribed concern for results, for caused consequences—either of their own acts, or of the organization that they serve, support, and defend.

We need to awaken members of organizations to their humanity.

How can organizational structures be humanized? How can a sense of personal responsibility within organizations be introduced or increased?

***

Certain responses—for example, the carrying out of threats—are regarded as negligibly likely because they would be irrational or self-destructive, and therefore useless.

However, the actors in question are *organizations*: states, bureaucracies, teams. These can arbitrarily and deliberately act in a manner that need not correspond to any humane qualities, even survival or aversion to massacre.

Thus, a threat of arbitrary, irrational, self-destructive or mass destructive behavior *can* be sufficiently credible *if it is organizational behavior.*

In an Authority situation, once an action has been identified as the required action—either by virtue of a specific order, or by calculation that this best meets the needs, interests, and desires of the Superior, Cause, or Mission—then every other course of action becomes "disobedient," or even "disloyal."

Responsibility in organizations is not defined by, or correlated with, what you caused or helped cause to happen, but by what you did relative to what you were authoritatively *supposed* to do. This is at the heart of the admonition, "do your duty."

"Doing one's duty" is determined by one's station in life, one's boss, and what will prevent you from having guilt, shame, or blame attached to you.

Part of the social contract that applies to leaders of organizations and causes is this: if an official can show that his choice was "reasonable" or "best" under the information given or permitted to him by his organization's position (including "official estimates" and prescribed beliefs and values), he is "covered"—no matter what happens to whomever.

Hence, the need for "memos for the record," as well as the preservation or destruction of files, when one foresees that a question may be raised.

One aspect of the appeal of authoritarian regimes like the Soviet Union is that *no one is responsible for anything*. It is a way to manage and allocate guilt, shame, responsibility, self-esteem, membership, and standing.

***

Sometimes it seems that the violent always inherit the earth, and the meek are subject to genocide.

Pat says our foreign policy is based on collective psychosis. An individual behaving this way (for example, Charles Manson) would be institutionalized. But since it is collective, it is considered sane. This insane policy being made by men in a male enclave is, as Pat says, "unacceptable."

What was unclear to all who looked favorably on Herman Kahn's proposal of "thinking about the unthinkable"[34] was this: his subject was not the possibility that a nuclear war *might happen to us*, but that *we might start one*. We might plan, prepare for, and *initiate* nuclear war.

In the book *In Flanders Fields* (1958), Leon Wolff said:

"It remains to be said, as usual, that the war ended on the eleventh hour of the eleventh day of the eleventh month of 1918. It had meant nothing, solved nothing, and proved nothing; and in so doing, had killed 8,538,315 men and variously wounded 21,219,452. Of 7,750,919 others taken prisoner or missing, well over a million were later presumed dead; thus the total deaths (not counting civilians) approached 10,000,000. The moral and mental defects of the leaders of the human race had been demonstrated with some exactitude."[35]

***

The Bhagavad Gita on Karma Yoga (from Zimmer, page 386)[36]:

Krishna says, "The individual should continue carrying on his usual duties and activities of life, but with a new attitude of detachment from their fruits—that is, from the possible gains or losses that they will entail ... Consider pleasure and pain, wealth and poverty, victory and defeat as of equal worth. Prepare then for combat. Acting in this way, thou wilt not be stained by guilt."

This is to say to oneself (and to others) that other people do not count with respect to one's duty—which may be to destroy them (see Arjuna) or to ignore their suffering.

Krishna continues, "Give thought to nothing but the act, never to its fruits. . . . For him who achieves inward detachment, neither good nor evil exists any longer here below."

(But what about "doing one's duty" as an oppressor? A torturer?)

Krishna again: "Thou dost feel pity when pity has no place. Wise men feel no pity either for what dies or for what lives."

(*After famine? After a massacre? After a nuclear bomb?*)

Much suffering is caused by actions rooted in the ignorant cravings of *others*—especially of organizations, elites, and government officials.

Instead of Buddha's Eightfold Path, we need a "Ninefold Path" that includes *Right Resistance*.

***

American traditions are steeped in power, empire, racism, and paranoia. However, our traditions also include freedom, tolerance, and self-determination.

Social change (toward freedom, ending poverty and hunger, ending slavery and torture, and ending war and the fear of annihilation) *can* and *must* be achieved without violence, revenge, terrorism, and massacre.

Gandhi says that violent struggle for justice is second-best to nonviolent struggle. Cowardice and passivity are worse.

We need courage in the service of compassion.

***

Why did I do it? Why did I release the Papers?

In May 1969 I saw that what we were doing in Vietnam was indiscriminate, random murder. I also saw it as an error that could only be corrected from outside the Executive branch, not by the President or his subordinates.

To ask me to justify what I did is, really, an extraordinary reversal.

I obeyed my oath to the Constitution and to the Code of Ethics.

I exposed lies, crimes, aggressions, and treaty-breaking, all with consequences of mass homicide, ecocide, and subversion of the Constitution.

I didn't put "obligation to my team" higher than my obligation to the truth.

No convincing evidence was ever presented that I harmed National Security in any way; what I exposed had harmed *us*, and was continuing to do so.

In this country, I broke no laws, and I did nothing that had not been done before and since, almost always to good effect.

The promise of secrecy cannot, Constitutionally, be a promise to conceal crimes from the courts and Congress.

***

Who are my tomes of moral outrage, shock, and horror directed to? For what?

Am I saying that "They" are/were different from "Me" in their immoral actions?

I did blind myself to what was happening. Am I defending myself for believing blindly in the groups/institutions that I was part of?

Like other whistleblowers, I thought my release of the Papers was a fairly natural thing to do and the only right thing to do. I hoped it would encourage others to take similar actions.

Perhaps I and other whistleblowers are more unusual than I realized.

One painful consequence that I failed to anticipate: being permanently distanced from my friends.

My non-negotiable requirement for groups that I join is, "Do not torture, massacre, or destroy democracy."

***

IN SANTA RITA JAIL[37]

"It is ironic for someone so obsessed with the evils of bombing as I am to have become associated so closely with bombing plans and campaigns. If you sell yourself to the System, whatever your purposes, you will serve its purposes—which are not what the System says, not what you understand, and not your own purposes."

Shortly after the talk in which I made the above comments, the man next to me turned to me and said, "It must be that you feel some guilt for what you did in the Pentagon. And I want you to know that I forgive you."

No one has ever said this to me before.

We need to forgive ourselves—for Tokyo, Hiroshima, Nagasaki—in preparation for repentance, investigation, learning, and change.

In the Trident blockade, I painted the name on my boat, "Nagasaki Phoenix." As a child of genocide, I felt a sense of being reborn from the ashes of Warsaw, Shanghai, Rotterdam, London, Hamburg, Cologne, Dresden, Tokyo, Hiroshima, and Nagasaki.

At Dulles Airport: Why do I cry when I begin to describe Dick Korn's poem "Things didn't turn out quite as I had planned"?

Hypothesis: I identify with the speaker, as of pre-1969 and pre–Pentagon Papers: my compromises, my complicity.

A feeling of redemption arises in the later poems. It is not too late for forgiveness, self-forgiveness, and repentance.

"Come home, America."

1984

Groups do not have a tendency to "mature," to "grow up."

Model of Group Evil:
 Subordinates feel part of an omnipotent organization or team—righteous, protected, and safe from criticism or judgment. Hence, they are free from constraints against hurting others, free of the fear of retaliation, and free from a personal sense of judgment or failure.
 Leaders feel themselves to be servants of the Cause, serving the organization, team, or State. They, too, feel diminished and take no personal responsibility for policy. They see themselves as being responsible to stockholders, the organization, or voters, in a way that "leaves them no choice." Hence, they are protected from the constraints of personal conscience.

Leaders and Insiders use secrecy, deception, and silencing of dissent to avert reproach and quell doubt about the brutality and recklessness of their policies.
 Meanwhile, the abuses said to have been carried out by "the Enemy" are greatly exaggerated.

The effect of all this is brutal indifference to "collateral damage" and the killing of "innocents," as well as oblivion to realistic dangers and an underrating of the damage inflicted.

***

How would postwar history have been different without the Atomic and Hydrogen bombs—or without use of, and reliance on, these weapons?

What if the U.S. had had a real desire to ban nuclear weapons, rather than using them to intimidate the Soviet Union?

***

How to get humans to serve non-compassionate, inhuman ends?

How to get humans to serve suicidal, species-homicidal ends?

Humans have the ability to adopt severely restricted loyalties and concerns (with "compassion" only for leaders, for "us," for elites).

One is expected to shed other loyalties, since concern for others is seen as reduced attention and concern for leaders.

Thus, to "shed one's humanity" is to set aside our ability to empathize widely among humans, beyond family and tribe.

If preparations for war are seen as necessary to drive the national economy, then an "Enemy" is needed to justify this effort and expense. The dispute may be a rivalry for the same interests or territory, or it may simply be rooted in and justified by a fear of the "Other."

An identified External Enemy can serve as a useful sacrifice to the Religion of the State. The Nation-State externalizes enemies as a basis for achieving national unity. "It is 'Others'—our 'Enemies,' who are responsible for our problems, frustrations, and suffering."

With scapegoating, our vulnerability, disunity, and weakness are blamed on the presence in our midst of a foreign, unassailable element, perhaps with ties to foreigners (such as the Jews in Germany, Arabs in Israel, or ethnic Catholics in the U.S.). People are urged to "unite" in opposing this single targeted element—hopefully, one that cannot or will not retaliate.

In expressing all our own impulses to violence, we are asserting our status and self-worth—just as, say, Klan members (white, Christian, men) do in calling themselves "free peoples," "law-abiding citizens," or "property owners."

***

Violence is dangerous, costly, and destructive. It often leads to unanticipated side-effects, especially its impacts on the "innocent."

The elites, whose job it is to "choose war" and conduct it "when appropriate," perceive and evaluate these relative costs and dangers less acutely than most of the public.

One of the consequences of preparing for war is to inculcate this inevitability, this insensitivity or blindness to human collateral damage. This leads to reprisals and escalation: a cycle of initiation and reciprocation.

If you want peace, prepare for peace.

There are moral and practical risks in preparing, threatening, or consciously choosing to heighten the risk of war or organized violence.

If you want to avoid war, plan and prepare to avoid war, not to make war. Reduce and oppose all of the various motivations and impulses to make war. Imagine and prepare alternatives to war-making and war-preparing.

The Gandhian sees preparing for war—physically, psychologically, and organizationally—as the best way of *ensuring* the occurrence of war and undermining alternatives to war. Confrontations and crises will occur in which one's own elites/leaders and public will *perceive* war as a "solution," "the only way out," or "the best or only alternative."

***

As an escalation strategy, disproportionate threats are regarded as less risky because they are more effective—and because "we can always back down."

Yet the risks of commitment to "disproportionate destruction" are understated. Leaders underestimate the risk that the opponent will not back down, as well as the likelihood that the threat will be carried out.

Every reaction creates new context for going further.

There is an incentive not to "back down," not to admit failure, error, or wrong tactics.

Instead, there can be a temptation to believe that more force will succeed, that the enemy is near the edge, near a breaking point.

There may also be an incentive to justify past use—or to routinize, institutionalize, and set a precedent.

Further risks arise from command-and-control failures, the breakdown of controls in the field, and the fog of war.

There are unthinkable thoughts in the White House, but nuclear threats and nuclear wars are not among them. However, "surrender" is.

Our "nuclear superiority" makes failure less imaginable. National defeat and failure would be all the more humiliating and unthinkable because of our power.

***

A Vietnamese civilian's comment to Dan Berrigan:

"We can handle anything but nuclear weapons. It is your job to stop those."

***

Humiliation provokes violence because it creates an obligation to react violently. Impulses toward reciprocal violence multiply as commands—even requests, assertions about preferences, desires, and pains of others—are expressed by those seen as "inferiors," such as troops, children, women, blacks, or former supposed superiors.

The prior act is perceived by the violent actor as a provocation, a humiliation, a violent act to be answered with violence. This violent response is seen by the reactor as retaliation or reciprocal violence, although it may be perceived by others as escalation or even initiation of violence.

***

There are no limits to obedience when:

- —there is not sufficient internal critique, questioning of orders, or monitoring of legitimacy, legality, and proportionality of means and ends.

—no one feels the responsibility or the right to question what is being asked of them, nor do they feel safe in doing so.

"A people that wants to be both free and ignorant wants what never was and never will be." —Thomas Jefferson

The notion of "rational choice" neglects and mis-predicts the nature of our decision behavior in a hierarchical setting, as well as the content of our actions in such a setting.

We tend to judge ourselves, our goodness, by our *personal* desires, values, aims, and restraints; by our proposals, stated initiatives, and feelings; and not by our *actual actions* in an organizational authority setting—whether as subordinates, passive citizens, or responsible leaders.

Humans are not aware of, and often misunderstand, the influence of authority on their choices and their behaviors. Thus, they can easily surprise themselves or blind themselves to what they end up doing, or to what others do—both leaders or followers.

Some things become "unthinkable," because thinking is associative.

Thinking arouses associations and awareness that affect hypotheses, pattern recognition, response thresholds, fears, and desires.

Thus, to think about one thing can be dangerous. It can lead to thinking about other things, and to feelings and fears that are unsayable, not to be explored or investigated, and not to be subject to explicit agreement, contract, or consent.

***

There is a persistent, large-scale, highly organized, coherent, and purposive pursuit of short-run aims in bureaucratic structures, which is as irrational, reckless, illogical, murderous, and suicidal as that observed in crowds.

This is an aspect not only of anarchic mob uprisings, but also of "sober" governmental bureaucratized processes.

Bureaucratic obedience brings no responsibility for overall ends and possible consequences. A follower is not accountable to outsiders, or to his conscience, independently of orders. He is accountable only to his boss and his organization.

Organizations can develop structures of beliefs and values and a sense of available alternatives that are fantastically removed from reality, yet are not subjected to reality testing or treated as uncertain.

Two people can be subject to a *folie à deux*, especially if one is the "beloved leader."

Grandiosity may arise from holding a superior position with power over subordinates. Or, someone in a leadership role may evolve "crazy" ideas to justify taking actions to preserve his position of power.

Why is all of this so predominantly male: observing and maintaining hierarchy and authority, being guardians of social difference?

Hypothesis: Males are more accepting of hierarchy. They're also on alert against enemies. Their gender identity is rooted in "otherness."

***

"Forgive yourself. Forgive that part of you that so rages at another part of you that it wants to destroy it."

Forgiveness: "I absolve myself of the obligation to avenge myself. I will not feel obliged to hate or hurt you. I will not feel ashamed for not seeking revenge."

***

"Fear alone is not a sufficient basis for politics."

"We need a 'liberation theology' for the First World." —Noam Chomsky

Nonviolent resistance has a special power to raise the question "What can I do to change this situation?" I have felt that power in my own life.

With nonviolent resistance, it is best to catch one's opponent unawares by a novel challenge, when he is without psychological defenses to deny unwelcome truths. The element of surprise can shift the focus and expose his habitual bases for action.

***

Corporate investment in South African apartheid will no longer happen with our consent. It will not happen without public challenge, and without arrests.

This policy has depended on invisibility and public inattention. To remove that protective cloak is more than a symbolic act.

We withdraw our consent. If this institution continues to seek profit from apartheid, it must do so over our own bodies.

***

We are in a crisis. Open up the options. Think radically and creatively.

What can we do without? What resources, processes, and ways of being can we sacrifice? Wars? Imperialism? Hierarchy?

The alternative would be to give up freedom, dissent, democracy, concern for others, and any sense of the "human family."

Ellen Klaver [from Rocky Flats Truth Force] says we must "work with those forces that are creative, purposive, mindful larger than human—forces that favor human existence, freedom, and love."

1985

Pat and I first went out April 27–28, 1965. Our Ganges trip was later that year, in December.

How I explained my government role to her: "I'm trying to stop the bombing."[38]

My change was not from simple "hawk" to simple "dove." I was never a bombing hawk, nor did I want to see the U.S. be "defeated." I wanted to bring attention to: the U.S. bombing and the lack of our right to do this; the poor prospects for success; a growing nationalism; Nixon's real plans to continue the war; and the inexorability of war as an instrument.

From 1968 to 1970, I was trying to head off the escalation of bombing; the invasion of Laos, Cambodia, and North Vietnam; and the use of nuclear weapons.

In September 1969, I gave up the goal of mutual withdrawal and turned to unilateral withdrawal, accepting nearly all the social costs of espousing pacifism. These costs included pressure on RAND, pressure on my clearance, pressure to resign, and a feeling of isolation from friends and colleagues.

After June 1969, my RAND colleagues shared my belief that we should get out of Vietnam. But they did not feel it as urgently as I did, and they differed from me in what to do about it personally.

As for me, I no longer wanted to be a "President's man."

***

In 1969, Wohlstetter[39] said, "Get out of Vietnam—but not now."

Well, *when*? After certain uses of our presence have achieved their purpose? When we can do it "gracefully," without causing shame or reproach or a loss elsewhere?

In the fall of 1969, I heard from Mort Halperin that Nixon wouldn't change his policy, nor would North Vietnam. Reading the Pentagon Papers, I learned that this had gone on for four previous Presidents and would likely continue after Nixon.

Clearly, it was time to give up hope in Presidents, something that had been part of my identity for at least 15 years—and even earlier, as far back as FDR.

With the loss of the President's authority, I was free—like the Accident. Having given up on the possibility of the Presidency changing Vietnam policy, which had been my only apparent basis of hope, I was free to search for other approaches.

My newfound freedom opened a door for me to discover new values, the pursuit of which had previously been contradictory to my attachments to security, identity, possession, and membership.

I was free to share and reveal certain information; to work with new people and institutions; to think new thoughts and follow new logic; to have new heroes and role models; and to take actions that risked my job, clearance, career, and time in prison.

"Freedom's just another word for nothing left to lose." [From "Me and Bobby McGee" by Kris Kristofferson, popularized by Janis Joplin]

Note that I was not in a subjective state of despair, hopelessness, or depression in fall 1969, which is all the more clear to me now that I *have* experienced depression. Rather, it was a time of high energy, initiative, determination, and intellectual activity. I was calm, resolute, and active.

Almost surely a factor in this: after meeting Janaki at War Resisters' International the previous year, I had become aware of an alternative approach: a new set of values, models, heroes, authorities, and political friends and associates.

I was not alone.

***

War, or the possibility of war, is viewed as a legitimate, "sometimes necessary" activity—an option that is to be prepared for and threatened, or pledged as in an alliance, or imagined and rehearsed approvingly while dwelling on its virtues and benefits.

Nothing is as infuriating to the "volunteer gladiator" as the "nervous Nellies" who not only make it more difficult for him to face down his opponent, but who also challenge, question, and undermine his credential-establishing contests, his rituals to establish masculinity.

The "hero" is seen as male, with a need to test and prove his fitness as a male.

My need to prove my manhood was satisfied in Vietnam. Did this make me more open than others to "accepting defeat" starting in 1967?

My experience in the Marines was that, although I was not interested in killing, I reveled in the excitement of being hunted, of risking, of being tracked and attacked, and of resisting and escaping successfully.

***

The elites drank coffee, smoked tobacco, and ate sugar—while taking over the world to plant coffee, tobacco, and sugar.

People were enslaved to grow these crops. The crops were bought with guns and rum, which incentivized local despotic regimes in Africa to participate in this trade.

The elites making policy judgments are reassured by a long tradition of elite consensus, raising little moral concern or doubt. As long as they maintain and act on these "consensual" beliefs and priorities, they are insulated by personal experience and position from feeling the full impacts and dangers of their actions:

—They are insulated from legal concerns due to secrecy, compartmentalization, and "national security imperatives."
—They are insulated from challenge, whether from elites or non-elites, by having executive control of foreign policy.
—They control media and education, and they have in turn been influenced by these, both in their upbringing and currently.

***

Dad's shift about nuclear weapons came not from me, but from a "trusted authority": *Tau Beta Pi Magazine*. I hadn't mentioned the concept of nuclear winter to him, or the likelihood of a "prolonged period of suffering preceding extinction" . . . akin to "an old age for our species." Dad's words about the article were: "peculiarly awful, credible, and near."

I came to accept a new idea from Dad: that possession or *any* use of nuclear weapons is unacceptable. Although I had been exposed to this idea from others before, when I heard it from him in this moment of despair, I accepted it.

Until then, I had been in favor of using nuclear weapons, in the sense that I accepted the need for deterrence—and therefore, the possession of these weapons. This notion was similar to the idea that the U.S.'s intervention and presence in Vietnam was legitimate, necessary, and important in order to maintain a minimally adequate "credibility."

Possession of nuclear weapons is an activity, a process—a continuous, institutionalized engagement in behavior. It requires investment in modernization and maintenance to "enhance credibility."

This process displaces other activities such as peacemaking and meeting other human needs, thus precluding exploration, creativity, imagination, and the generation of alternative approaches to peace, justice, and freedom.

It is risky to raise fears in the other superpower, given the various possible dangerous responses. What is needed is *mutual* security, *mutual* reassurance.

The use of tactical nuclear weapons is more likely than most people realize. This is due to the probability of U.S. intervention, and then of large resistance, as well as the likelihood of Presidential threats, the probability of rejection of the threat, and the resulting probability that the threat will be carried out.

All of this means that the dangers of preemptive weapons are wildly underestimated.

Somebody may begin a nuclear war in self-defense. Preparations for self-defense fuel the cycle of conflict, as they are ambiguous and provocative.

"Self-defense" is used as a rationale for any amount of violence and aggression—up to and including damage-limitation and preemptive nuclear war.

Plans are frequently ordered to be implemented in circumstances other than those originally intended. This brings results that are quite different from those that were desired or foreseen—although they were foreseeable, given the circumstances.

***

My country is sleepwalking toward an abyss.

The future is not some place we are going to. The future is what we are creating every day. If we continue to prepare and plan for thermonuclear war, that is what we are going to get.

We must stop testing nuclear weapons and start testing the Russians.

Don't delegate conscience.

***

On Civil Disobedience:
One way of calling attention to a danger or an illegal practice is to take an action of obstruction, or symbolic obstruction, that will lead to your

being in court. Once there, in the context of your defense you can raise issues of illegality, criminality, constitutionality, and danger.

From the trial testimony of Carol, a White Train protester[40]: "I vigiled in protest of the White Train. It is hard for me to admit that it took so long to act. Part of me doesn't want to believe that those trains are coming... and that it depends on people like me to try to stop them.

When I saw the trains, I couldn't help thinking of the trains at Auschwitz and Dachau—only these trains were carrying the ovens."

Heard at the White Train trial, Bangor, Washington, 6/19/85:
"I plead innocent of this crime, by reason of sanity."
Q: "Are you ready to go to jail?"
A: "Yes. I don't look forward to it."
Q: "What gives you the right to do that... to choose which laws to obey and which not?"
A: "No law compels me to endanger human life."

***

"One must not give up hope."

In whom? In what? Humanity? God? The U.S. government? Presidential elections? The Democratic Party? History? The working class? The people? Military strength? Science? Reason? Prayer?

I discovered hope—with no past experience of it or evidence supporting it—in previous adversaries: Congress, the public, radicals, and pacifists.

Freedom lies on the other side of despair.

It may be that a willingness to give in to despair—even in what appears to be the last hope, the only chance—may be necessary to bring about the discovery of new approaches through a re-examination of things that were not previously questioned: premises and tactics that were not in one's consciousness before as being relevant or potentially useful to consider.

In addition to personal transformation, we need societal transformation. The bomb has made moral and spiritual evolution not merely Utopian, but practical and necessary.

We must extend our personal values to include the truth that we are one family of humanity.

***

My Chosen Epitaph: "He helped to end the Vietnam War, and he struggled to prevent nuclear weapons from being exploded ever again."[41]

1986

Brainstorm of Ideas for Book Title: "The Nuclear Mousetrap: Build a Better Mousetrap" ... "Vicious Cycle, Degenerative Spiral" ... "The Quagmire Myth" ... "What Did They Know, and When Did They Know It?" ... "What Did We Know, and When Did We Know It?"

My task is to explain, compassionately and dispassionately, how elites, right now, can be working toward World War III despite all of the warnings—and how the public can be letting this happen. I will describe the human and organizational patterns that make these choices probable, or not unlikely.

***

The willingness to threaten, prepare for, and risk the initiation of nuclear war when other means fail is madness that falls far beyond "normal madness."

It is one thing to be once on a roulette wheel, with all of your assets on the table. It is another thing—as long as you win or break even—to let your bet *ride indefinitely*, spin after spin.

A Game of Chicken: What if the Soviets' response is neither to back down nor to preempt, but to raise the risks still higher?

Brinkmanship: we are using shared risks of mutual catastrophe, instead of minimizing them cooperatively.

How to bring a long-range perspective to bear on policy, considering that, unlike past wars, one failure will be fatal?

Forty years of no nuclear war is like nine "safe flights" of the *Challenger*, until unprecedented cold—together with officials' desire to launch without delay—brought disaster.

***

My colleagues were my friends, my fathers, my brothers.

However, I found Herman Kahn's work particularly dangerous. He was eroding barriers and inhibitions to atrocity . . . tying down safety switches . . . muffling alarm bells . . . encouraging preparation to create a catastrophe.

***

The history of catastrophe is the history of leaders who ignored warnings and kept them secret, choosing instead to gamble on the avoidance of possible disaster.

It is also the history of people who "stayed within channels," who warned their bosses but agreed to keep silent to outsiders, or even to their fellow employees. By "swallowing their whistles" instead of blowing them, they protected their own cachet and identity as Insiders—at the cost of potential catastrophe.

Plausible Denial: the President can use the excuse of non-culpability due to ignorance of a situation. This was the approach used by Eisenhower and Reagan. For this to work, one needs responsible subordinates who are in control, so they can be blamed if things go wrong.

In contrast, JFK and Carter cultivated the image of total personal control.

***

No one, in any country, likes their patriotism to be questioned.

The best way to avoid having one's patriotism questioned—in fact, to *assure* it is unquestioned—is to be *unquestioning* of the regime in power. This is especially so in its dealings with foreigners.

One exception to this: as an expression of being "super-patriotic," one *can* question government policies or leaders on the grounds that, when dealing with foreigners in pursuit of U.S. interests, they give *too much* consideration to:

- the rights or interests of foreigners
- moral, political, or legal constraints on the use of violence
- the demands of international law and treaties.

Thus, to be seen as "unquestionably patriotic," it is safe to talk and act as if:

- foreigners have no rights that an American President or military commander is bound to respect
- foreign states have no legitimacy or sovereign rights
- foreigners are less than human, in the sense of not possessing fundamental human rights such as the right to live free from the fear of being terrorized by us.

Embassy officers said, "We may make mistakes, but the other side is ten times worse." This attitude, this justification, is all it takes to understand any atrocity: it was done to people who are defined as either "enemies" or "sub-human."

***

In the words of conservative commentator Pat Buchanan to me in 1983, "Why do you keep doing these penny-ante actions?" He was referring to the fact that I had just come out of a circus tent, where Livermore Lab nonviolent protesters were housed in makeshift overflow quarters.

I ask myself, "Why am I drawn to civil disobedience? Why can't I stay out of jail?"[42]

True, there are rewards. I meet wonderful people. In a sense it is a place for renewal . . . a place of hope . . . and no telephone!

On the other hand, I am away from home. The trials are tedious.

Further, it is troubling that doing civil disobedience damages my credibility as an expert. In many quarters I am deemed "unserious."

Pat commented to me, "You're not *married* to a martyr, that's for sure. Anyway, you are a prophet, not a martyr."

***

Nonviolent civil disobedience does not eliminate moral dilemmas, costs, consequences, and lesser evils. However, it does inspire a search for new ways of behaving, seeing, feeling, and being.

Unless you have a sense that what is offered currently as a "best bad" is still evil, you don't search desperately, nor do you undertake painful change.

"To speak practically and as a citizen—I ask for, not at once no government, but at once a better government. Let every man make known what kind of government would command his respect, and that will be one step toward obtaining it." —Henry David Thoreau

"Cast your whole vote, not a strip of paper merely, but your whole influence."[43] —Henry David Thoreau

In 1978, I found myself sitting on the railroad tracks at Rocky Flats. I loved the simplicity of this action: *just sitting*.

Sitting is everything in Buddhism. Sitting and being present is all you have to do.

But Gandhi's extension of Buddha's insight is: it does make a difference *where* you sit.

1987

Up to the moment of Kottler's assessment, I was fated to be a "loyal pianist."

I did not revolt or protest his finding.

The fact that I didn't fight it doesn't make me causally responsible for what followed. Even if I had fought it, that would have just been denial.

Until this morning, though, I still hung onto my feeling of responsibility—which was just inadequacy, not revolt. And bad teaching!

A friend said to me that after Kottler's judgment and my acceptance of it, my mother was perhaps suicidally reckless—and more attached to her brother than to me, my career, our family, or her own life.

My lack of power to prevent the Accident permanently lost me my Good Mother.

Just as "*the other person's* guilt" is preferable to "*my* guilt," even "my guilt" may be preferable to "my *shame*," or its basis.

Guilt is less terrifying than shame. Shame is associated with fear of permanent loss of essential relationships. It shapes our behavior so as to reduce this risk, and it increases our desire to repair and restore the relationship.

Hypothesis: shame is aroused most by threats to the relationship with a caregiver or parental figure—the person on whom one is dependent for basic self-esteem or survival.

Me: "I was causally, but not morally, responsible for the Accident. Dad was both, of course."

Pat: "But your mother was mainly responsible."

This was my first inkling of this possibility—the first mention by anyone.

Pat thought it was self-evident. She thought I saw it when I described Mother's pressure on Dad.

Yet I never did—a spectacular case of Decision Theory![44]

A possible point of view: Mother's death was certainly not my fault, was largely accidental, and was not necessarily the model for the end of civilization.

***

The Accident turns out to be one more case where an apparent accident was preceded by clear indications of danger, and also by warnings and protest and alternative urgent recommendations by a "subordinate," my dad.

The decision was made by Mother to push on in the most dangerous mode—the only one that could, with luck, meet her objective of getting to Denver before July 6th to avoid the humiliation of missing the event.

I had thought that my father killed my mother and sister in his anger and depression. I came to hold him as responsible, as if he had been in charge, or as if he had made any of the decisions—or even as if Mother had warned or suggested or demanded he not continue to drive. In my mind, he had ignored or rejected alternatives such as Mother driving, pulling over, or stopping at a motel.

In fact, he *did* protest, offering alternatives that Mother rejected.

He was not in charge, and he was mostly obedient. He was like those in the Milgram experiment with real authority who protested against the experiment, but ultimately continued on.

So, it was *Mother* who demanded that major, obvious risks be taken with all our lives. Yet I have never thought, "Mother was suicidally reckless. She risked us all and lost her life and Gloria's." I have focused on those like Dad, who knew better but obeyed. I inferred that I didn't want to be passively reckless, like him.

What I didn't infer: "I didn't want to be like Mother, or to obey Mother, or fail to warn others of a President . . . like Mother."

It is terrifying to perceive that one's primary caregiver or mother does not care enough about you to avoid or forgo the risk of terminating the relationship.

I would prefer to believe that Dad was reckless, and that I helped set these events in motion with my efforts for independence, defying Mother's wishes on piano, which led to her total loss of interest in the family, Dad's depression, and hence his recklessness.

I had not come to terms with Dad's simple obedience and passivity, which pointed to *Mother* being responsible.

She not only risked her life; she also risked my life and the rest of the family's lives.

Ken Wilber says the absence of "the good mother"—a loving, supportive, appreciative mother—may involve a mother who is physically absent, or if physically present is not good or not emotionally present. This occasions not only rage and frustration, but also shame at one's evident incapacity to control oneself so as to assure her presence (a Magical Assumption!). It might also engender denial to avert the shame or terror at the prospect or reality of the permanent loss of the Good Mother.

***

When I broke up with someone I loved, I didn't feel consciously depressed; I just took big risks.

Now I am studying desperate, reckless choices by Presidents.

The experience of betrayal may be associated with shame, rage, resentment, and terror at the rupture of the relationship with, or loss of trust in, the Good Parents.

Similarly, the President's deliberate, conscious risk-taking threatens us, bringing up fear and terror at the lack of control we have over him, given his lack of concern for us. We are uncertain if he will be present for us and protect us.

***

I am an expert in several fields, a former high-level insider who differs quite sharply from most of my fellow experts in that I believe the public's apprehension is right, and that certain kinds of catastrophe in my fields of expertise are very likely.

Now, and earlier, it is nuclear war that preoccupies me.

I am like a ship designer or engineer before 1912 who could imagine a wreck like the *Titanic* and could see problems in the *Titanic* itself ... or like an official of the courts of Russia or Germany or England in 1911.

Here are three really complex, difficult questions:

—Who was and is responsible for the Cold War?
—Who was responsible for World War I?
—Who was and is responsible for the Arms Race?

Each side tends to reject any responsibility, any role or motive except self-defense. Both sides have this feeling.

It may be more important and useful to focus mainly on the motives, intentions, responsibilities, and lies of *one's own side*, although not exclusively.

***

There are some policies that can't be legitimized by democratic processes—such as Mutual Assured Destruction, ecological destruction, and strategic bombing.

The history of U.S. entry into wars in the 20th century teaches us to regard as suspect any officials who urge on us reasons to go to war.

Statesmen, leaders, and staffs should not be trusted to keep us out of avoidable, unnecessary wars, or to end them when they should. Nor should they be trusted to tell us the truth about what they are doing or why, or the costs and risks.

We should, by now, assume we are being given a radically false picture of the issues that government officials actually prioritize, the issues they see at stake, the risks and costs they foresee, why they regard this course of action as worthwhile, and the pros and cons of possible alternatives.

The capacity to wage nuclear war has been prepared, threatened, and chosen at the highest levels.

At present it is the intent of the U.S. President and NATO to initiate limited, hopefully unilateral nuclear war under certain circumstances that are understood to be possible, even likely over a long run—circumstances that have repeatedly come close to occurring in the last 40 years.

This combination of readiness, threats, and Alliance commitment poses the greatest risk of all-out nuclear war in the world, given the reliance on these threats and the nature of the strategic arms race that results from efforts to make these threats credible (and, on both sides, to match opposing capabilities to assure at least parity, even at the price of instability).

Big thermonuclear war will probably come about as the result of accident, miscalculation, or loss of control.

It may have been intended to start, and intended to be limited.

No one will have desired or intended this outcome.

***

In 1961, I saw South Vietnam as a quagmire to be avoided by the U.S., and at any rate by me personally. I felt no compulsion either to participate in that failure or to warn the U.S. out of it.

When I was assigned to work on Vietnam in 1964, I found my forebodings confirmed.

Both in Vietnam and in Washington, I did what I could from the inside against the obvious odds, with the hope of eventually winning "in a decent manner" or getting out. No real prospects of winning "indecently" were vivid enough to tempt me, though other people succumbed to the line of bombing or "counterterrorism."

When these efforts showed themselves to be failures, I foresaw the likelihood of catastrophic continuation and escalation, much of which did occur. Yet the worst possibilities were averted by the public mobilization in which I eventually played a role. There was no invasion of North Vietnam and no use of nuclear weapons. An additional decade of bombing, torture, and massacre by the U.S. was averted.[45]

I count it a success that we did not continue to take on the role of the jailers of the Vietnamese (even though our departure did not liberate them).

After a U.S. official reported atrocities being committed by a Vietnamese official, his boss said, "If you don't have the stomach for this job, you can leave and go to another post." Had he done so, it would have killed his career . . . and he was still paying for his divorce.

So he stayed on for two more years.

Someone said that up-country in the Delta, 98% of the night patrols reported by case officers were fabrications, but "If there were no tension, no great conflict in the world such as that evidenced by our own military operations, *how would we justify our arms spending*?"

Those who lie a democratic country into war deserve the worst contempt, reproach, condemnation, and punishment that society offers. They have done what our democratic system was intended to prevent.

***

People accept job parameters that include a designated responsible person. When an ambiguous situation arises—a circumstance not covered by rules—people will defer to the judgment of the boss or his designated representative, someone who knows from past experience "what the boss wants."

Bureaucratized conscience: individual conscience and inhibitions are no more allowed or legitimized to operate in a bureaucratic setting than are purely personal goals, prejudices, preferences, and impulses.

[In their research on decision-making,] Kahneman and Tversky discovered that risk-takers "hear" the voice of *uncertain* possible future outcomes to themselves and society and others "more faintly" than they "hear" the *certainty* of short-range failures or humiliations for themselves.[46]

Hypothesis: Quitting is worse than losing.

We are socialized to accept the judgment "He can't quit" and "You can't quit."

"Quitters never win; winners never quit."

Michael persists at the piano lessons that he dislikes because he "doesn't want to be a quitter." In the same way, Presidents don't want to be "quitters" and have the country "lose a war" on their watch.

Worst of all is to lose without "trying everything" to prevent it, short of nuclear weapons.

***

At Treya Wilber's Cabin:

To me (vs. Treya[47] and Barbara [Marx Hubbard[48]]), to say either "everything is for the best" or "everything will turn out for the best," even "ultimately" or "on balance," is both untrue and dangerously misleading. That way of thinking makes catastrophes more likely.[49]

To assume that "everything will turn out for the best" is a cop-out, a denial of one's responsibility for or complicity in past, present, or future catastrophes.

We have the need and the ability to change or avert catastrophic situations. Thus, we have the responsibility, challenge, and obligation to do so.

***

A nuclear power plant produces power for decades; the nuclear waste it leaves behind will remain lethal for 10,000 years.

***

Do we opt for nature's wisdom as the solution to our problems? Or do we go with human cleverness?

It is not that humans do not learn faster than Nature; we do. It's just that Nature has been at it a lot longer.

Our civil disobedience is rooted in the Judeo-Christian value of *stewardship*. We are acting as stewards to re-sacralize life (not just human life)—to preserve life and the conditions for it.

Does a citizen have a right—or sometimes, even a duty—to interfere with, resist, challenge, "indict" authority that is criminal and immoral—*even if* this is done in ways that violate traffic, trespass, or secrecy regulations, or interfere with the rights of others to free speech, free passage, and free access to work and commerce?

I think the public's intuition is right that my fellow experts are not giving advice or leadership that serves to diminish the likelihood or scope of catastrophe. Quite the contrary.

Thus, public criticism, creativity, and pressure are essential.

I believe, against most but not all historical experience, that popular sovereignty can be achieved and can avert the worst.

Unlike equally disillusioned insiders, I did not walk away from our Vietnam involvement in 1966 and simply distance myself from the catastrophe, as I had from its prospect (from 1961 to 1963). After 1969, I devoted myself to the only game in town with any prospect of succeeding: public pressure on Congress.

Speaking and acting from my Inside knowledge led to my exile from the Inside forever, both socially and psychologically.

Still, I remain nostalgic in dreams—such as last night's, in which I attended a luncheon meeting at Wohlstetter's home.[50]

***

In the last 20 years, every President has come to see democracy as part of his problem, while I have increasingly come to see it as part of the solution—with civil disobedience an essential element.

I was not moved to give the Pentagon Papers by those who vigiled. However, I *was* moved to join in a vigil for Quaker draft resister Bob Eaton. This was a critical step that opened me to Randy Kehler's subsequent example.[51]

Randy first took part in an Oakland sit-in. Then he joined War Resisters' International.

Both Randy and I were changed by "small" actions. Then we were ready and available to be changed by "big" actions.

A story on Derrick Bell today in the *Globe* had this quote on civil disobedience:

"When you put your person in the way of oppressive power, it does not mean you will get your way. But you can feel good, and those who are doing bad will feel less good—and sometimes you inspire people who *do* have the power to change things."

Questioner: "Obviously, civil disobedience is appropriate, given the disparity between executive policy and what is needed. But what if these executive values are shared by the majority of the public? Is civil disobedience the right response then?"

Me: "All the more! Challenge and obstruct the majority to protect the rights of the unrepresented and underrepresented. Live your values and act on conscience."

1988

I am a former defense intellectual and national security analyst. Now I am a peace intellectual, international security analyst, and activist.

I was 10 in 1941, in the time of the U.S. vs. Hitler, the Japanese, and Mussolini.

My images of war were formed from: Pearl Harbor, my half-brother Harry, Dad's work, my uncle Ned[52] and his books, Americans and British in the French Foreign Legion (vs. Arabs in South Africa), [Gen. Edward] Lansdale,[53] *Banks of Iwo Jima*, "The Saint" movies (= James Bond, for JFK?), and *For Whom the Bell Tolls* (Spain).

When I learned about the possibility of nuclear accidents, false alarms, and unauthorized access, I was alarmed to discover that the President lacked the flexibility *not* to respond by hitting Chinese cities and Moscow.

One day, in the spring of 1961, I held in my hand a piece of paper I had thought did not exist. It was a graph with numbers on it, responding to a question from the President, a question I had drafted believing it could not quickly be answered. It showed the number of people that top U.S. military leaders expected to kill if they launched a nuclear first strike against the Soviet Union: *600 million*.[54]

I had thought this number didn't exist. *That* was what I had proposed to expose.

They knew. Then, *how could they?*

How could they be so ready to threaten, prepare for, plan for, and carry out coercion, using massacre and torture as instruments of policy?

How could they continue in this course, even when it was clear that it was not working, and even when it was likely to lead to social catastrophe?

And how could they be *obeyed* by those who had come to realize the hopelessness and wrongness of what was happening?

For 25 years I have been trying to understand, so as to prevent, a catastrophe: nuclear war.

How could this possibility have been permitted? The very possibility of murder on this scale, which seems unmistakably real, is a mystery that I am trying to investigate: a *mass murder mystery.*

If nuclear conflagration comes, it will come at the hands of humans. It will be called a "tragedy," an "accident," an "error." But it will be a crime as well—one of almost unimaginable proportions.

***

In today's State of the Union address, we will probably hear some personal stories. President Reagan likes to discuss his own policies by pointing to individuals who are affected by them.

None of these stories will involve people who have felt the impact of U.S. aid to the Contras in Nicaragua, aid that the President will be asking to increase. I doubt his staff has brought any stories of this sort to his attention.

As for me, I have very vivid pictures in my mind about what that aid means—how that money is used—from visiting Pearl Lagoon, a village on the Atlantic coast of Nicaragua, a few days after it had been hit by a band of Contras who were paid and organized by our government, with boots and weapons from the U.S.

I don't know what the little girl, Idita, looked like, but I "see" her in the picture she drew in her arithmetic notebook, which I found in the rubble.

I don't describe what the U.S. concussion grenade did to her—but you can get a pretty good idea of it from what it did to her doll that was in the room with her.

This was no "irregularity." This is pretty much it; this is where the money goes.

It is intolerable that Congress is asked to authorize money to pay and equip people to do this.

The word for what the Contras do is "terrorism." It is intentional, state-sponsored terrorism. No budget authorization by Congress can make these activities legal, under the international charters and treaties that the Senate has ratified. It can only make Congress complicit, which is what Presidents want.

The truth is that terrorism is just as bad as President Reagan says it is—and he should stop supporting it.

***

Many Americans believe that in the Third World, the U.S. favors, supports, and pursues democracy, development, self-determination, independence, and human rights.

Myths: The U.S. as different, unique, the good guys, anti-imperialist, recognizing the legal equality of nations.

Yes, the U.S. *is* exceptional—in our experience of war (World War I, World War II, Korea, Vietnam, Iran, Iraq), our airpower and nuclear weapons, the extent of our own sphere of influence, and our denial of our role and influence.

"Self-defense" is actually the defense of U.S. indirect empire or rule. The seeming independence of an "ally" is a cover for U.S. informal rule—in other words, a sham.

In fighting abroad, what is being opposed? A potential regime that is not dependent on us, not subordinate or deferential to us.

***

I had become disillusioned with the power of the U.S. and the President to change or stop the war.

For me in February and March 1968, the challenge was to prevent further escalation after Tet and the failure of the "war in South Vietnam" strategy.

My March 1968 leaks were to prevent deployment of 206,000 troops.[55]

In 1972, I tried to forestall the mining of Haiphong and the potential use of nukes. I helped block it from inside in May–June 1965—one of my few accomplishments! That is the advantage of access and status.

The problem for me was never what the public saw. It was to forestall or expose secret new U.S. aggression and terrorism, which was—unknown and unguessed by the public—being prepared and secretly threatened, and not as a bluff.

At the War Resisters' International (WRI) conference, I took part in a vigil, an actual act of resistance. This act jeopardized my Elite (advisor) status.

Participating in the vigil led me to identify with young antiwar activists. I came to care about them, just as I had come to care about the Vietnamese.

After the vigil, Civil Disobedience was available to me, but it did not yet feel relevant. Other things looked more effective at that time.

From knowing Janaki and others, I had begun to view our violence as a pacifist does: it was cruel and wrong.

I was not at the War Resisters' International conference as a civil resister, but I wanted to meet those who were. After my year of reading, I wanted to meet others.

My career was at its peak. Still, I was ready to be challenged, ready to have my life subverted. Although I didn't expect what happened to me, I didn't just *happen* to be at that place at that time.

War gives soldiers the occasion to find out if there are things they would die for, while civil disobedience offers civilians the opportunity to find out if there are things they would go to jail for.

More specifically: are there things for which people would risk giving up their relationships? image? status? job? career?

I may have dropped my insider access too quickly and completely. I did this so as not to put my associates at risk of further controversies.[56]

There is a dark side of the integrative impulse/the instinct and desire to belong.

Few people realize the force of the desire to belong, to conform, to be accepted if not admired.

Wrongful, catastrophic courses usually depend on a widespread, prolonged conspiracy of silence. This includes silence about prior foresight, warnings, and dissent. Loyalty, patriotism, and trustworthiness to one's team and boss are equated to maintaining silence about recklessness, lies, and crimes.

I am a Revelationist, telling truths to enlighten and empower.

It is not enough to speak up candidly inside the hierarchy.

Beyond "Speaking Truth to Power," we are called to "Tell the Truths That Power Does Not Want Told." This means speaking up to expose what is wrong, harmful, and dangerous.

***

Questions to Myself:

Why didn't I distribute the Papers secretly?

Why did I take off the Top Secret markings when I copied them?[57]

Whistleblowing is not so much a conversion to something as it is a *loss*—the death of an identity and one's ego-ideals.

National security whistleblowers fall out of love with their organization, as well as with their old identities, ideals, and goals.

The consequences of whistleblowing can be difficult for a spouse. This can lead to tension at home that makes the whistleblower feel even more isolated.

I was not "unique," although I was unusual.

My act was highly publicized due to the injunctions, the scale of it, my background, the potential penalty involved, and my motive in taking an action of value to the public.

I was not a martyr. I did take my risks into account—but *not only* my risks.

***

There is a great gap between our private ideals, values, and constraints for ourselves, and our actual societal performance, which is partly covert.

Most people aspire to *be* good, but this does not necessarily mean that they aspire to *do* good to all others. They may think that some people have to be sacrificed "for the good of others," or as "cautionary examples" to encourage others' obedience to authority.

Thus, so-called good people can do harm. Indeed, most evil is done by "good" people.

I worried about the President's crisis decision-making when experiencing rage, humiliation, or the risk of losing an election.

Nothing evil is done "for the first time." In the eye of its author, there is always a reassuring or legitimizing precedent.

***

Thoughts on Genocide[58]:

Humans' fatal flaw: we do not have instinctual restraints on violence within our own species. Such restraints are a useful social construct.

Humans' total flaw: the readiness to kill or torture other humans without limit, for a variety of reasons that include protection from ego-loss, humiliation, shame, defeat, loss of status, pride, or danger to image or self-esteem.

Everyone loves a mystery, especially a murder mystery. But *mass* murder is mysterious in a way that induces dread, anxiety. It is senseless, savage, and indiscriminate.

Why did Nazi guards behave so cruelly, contemptuously, indifferently, and inhumanely? Because they were ordered to. Such orders are obeyed without much problem or delay.

Whatever shame or anxiety is evoked is turned on the victim, who is seen as "compelling" this behavior, occasioning it, or "deserving it." See, for example, overworked prison guards who may be frustrated, humiliated, fearful, anxious, tired, and angry. Prisoners are people toward whom they can express anger, cruelty, hatred, indifference, and contempt to a virtually unlimited degree without facing retaliation or rebuke. Their power is absolute—just like, in earlier times, men who had power over children, women, and slaves.

Doctors and generals demonstrated their status (as members of the Master Race) and their adherence to, loyalty to, and identification with Nazis, Hitlerian doctrines, ideals, and values by acting as if Jews were bacilli, vermin, a lower form of animal. They were not immobilized and made maladroit by anxiety, dread, or shame at behaving cruelly. They saw themselves as "real men," "real Nazis."

***

Israel, this week, is in a struggle for its soul—for its character as a nation, for what it will be, what it may become.

Can Israel continue to rule the Arab population of Gaza and the West Bank as occupiers, and remain a true democracy?

***

Power corrupts and addicts. The corruption of Power is proportional to its degree of concentration.

"Corrupt" means used for personal, self-serving ends.

Absolute power, perhaps because it is secret, is unmonitored and unaccountable. There is no superior, no monitor who can observe and control.

For the Power Holder, having Power magnifies the motive of retaining that Power. The Power Holder fears, and is concerned to avoid, losing any large part of his power: any part that might lead to unraveling, dominoes, loss of mystique and credibility, loss of the aura of legitimacy—and thus, efforts by those dominated to become less dependent, allying with or relying on others.

Retaining power may come to seem as important as retaining one's life . . . and *much* more important than protecting others' lives.

Thus, small organizational or national losses that mean loss of power for individual leaders are treated as the equivalent of social catastrophes. Huge risks may be taken to avert the certain loss in the near term, in order to prevent personal catastrophe for the Leader.

The majority of the U.S. public does not feel that an individual can rightly be held responsible for obeying unlawful orders of an otherwise legitimate authority. They believe that the Authority should be held responsible and should accept full responsibility, as part of an implicit contract that assures subordinates' unquestioning obedience.[59]

***

People don't realize the personal and social pressures that Presidents face not to "be a quitter," not to "break your word."

Presidents can't predict even their own behavior under situational pressures and threatened commitments.

This morning, Senator Gary Hart, as he reentered the race for President, said, "There's no shame in being a loser. The only shame is in being a quitter."

***

Obstacles to the Public's Enlightenment:

The broader public widely assumes "It Can't Be" that the U.S. opposes democracy, wants other countries to be run by brutal military tyrants, likes people to be disappeared and terrorized, opposes nationalism and self-determination, plans and executes aggressive war, and desires revolutionary regimes that justify stronger repression.

It is not the case that officials *desire* or *intend* to do these things—or even that they *believe* they are working to achieve such things. They may perceive themselves as having worked on only "one case," for "complicated reasons."

There is no limit to what even the Best and Brightest[60] may do, or threaten, risk, prepare for, or advocate—even for reasons other than national survival, deterrence, reprisal-in-kind, or revenge.

One needs to be ready to tell secrets, break agreements and promises, lose, be humiliated, face failure, leave the team or leader, disobey authority, or break laws.

I draw the line at killing innocents (especially massacre), torture, concealing such crimes, launching and continuing aggressive wars, obeying unlawful orders, and lying to the public or myself.

Sometimes there is a need for Emergency Exits.

***

Colleagues' expectations play a huge role. Team members are keen to be seen as "on the same side" in relating to the task at hand. They do not want to be seen as "different," as disagreeing, challenging, accusing, or embarrassing their colleagues.

Most of all, they do not want their team members to feel "We have failed because of *you*."

The goodness of a person is to be judged by the foreseeable consequences of their actions to other persons, not just to Authority.

Note: it is necessary to let go of the desire, need, necessity, and love to work for Presidents. To tell critical inner secrets to the public is to lose this opportunity.

Needing a job is far from the only incentive to moral stupidity. It is enough to want to keep one's status, one's self-image (as a good person, as tough/manly, autonomous, obedient, loyal), and the good opinion of teammates, bosses, sponsors, constituents, and allies.

Self-deception is a process of canceling out the effect of evidence that would lead to an unwelcome conclusion or inference.

This can involve lying, which "comes to be believed" in part because it justifies doing things to increase the credibility of the lie to others, or to make it less vulnerable to exposure. This makes it easier to come to believe the lie itself.

Thus, lying facilitates denial and repression.

Plausible Denial of Blame:

"It is, was, or will be the *right*, the *best* choice—given our aims and expectations, and given the alternatives."

"It was ordered by authorities, or we could reasonably believe that it was aligned with authorities' goals and expectations."

"I/he didn't make the choice. It was delegated to others, or it was unauthorized."

"My capacity to choose wisely was diminished for reasons that were not my fault."

"There was no choice to be made. No acceptable alternative existed, and there was overwhelming consensus to proceed."

Be skeptical and critical of calls for help as a valid basis for violence—especially across national borders, and especially violence directed by a Superpower.

The options of refusal, withdrawal, disobedience, exposure, revelation, and resistance are always available in some form, and with a chance—probably underestimated—of some useful effect.

This will be at a personal cost, the probability of which is *not* underestimated.

There is a *big* gulf between getting ready to stop/tell/resign, getting near the threshold, getting close to it . . . and *actually doing it*. That gulf is usually never crossed, although the existence of "the line," the potential option and the consideration of it, can be important to one's sense of self-esteem and character.

An Exchange:

"We need to teach people not just to disobey, but to break their promises when appropriate—including promises to their bosses to obey or to keep secrets."

"Well, doesn't *that* make your flesh crawl?! That would mean *Anarchy*!"

The U.S. may have been closer to a right-wing coup, more often, than is generally realized.

See Nixon and Mitchell's warnings on Wallace: "This country is going to go so far right that you won't recognize it."

Moral: *It can happen here.*

We are in a struggle for the soul of this country.

Our resistance, no matter how small or symbolic, can be a needed "alarm" for others.

For me, major influences about nonviolence have been: Janaki, King, Deming, Bondurant, Dellinger, McReynolds, and Thoreau.

We need to cultivate global compassion and a recognition of the fellowship of Humanity.

A broader compassion is less easily manipulated.

Consider your impact on others: their welfare, their desires, their interdependence with you and all. This includes the future, one's grandchildren, the Earth, the human family, and all of Life.

***

For most people, "the environment" is "the Other." They view Nature as a garbage dump and a source of resources to exploit. They don't have a felt sense that their very flesh and blood is created from Nature and is wholly reliant upon it. They also have a reckless disregard of our environmental future and the people who will be living in it.

***

Does the joy of the mystical experience compensate for suffering, more than anything else one can do?

The human problems of the great teachers have looked really problematic. Perhaps this is part of the answer to the question "Why seek Nirvana?"

Why "seek" Spirit, as if it weren't already there?

To seek the Tao is to miss the fact that it is everywhere.

Are we merely to accept that we are already "one with God"?

What room does this leave for spiritual development or motivation?

We try to understand the nature of Illusion so that we can become free from it. (Is this the only reason?)

You stay at a particular stage until you see the silliness of it, until you laugh at how much you think you are accomplishing, until you get the joke.

***

I am crying after just reading the end of Janaki's speech at War Resisters' International.

What makes me cry? (Like Saturday, during the oral history interview on Vietnam?) I cry at the thought of my own past foolishness and complicity.

***

"Can't one ever get over one's childhood? Enough already! Have done with it! Forgive! Move on! Isn't it time?"

***

Questions for Whistleblowers:

What about you and your life changed? When did these changes start?

What do you see and understand now that took the longest to learn?

What do you see and understand that you learned, or could learn, only through taking action?

Q: "What made you think you had the right to lie?"

A: "What made *you* think you had the right to keep silent?"

"I'm glad I didn't know what the consequences and costs would be when I made the decision to leak, or I might not have done it. Still, the experience has changed me in a way that I am grateful for. I would have missed out on unforeseen benefits that I could never have imagined, given the social influences I was under then." (*Unnamed Whistleblower*)

1989

Did I not have an attitude after the Accident that I had been both *spared* and *liberated*, even if in "Monkey's Paw" fashion? The Accident was the *only* way I could have been freed so soon.

After surviving the Accident, I felt that I "owed a life," and I felt that I was living on "borrowed time." Hence, my life was available to be expended for a worthy purpose. Had I been spared for some big achievement or contribution?

My continuing with piano practice out of respect for Mother's memory and wishes was like the restraint of a widower who does not take up with a young lover immediately, thus demonstrating preoccupation with who one has lost rather than expressing relief or excitement at new opportunities.

***

My intellectual life is a succession of problems on which I obsess.

Among my preoccupations:

How is it reasonable to act when the consequences are uncertain, and when obedience, or living by the duties and values of your ascribed inherited identity (i.e., following Krishna's advice to Arjuna) means being a slave, untrue to your own sense of real identity or your authentic desires?

How is it reasonable to act when the alternative to which you are drawn—asserting independence, rejecting assigned identity, following your own desires, and disobeying/defying Authority, Mother, lover—risks catastrophic results, possibly including the end of the vital relationship on which your status, identity, and purpose have heretofore depended?

***

From the *Bhagavadgita Gita*:

"The Lord said, 'I am Time grown old to destroy the world, embarked on the course of world annihilation.'"

"If in the sky the light of a thousand suns were to rise at once, it would be the likeness of the light of that great-spirited One."[61]

***

Janaki said, "I went to Catholic School and hated it. I rejected the Catholic/Christian notion that there is a stain on the soul when you sin, a stain that is indelible and must be burned out of you in Purgatory."

She wouldn't use a Roman Catholic or any Christian formulation, as they felt inauthentic to her. However, other Gandhians believed in doing so, in order to communicate with others who held that world view.

Janaki said, "Gandhi does use the word 'evil,' and he does distinguish between what people *do* and what they *are*. Remember, there is goodness in everyone. Look for that. There is no person who *is* an enemy, although they do bad things. They can be reached. There is something in them that can expand."

***

"The Germans are reuniting! Berliners celebrated history's largest, happiest *family* reunion!"

It's time for all the palisades of missiles and barbed wire to come down.

1990

We need a term for "wartime genocide"—genocide that is used as a form of warfare, a "tool" used to win a war.

Violence not only evokes violence in response, it legitimizes violence in response. Then new violence is legitimized in response to the violent response.

The same can be said of the threat of violence, preparation for violence, exhortation to violence, and authoritative consideration and recommendation of violent options.

All of this institutionalizes the preparation for, threat of, and execution of violence.

Even if threats and preparations and demonstrations of violence do deter and avert violence in specific confrontations or crises, the institutionalization assures some level of violence. It makes it hard or impossible to reduce this below a certain level, which keeps open or enlarges the risk of massive escalation.

The Enemy Within: An internal enemy is identified as a cause of our national failure or humiliation. This identified "them" may be "the Jews," "the Communists," "the libs," etc. Such "internal enemies" may even be suspected of collaborating with foreign enemies.

***

A Call to Moral Courage, Now:

You only need one example. Even better: two or three.

Ask yourself, "Where is the environment where I can be showing moral courage now? My work? My family? My community?"

Find the strength and the moral courage to do what is right, without knowing what the outcome may be.

It is not possible to know what effect your actions may have. For example, I couldn't have foreseen how my release of the Papers would eventually contribute to Nixon's downfall.

1991

Zen is perpetual one-upmanship. It is very male and intellectual. It is "*Awokemanship*."

What is the *real* relation of mindfulness practice to social change?

Contrary to some people's opinion, it is *not* a substitute for other forms of resistance. Nor is it an absolute precursor. Activists don't need to be "enlightened" to make change.

***

Pat says, "In civilized states, the collected universal taboos of primitive society are called 'foreign policy.'"[62]

You must *learn* to kill. You must learn to kill fast, without thinking... even at nighttime. Both sides "practice" this for months.

I watched the 500,000 people on our side practice killing, hate, and violence—then go back home to their wives, children, parents, and friends.

***

There is a time when silence is a lie, when silence is complicity, and when silence betrays our troops, our country, and ourselves.

We owe it to our troops, as well as to other potential victims of this war, to speak the truth about ourselves: what we believe, what we reject, and what we want.

The truth for me—is it not for you?—is that it was wrong to start this war, and it is wrong to continue it.

We demand that this war be ended now, before a ground war and other escalations take the lives of thousands of Americans and hundreds of thousands of Iraqis.

This is the time. The continuation of this war is a greater evil and a greater danger to this world than any of the plausible diplomatic agreements that might end it.

***

"We need vision to see the ordeals of this generation as the opportunity to transfigure ourselves and American society." —Martin Luther King Jr.

1992

Why was I preoccupied with the notion of a "good death," even before the Accident?

I imagined meeting my end through self-sacrifice while saving a life, secretly, unrecognized, although revealed later.

***

An interviewer asked me how I could have worked on SIOP, the U.S. plan for implementing general nuclear war.

Do analysts now think of themselves as working on nuclear first strike plans? I didn't.

***

"If you speak forth what is within you, it will save you. If you do not speak forth what is within you, it will destroy you." —Gnostic Gospel of Thomas, Verse 70

1993

Trauma is an interruption of consciousness that is not assimilated.

As Freud described it, trauma is experienced just *after* an accident, "a moment too late." Initially the experience is missed, but then it is repeated and relived endlessly—especially at night, in nightmares. One wakes from the dream in a state of fright, uncomprehending, surprised to be alive.

To awaken from the dream reawakens the trauma of having survived.

Cathy Caruth[63] says that trauma survivors have a sense of *failure*: failure to foresee, failure to control events, and failure to protect or warn others. This is called "survivor guilt."

Survivor guilt is irrational—in contrast to a *lack* of guilt for an *actual* sinful act that did not "fail" and did not lead to exposure, failure, crisis, trauma, or punishment.

Note that this exaggerates the survivor's ability to foresee or control events. Could he have been Godlike? Did he *actually* have the power to have averted the situation?

The survivor's need to "bear witness" is part of doing penance for the trauma or crisis.

My hypothesis: survivor's guilt is a cover, a rejection of a more frightening conclusion: that life is meaningless, random, unpredictable, and uncontrollable.

With respect to "trauma," there is new interest in *resilience*, not just breakdown.

***

When Robert Jay Lifton[64] went to Hiroshima, for the first few days he was overwhelmed. He thought, "Perhaps I'm not the person to do this project; I should go home." But in time he was able to draw back, listen to statements, question, and analyze.

Lifton describes himself as a "witnessing professional" who is in service to the continuity of life.

Russian-British philosopher Isaiah Berlin said that nationalism comes from a *wound*, a loss—for example, of a medieval worldview, which nationalism then replaces.

I have witnessed the capacity of so-called ordinary people to do evil.

It is commonly assumed that the Nazis in general were unique, that Nazi doctors were "a specific form of professional evil," and that we and our leaders have nothing to learn from what happened in Nazi Germany.

I don't see it that way. I believe that many Nazi doctors were no better or worse than many of us in this room, who likely would not have resisted had we been in that situation.

After being present at an execution, Tolstoy wrote, "After witnessing such a thing, I will not just never attend such an event again; I will never serve *any* government, anywhere, again."

***

Why would anyone want to be in the Government? For me, it was the excitement . . . being in the know . . . having the Inside Dope . . . experiencing a different, higher, and seemingly "more real" form of reality.

***

President Carter started out as an opponent of nuclear systems. Then in 1979 came the Pershing II, cruise missiles, and Presidential Directive 59.

What happened is that someone who opposes nuclear weapons "cannot be President."

We need to leave radioactive materials where they can be monitored and guarded while we await a better method of dealing with them, rather than burying them. These materials will remain radioactive for 10,000 years.

The only appropriate reaction to this situation is, "Holy shit!! 10,000 years!! That's incredible!"

Put on a blackboard the date that the EPA has determined these materials will be safe: *the year 11,942.*[65]

How are we wedded to combat and unable to end nuclearism?

We're not on solid ground. We are like The Old Man and the Sea, huddled in a small fishing boat next to a very large fish.

***

Some of the most agonizing conflicts of the century have occurred in divided nations such as Vietnam, Korea, Ireland, and India-Pakistan.

Often, tragic situations are only made worse by U.S. military intervention.

Be extraordinarily wary of interventionists who overestimate the degree to which political will and benign intentions can be translated into effective political action. When these "benign interventionists" recognize the limits of their public support, they are likely to pursue bombing or arms sales.

***

"Looking from outside, ours looks like *the* species whose mission or purpose is to destroy life on Earth." —John Mack

Of course, this is not our intention. But is it our inadvertent, unforeseen destiny? Look at all the planning, the degree of foresight, the priorities around which society is organized.

***

A psychiatrist said to his patients, "Don't tell me your problems—money, sex, power. These are universal. Tell me your *solutions.*"

Events of the last five years would have seemed impossible ten years ago: the reunification of Germany, the liberation of Eastern Europe, Nelson Mandela's release from prison, and the repudiation of apartheid by South Africa in a voluntary process led by President de Klerk. These events could not have been envisioned ten years ago; they would have seemed too absurd even for the Theater of the Absurd.

Thus, we don't know enough to be pessimistic.

1994

There is a hierarchy of secrets. The higher ones are only available to, and can only be told by, higher officials who have been tested by years of protecting lies and keeping lower-level secrets. Many of these should not have been secret; they needed telling in order to save lives and avert wars.

I was not a temp who saw a drawer full of secrets.

The belated honesty and courage of those who reveal Big Secrets must be welcomed.

1995

Who was the real murderer? Who was responsible?

Was it Dad? Me? *Mother?!*

It wasn't Gloria. But *she* took my place!

If Mother was not trying to kill herself, risking everything while in depression over me—if she had a strong, not trivial, reason to get to Denver on time such as a party in her brother's honor, not just a housewarming—*then I am not guilty*.

***

I wanted to be in Washington full-time, where my friend Harry Rowen was a Deputy Assistant Secretary. I wanted to be part of the *New Frontier*.

"Ah, this was it," I thought to myself, as I recalled the week in 1962 that I spent in Washington soon after finalizing my thesis. One night, I was up all night re-drafting and correcting Walt Rostow's BNSP [Basic National Security Policy], guidance for the possible U.S. use of nuclear weapons.

Then I was up very late another night, commenting on the new JSCP.[66]

Overall, it was an amazing week of feeling influential, needed, and in-the-know at the highest levels.

From there, I went to my Harvard graduation wearing a PhD gown. Then I attended my 10th reunion with the satisfaction of having fulfilled my pledge in the Alumni Notes: that I would get my PhD in June.

***

The classified info that I read on nuclear weapons from 1958 to 1961 persuaded me of the need for deterrence, coercion, and war-fighting ability. It reinforced my support of the Administration's policy.

In contrast, the classified sources that I read on Vietnam had the *opposite* effect. They made the government's policy seem foolish, reckless, and incomprehensible.

***

We must *unlearn* the moral lesson of Hiroshima. It was a moral catastrophe.

Before Hiroshima, who would have thought that killing 100,000 civilians could be justified under *any* circumstances? Who could have imagined that this would be viewed as anything but a major crime?

However, after 1945, most Americans believed—and still believe—that the existing circumstances *did* justify such a slaughter, and that this action was justifiable and successful because, they believe, it "saved a much larger number of lives."

I am going to fast on water from 8 A.M. on August 6 to nightfall on August 9, in memory and repentance for all those victims who were slaughtered by governments since I was born. As an American, it will be particularly for those slaughtered by my country between March 10, 1945 (Tokyo) and August 9, 1945 (Nagasaki).

***

I dreamed of Vietnam. There had just been a terrible battle, and all of our units, together in a large plain, had been destroyed simultaneously in a "failure of security."

I was struck by the fact that I saw no blood and no bodies on the battlefield. I imagined going into the field to look, taking home a blade of rice—stained with dried blood—as a souvenir.

Now, after the dream, I recall the sharp-edged shadows of rice leaves across the bright face of the moon, reflected in rice-paddy water in Rach Kien as we moved into position to attack a tree line at dawn.

***

It is time to tell the truth about nuclear weapons: that they are instruments of mass murder that should be globally banned, like chemical weapons and biological warfare.

What would it take to "make new law" on nuclear weapons—legally, politically, psychologically, and ethically?

***

In boot camp, the new recruits are taught—by orders, intimidation, discipline, and the example of others—to obey absurd, arbitrary orders, even if given by someone they hate and fear. This develops "good habits."

The other day I recalled telling my Marine platoon, "If you don't train and practice profusely, you will not suddenly 'get the message' when you are under fire."

***

Last night I dreamed, as usual, of being at RAND. It has been several nights in a row now.

***

When the nuclear documents were lost and I couldn't put them out, I felt like a failure . . . a loser . . . a *schlemiel* . . . a schmuck.

I've waited too long to tell the story. My memory is shot. The memories are gone, leaked out, dried up.

(Me, the "Great Leaker"—*ha!*)

***

Thay (Thich Nhat Hanh)[67] says, "To love is to want to make the other the gift of one's true presence. This is the greatest gift you can give. It is the gift of being fully there."

What a way to live: to be mindful of all the things there are in the present moment to appreciate . . . to be happy that they are there.

More from Thay: "We must learn the art of being still, and of looking deeply."

I try to imagine pausing at the beginning of my talks, or my questions, and "looking deeply . . ."

1996

We search for the ideal Mother who will give us unconditional love, without our having to edit out parts of ourselves.

When a child tries to express themselves in an authentic way, they find that their mother is only willing to accept certain parts.

At some point, the need to tell the truth becomes so strong that you do it anyway.

A month after the Accident, I was trying not to remember the trauma of it. I believed dwelling on it would only weaken me and make me less attentive to the here and how. So I organized my psyche around *not* feeling or thinking about it.

"I'm not going to die. I'm going home, like a shooting star." —Sojourner Truth

Reading these words, I cry for Mother and for Gloria.

"Thank you, Mother, for birthing me and Gloria. I love you, Gloria. I love you, Mother. Thank you for loving me."

Tears fall from my eyes and bounce off my cheek as I write.

***

I have lived through, participated in, and then actively resisted two processes—the nuclear arms race and Vietnam—that can be seen as mad, evil, criminal, wasteful, counterproductive, hopeless, catastrophic, and escalating stalemate with the potential for Apocalypse.

I was part of the antiwar movement that helped stop the U.S. war against Vietnam. Like tens of thousands of Americans, most of whom were young people, I did everything I could think of—non-violently and truthfully—to help end the war. That was the right thing to be doing, although from late-1969 to mid-1973, I expected to receive a long prison sentence as a result.

***

I very much regret certain unavoidable consequences of releasing the Papers. My regrets include the result for McNamara, Gelb, RAND, and Harry Rowen.[68]

Did they see me as simply obeying ideology, or gaining fame as a martyr at their expense, their harm?

My action was the only available action that could accomplish what was needed to save lives and save democracy.

***

Journalist Bryant Gumbel asked me, "How do you feel about being regarded as a traitor?"

I've been a patriot all my life, so I do take that as a very serious slander. People who believe that don't know much about me, and they don't know much about this country and the differences between this country and others in what it takes to be a good citizen. They think they're under the rules of the Empire we broke free from, where officials take an oath to the King.

I took an oath to uphold the Constitution. That's what I was doing when I gave the Pentagon Papers to Congress, and later to the sovereign public.

In truth, it is terrible to be seen by even one American as a traitor. I come from the World War II generation. In quite conventional ways, I am patriotic to my core.

This country was founded by so-called traitors, including anarchist Tom Paine and radical firebrand Sam Adams. They forged a country in which it is not treason, and not even a crime, for a civilian to tell the truth to his countrymen, to tell secrets of state that embarrass or incriminate a boss in the Executive branch—even a President—despite what he has been ordered to do and has promised to do.

However, any bureaucracy, such as the Executive branch, has many ways to punish an insider who tells its secrets without authorization. Even if Congress seeks to protect whistleblowers, it can't stop that.

***

In *Eichmann*, Arendt is saying the problem was not just Eichmann, the man in the glass cage. The problem was "banal" in the sense that it was *everyone*.

It is not *only* that others *could and would* have done the same jobs; others *did* do the same jobs. The work was widely shared. Thus, the problem would not have been dealt with simply by hanging Eichmann.

All of us have our hands dirty somehow.[69]

***

Someone asked me, "Do you regard yourself as a hero?" That is not a word one awards oneself.

I'll not pretend mine was a routine decision, though. To do what you should do at great risk to yourself is routine in combat, but this is not always done in civilian life. It does require models, examples. I benefited from and needed such models, and I hope my actions help others who find themselves in similar situations.

The lesson of Robert's book, *All Saints*, is that these people's life stories, their examples of sanctity, are healthy to contemplate now, in the late 20th century. These were whole lives of change, not just moments or isolated acts.[70]

Many of the saints were not perfect; they were not irreproachable in all aspects, all the time, all their lives. Doesn't that make their lives all the more exemplary and inspiring for us?

***

I want to change morals and norms with respect to bureaucratic obedience, secrecy, obligation, and loyalty.

Risking one's career or freedom (as with civil disobedience) provides an example of courageous action. It shows the power of truth-telling to change opinion, behavior, affiliations, and lifestyles.

Quotes by Rabbi Abraham Heschel[71]:

"In a free society, some are guilty, but all are responsible."

"To speak about God and remain silent on Vietnam is blasphemous."

"Be sure that every little deed counts, that every word has power."

The struggle against the Vietnam War was long and hard, like a relay race.

Be in the right spot and be ready to receive the baton.

Do your best, then pass it on.

I was grateful to those who handed me the baton, and I did my best with it.

I'm glad there are others now to pick it up and carry it forward.

1997

I was trained and reared to be (and in fact, was realistically headed to be) one of the top 100 best pianists in the United States—similar to the rankings for golfers and figure skaters.

Did I keep practicing after Mother died to keep from seeming to accuse her of coercing me?

Did I keep practicing to keep *myself* from the shame of admitting to myself that I had gone along with her coercion?

***

I developed a talent for risk-taking, and for calm, competence, and grace under pressure when assessing and reducing risks.

John Paul Vann believed it was crucial to take risks, preferably small ones. I practiced this—for example, driving the rural roads in Vietnam.

We were "taking back the roads" . . . "standing tall" . . . "showing command presence." The point was to make it routine, a habit, an example.[72]

Courage is a choice. It is trainable, manipulatable, and subject to group influence, exhortation, and practice.

***

It can be hard for people to grasp that I am and feel both Jewish and Christian-Protestant.

I was raised as a Christian Scientist. My parents always said that we *were* Jews, and that we were Christian in our *religion*.

Were we Jewish Christians? Christian Jews?

Erik Erikson, Robert Jay Lifton, and Ken Kenniston started the yearly Wellfleet[73] gatherings. Our idea was that we would pin down psychohistory ... make it a "real" field, although Erikson hated the word "psychohistory."

What I *didn't* want was for us to become an arm of the Academy. Some people wanted us to "train" students, but we wanted to be able to speak freely with each other.

***

Why distrust Conscience? For the same reasons not to trust Authority.

Individual Conscience is shaped, educated, and installed by Authority, through interactions with parents, peers, and societal authorities. Thus, it gives excessive priority to Obeying Authority.

Conscience is easily duped and put to sleep, or overridden. People are too easily persuaded that alternatives to Great Evil would be even Greater Evil.

Actually, much Great Evil is done with the *active help and instigation* of Conscience. One feels impelled to Obey Authority and protect the group and nation in order to avoid guilt, shame, blame, remorse, social sanction, or legal punishment.

The threat of Shame gives undue weight to the opinions and interests of hierarchical society, and too little weight to resisting and rejecting Great Evils.

***

My personal ethic is that Evil is never to be done and cannot be justified. Any purported justification for it is to be distrusted and disregarded. It is to be warned about and exposed, not concealed. It is to be condemned, resisted, organized against, averted—even at the possible cost of self-sacrifice.

In the eyes of the President, bombing Hiroshima and Nagasaki was justified by one set of reasons; in the eyes of most Manhattan Project scientists, by another.

What the public was told: "One million lives were saved" by the use of nuclear weapons in Japan.

For officials and subordinates, the justification was: "We were following the President's orders."

"Humanity's willingness to do evil when instructed by authority is well known." —Hannah Arendt

***

Unauthorized disclosures are the lifeblood of a republic. Without them, it can't survive as a true republic or democracy.

If a leader can effectively block off the legislature from all Executive Branch information except what he authorizes, he is a dictator or a monarch, even if an elected one. In such a state, the notion of popular sovereignty or democracy is a hoax.

***

I wanted to expose the Pentagon Papers as the internal records of Empire.

One reason capitalism is popular is the widespread belief in "equality of opportunity." "Anyone can succeed," it is said. This has a lottery-like appeal.

Ignored in all of that are actual odds of "success," as well as the questionable means that are often involved in achieving it.

The power of the West has been its ability to mobilize a group of people into a community of violence, hatred, and fear against internal and external scapegoats.

What happened to "We're all one human family, sharing our one and only lifeboat?"

American government and society show scant recognition of the sacredness of life and the Earth. The Earth should not be sacrificed for national or personal purposes.

***

The problem with "problem-solving" is that it reduces life to a series of problems.

Stay with your ability to grow, learn, and respond with your whole self.
Cultivate joy.

***

Pat says that what sustains us as we get older is some kind of connection to spiritual values, vision, and experience.

For me, that was Gandhi. But I've gotten away from this.

In 1968, I was introduced not only to civil disobedience (self-sacrifice, disobedience, and jail-going) but also to the power of nonviolence and the truth of our Oneness. The underlying values of nonviolence spoke to me.

At this morning's talk, I am tempted to speak about Gandhi's influence on my life.

***

Titles:

"An Unclassified Life"

"The Making and Unmaking of a Cold Warrior"

"Eightfold Path for the Nuclear Age"

***

It was rational for my RAND colleagues to treat me as untouchable, banned, taboo.[74]

***

What if I hadn't had the Pentagon Papers? How would my life have been different?

***

At 4 A.M., in a hotel room in Princeton:

My notepads are filled with questions.

I am a Saul Bellow character, up writing questions at 4 A.M., after 36 years.

If I publish these questions and hypotheses, I fear/hear readers asking, "Why am I reading this? Why are you publishing this now, rather than waiting until you have the answers?"

I feel like a mountaineer on the face of a cliff, seeking handholds, a path up the East Face, needing greater skill and equipment and team than I've got—and also greater strength, endurance, hope, determination, and courage.

1998

Titles Brainstorm:
  "The Courage of One's Insignificance"
  "The Uses and Abuses of Honor, Courage, and Loyalty"
  "Memoirs of a Revelationist"

What happened to me? I was at the height of my—and RAND's—influence and prestige.

I had the equivalent of a religious conversion: I was "Born Again."

***

I was a disciplined Marine Commander who relished my autonomy as Company Commander.

A good Commander does not issue commands for *how* to carry out a task or achieve an objective. He leaves unsaid the details about how it is to be implemented; he does not over-monitor or over-control. He gives leeway and time and resources for initiative, flexibility, creativity, imagination, ingenuity, and exploitation of local or personal resources in carrying out his orders.

Marine fire-teams, like guerrillas, expect to be on their own, out of communication, and lost. They are expected to find targets without orders or direction, and then proceed to risk their lives.

***

A soldier is trained, rehearsed, and habituated to do brave, self-sacrificing things, things that are dangerous, difficult, and unpleasant.

These "virtues of a soldier" can also be used in defense of one's Constitution and country to oppose secret-keeping, illegal orders, Commanders, and Presidents.

The Moral of My Talk at Veterans for Peace Event:

As a citizen, situations may arise that challenge you to put at risk "all that you hold dear"—your career, family, membership in the elite, livelihood, fortune, reputation, and "sacred honor."

***

War is an "altered state," with values and norms reversed. Civilian authority becomes subordinate to military authority, which is to be obeyed without question.

The military habituates soldiers toward self-sacrifice, courage, and risk-taking: on order or when called for to support the mission—or, secondary to the mission, to support the team, unit, and friends.

The use of violence (and even lawbreaking) to maintain power may be viewed by leaders as "necessary," "worthwhile," "tolerable," "excusable," or "inevitable."

To kill, which was formerly taboo, becomes an *obligation*.

Even for a bad cause, there may be room for bravery, loyalty, dedication, patriotism, and decency.

Yet the existence of these doesn't make it a good cause.

Nor does a bad cause make the opponent's cause good, wise, admirable, or right.

There may be no "good side."

"Here dead lie we because we did not choose
To live and shame the land from which we sprung.
Life, to be sure, is nothing much to lose;

But young men think it is, and we were young." —A. E. Housman

***

Hypocrisy is viewed as shameful and embarrassing, so it must be denied and concealed.

We are hypocritical about our own hypocrisy, while condemning others' hypocrisy.

We lie, we lie about lying, and we lie about what we lie about.

***

Inaction may be a safer course, even for a President, compared to acting and failing. If you refrain from acting, catastrophic results are less likely to be attributed to you.

To act or speak out attracts possible blame, while *not* acting keeps one safer from being held individually responsible.

George Stephanopoulos said in *Newsweek*, "All Presidents should have learned that the cover-up is always worse than the crime."

Actually, *no*. Look at the examples of My Lai, Hiroshima, Dresden, Tokyo, Hamburg, El Salvador, Guatemala, Nicaragua, Chile, Iran, and Indonesia.

Many cover-ups continue because they conceal crimes of immense proportions, crimes that are still going on or are likely to be repeated in the future.

***

I'm not a *revolutionary*; I'm a *"revelationary."*

I'm a Loyal Mutineer. I believe that secret, covert, unconstitutional Executive practices—the Invisible Government—must be exposed from within.

We need a national and global change that is as dramatic and "miraculous" as the change in South Africa.

I would like to be able to love my country and love justice, too.

I would like to be able to *criticize* my country, in order to change it and make it more lovable.

1999

When Janaki and I first met, she was surprised by my work and curious about what I did. She was shocked that I would do such a thing as my earlier work.

She is still curious about the way I think. For her it is both familiar (Harvard, MIT) and unfamiliar (my knowledge about the government).

Janaki came from a nationalist culture in India, *and* she was brought up to serve the people. It was a paradox: the richness of her culture, but also the horror of it (the caste system). Her parents were very strict about being anti-caste.

Janaki told me that Mahavira, the first Jain, was a great man and great spiritual leader who lived about the same time as Buddha. He was anti-caste and communitarian.

Janaki and I talked about individual transformation, which was a key concept for her.

Hindu mythology focuses on shape-changing.

There are circumstances in which humans ordinarily, almost universally, behave very badly. Can this be changed?

Can human nature and bureaucratic behavior be changed?

Janaki says the word "enemy" doesn't allow for transformation.

When you say "He's a friend," it means that you have a possibility for change.

***

Given all my government-based experiential reasons and my conscious calculations and (perhaps unique) knowledge, and even meeting Randy, and my exposure to Gandhi, etc.: does it all add up to sufficient explanation for what I did? Or do you also need the element of childhood psychological trauma in the mix?

***

Q: "What changed you from being a Company Man?"

Good question.

In 1967–1969, all my friends were Cold War Company Men—and we *all* wanted the U.S. out of Vietnam.

I was a Company Man who exposed the secrets of the Company.

What if you come to believe, during a war, that as Henry V said, "The cause be not just?"[75]

For me, this moment came in September 1968, as I read early volumes of the Pentagon Papers and I shifted to seeing the war as a moral issue.

If you managed to talk to the right people in Vietnam, it didn't take long to learn that we were not going to be successful there.

You didn't have to be an ichthyologist to "smell the stinking fish." In 1961, it took me a visit of less than a week.

***

My survival in the Accident in 1946 was accidental, inadvertent. It was not through my initiative, efforts, or skill that I survived. It was not in any way chosen by me.

Nonetheless, at an unconscious level I felt guilt-worthy and blame-worthy.

Guilt . . . guilt . . . guilt . . . How to get rid of my guilt for Mother dying?

Actually, my mother was "guilty as hell" for the Accident and for her and my sister's deaths. Her insistence on going straight to the party—and not stopping at a motel so Dad could sleep—was a measure of her self-absorption.

She may have been depressed—and, as Dad said, "suicide-prone."

Still, Dad should have insisted on stopping.

He, like Mother, was guilty. It was time for him to disobey!

By the time of the Accident, I had already given up on a "piano career" and concerts. I was learning pieces that I liked, such as "Clair de Lune." I no longer needed to "wish" for my freedom.

Should I have *insisted* on the "Good Seat"—the one that turned out to be the "Death Seat"? Nah. That was random.

It was an accident that Gloria died, not I. It wasn't my fault, and I don't owe anything to anyone for it.

A friend said, "Forget about your all-forgiving attitude toward your mother. What you need is to get out your rage at her for being so self-centered, not seeing you, and putting her own pride and dreams ahead of you."

***

My secret had been that I was *not* going to be a pianist.

Later, no one knew that I had ever been a pianist, or that my mother and sister had been killed.

***

Someone who enters psychoanalysis enters a world where all rules of reason, all norms, all common sense have changed. The very nature and identity of authority and of reality are in question.

Likewise, his identity—all he knows about himself, his past, and his values, aims, and beliefs—is put in question and undermined. His understanding of himself, as well as his self-esteem, are at the mercy of another: a capricious and initially inscrutable Authority who cannot be induced to speak, to respond.

However, by conforming to the rules and responding to cues, he can win the analyst's approval, encouragement, and even hope of a cure.

***

No one understands fully, and/or accurately, their *own* family, marriage, neighborhood, town, country, state, nation, empire . . . or other people.

My secret is that I was raised as a Christian Scientist. By fanatics. In a cult.

I was taught that what others believe, and what all the "evidence" of the senses shows, is false . . . myth . . . ideology.

I don't want to be defined by others as either a "Jew" or a "non-Jew."

I revel in my singularity, "ambiguity," contradictions, and complexity.

***

In "normal" circumstances, including crises—*especially* in emergencies—I was a reliable team player. I was focused, disciplined, efficient, and deferential. I wasn't one to "fight the problem," "buck authority," or try to "do it my way."

***

What *did* send me over the brink, to work actively with Congress and the antiwar movement in ways that precluded the possibility of further work for the Executive?

The usual misunderstanding of my motives ignores and underrates the role of information from my friend Mort Halperin about Nixon's intentions.

Mort, not I, was a Kissinger associate, assistant, and student. He worked in the Nixon administration and was in charge of the Pentagon Papers.

Would someone else have acted similarly[76] who had the same experience that I had? It's hard to know, because *no one did*.

Would I have done it without my work as a RAND analyst for State, Defense, and the White House from 1958 to 1964? My research for my 1954 and 1962 theses? My 1958 Coercion notes?

Would I have acted the same from 1968 to 1975 if I hadn't *gone* to Vietnam after spring 1966? Probably not.

To leave out important, even crucial, explanatory or causal elements such as these is misleading.

2000

I grew up during World War II and the Cold War. That brought me a certain *vision* of America's role in the world, and a *vocation*: to serve the President in foreign policy.

Both of those took me into participation in Vietnam, and that experience cost me both the vision and the calling.

The war took these from me. These losses were painful, like an amputation. They still hurt today.

Fortunately, with the help of other Americans, the resistance to presidential pursuit of the war taught me a new form of courage and patriotism, as well as better ways of serving my country.

That is why I am writing a memoir now: to tell future officials, *don't wait*.

***

Courage in a Bad Cause: The Pentagon Papers described a war that was hopeless, unjust, and criminal. Does this dishonor our dead? Does it dishonor their courage? Their patriotism?

Neither side is necessarily "good" in a civil war, a colonial war, or even a war of self-defense.

How often is a just cause fought entirely by just means?

***

Previously, trust in the President was excessive, inappropriate, and misplaced for officials and citizens of a republic. This was a naiveté that we should not wish to return to.

2001

I was seen as unpredictable, uncontrollable, a loose cannon.

[My RAND colleagues] viewed me as the (self)-designated sacrifice, the volunteer to "bell the cat"—that is, to reveal secrets.

"Let DE do it. Let DE take the rap. But give us the quotes, and we'll analyze them."

No one who said to the President "Cut losses *now*" told the same thing to Congress or the press. Why? They had promised not to.

Don't waste your life speaking truth only to Executive power, to the President. Tell Congress and the press the truths that "power" doesn't want known about estimates, calculations, and plans.

Axioms:

1. Nobody knows confidently, reliably, or fully what we are up against or how best to deal with it—in both the short range and long range.
2. Beware of irrevocable courses of action.
3. Mistakes will be made, mis-predictions will be offered, and experiments will fail.
4. There is no sure protection against failure. This includes inaction.

***

What I was *not* was as important as what I *was* in shaping my response to Vietnam. I believed in Just War and limited war. Thus I opposed reliance on nuclear weapons in warfare or diplomacy, I opposed strategic bombing of cities, and I opposed massive retaliation and war with China.

***

Q: "How do you feel about being called a 'Traitor'?"

A: "Do *you* think I am a traitor?" . . . "How would *you* feel?"

I couldn't have done what I did if I had been terrified and paralyzed at the thought of being called names and slandered, even names that I hate—such as "Traitor," "Rat," "Snitch," or "Commie."

Too many people kept silent for too long, while too many men were being lied to death, their lives "wasted," for fear of being called names by their friends or bosses.

Those who call me "traitor" don't appreciate our form of government. They don't know how lucky they are to be citizens of a nation in which it is not treason to tell the truth to your fellow citizens, even though officials don't want it told.

Their sense of who loyalty is owed to is more suited to an absolute monarchy or a dictatorship than to a citizen of a democratic republic—or of a country that aspires to be so.

***

Lifton says, don't be proud of holding the power of life and death. Whatever you threaten, you will be threatened with.

We hold double standards for ourselves and for the regimes we covertly support. Why "covertly"? To sustain the image of ourselves as promoters of freedom and democracy.

As with Sen. Zell Miller's comment: "We are liberators, not occupiers."[77]

We do things that only make matters worse, such as Reagan's "arms for hostages" and support of contra terrorists in Nicaragua.

When the U.S. lacks national or strategic interest, it does not lift a finger to prevent genocide or mass atrocities.

"Why do they hate us?" Because they believe, with reason, that we have reckless unconcern for their welfare, which we worsen capriciously, casually, and cruelly.

***

"If you could cure all the world's diseases, at the cost of killing an innocent child, what would you do?"

A hypothetical question such as this can damn you for life. It can so distance you in your sense of what is morally possible, permissible, and justifiable as to corrupt and debauch you—like the first bribe you accept, or your first experience of an addicting drug.

***

We urgently need new capacities—a nonlinear, discontinuous leap in our ability to understand and change human social behavior.

Advice to the Left: quiet voices are to be encouraged.

We owe it to both our forefathers and our progeny not to squander our Constitutional inheritance in a moment of panic.

Maxim of a free government: entrust no one with the power to endanger the public liberty.

***

Written while flying United Airlines to New York in late 2001, the day bombing began in Afghanistan:

We are all passengers of United Airlines Flight 93. How will we use this precious time?

How will we use the rest of our lives, whether short or long?

By telling another, "I love you; I've always loved you."

2002

Humans can now destroy most human and other species by poisoning the conditions of life—including urban, "civilized" life.

"The unleashed power of the atom has changed everything save our modes of thinking, and we thus drift toward unparalleled catastrophe." —Albert Einstein

What change was Einstein calling for?

We need to use our human capacity for change on our own propensities—specifically, our readiness to gamble with catastrophe.

We need to change what it means to be human.

***

Don't inflict catastrophe, or the unthinkable, on societies—even if, by your calculations, it is the best or only option to avert a greater catastrophe. Always distrust and ignore such a calculation!

Nuclear first use would not be merely an error. It would be a crime against humanity. To threaten it, prepare for it, anticipate it—as we do—is to contemplate committing a crime against humanity.

To fail to do one's utmost to prevent this is to be an accomplice.

I was an interventionist Cold Warrior. I also was, and am, a Just Warrior. Hence, I advocate for bans on strategic bombing, nuclear weapons, torture, terror, military dictators, coups, empire, and disproportionate killing.

***

Violence is cruel. Cruelty breeds cruelty, fear, and hatred, which gives rise to revenge and reciprocation—setting in motion a cycle of violence.

Just Say No. Reject violence and cruelty. Withhold your deference, cooperation, and support. Refuse to be silent.

***

My book is an insider's account of how I and my colleagues faced choices. I neither defend nor wholly condemn my earlier choices and the underlying motives and values that drove those choices.

Title ideas: *Stolen History*; *Forbidden Truths*; *Thief of Truth*; *Stolen Truth*; *Higher Loyalties*; *To Help End a War*; *Revelationary*

I did something that is generally regarded as *always bad*: breaking a promise, an oath.

In my specific case, it was seen as "treasonous" by many, including the government.

Actually, I wasn't a thief—I *copied* the Papers; I didn't steal them.

Was it a transgression? A crime? A prophetic transgression?

There is no good-sounding term to describe making an "unauthorized disclosure."

I acted out of *responsibility*, not guilt. I knew more than most because of my close involvement, in both Vietnam and Washington. I felt that I should help clean up our mess.

***

It takes a lot to make a person break the group solidarity that is the main basis of their happiness.

Fear of becoming separated from one's own group is one of the fundamental human fears, virtually equivalent to the fear of death. Even to contemplate such a separation evokes feelings of loneliness, isolation, unworthiness, and meaninglessness.

It is absolutely *banned* to make unauthorized disclosures that hurt institutions by lowering their authority or prestige, thus "weakening" them in the eyes of rivals.

Also, one may be motivated to remain silent about an institution's past or present crimes because of an altruistic fear of hurting a "good institution" and its people, as well as those who depend on its work.

***

If you want to be entrusted with secrets, you must be willing to lie convincingly and conceal things from your family, friends, close associates, and teammates.

Information Theory: Lying involves *compartmentalization*. It is essential to maintain watertight compartments with no "leaking" or "spillover."

See the *Titanic*, which sank because multiple compartments were ruptured. If the rip had only been in the middle section, it wouldn't have been a problem.

***

In decision-making, there is little to no consideration of "best case" outcomes.

Consider "miracle" events that had been seen as "impossible," or had not even been imagined: the Missile Gap turning out not to be real; Iraqi "weapons of mass destruction" not found; the end of the Cold War; and the South African revolution.

Are history's "Hinge Periods" ever recognized as such at the time? Such openings often precede foreign policy "miracles."

***

The written—and now, taped—record is part of a process of blame-avoidance. Ignorance is an excuse; it is the primary defense. "I didn't know . . ." "I never dreamed it would . . ." "No one could have . . ."

But a *document* proves that *someone* could, and *did*, know . . . inquire . . . guess . . . fear . . . warn. Documents are needed to hold leaders to account.

For oral histories, ask the person, "When was this document written? To whom? Who really wrote it, and with what guidance? What did it mean? What was it meant to achieve or evoke? What was it arguing against? What did it conflict with?"

"Plausible denial" says: "it didn't happen"; the U.S. had nothing to do with it; the President had nothing to do with it; it was done for a compelling reason; the President had "no choice"; there was "no alternative"; and "no one could have foreseen" the resulting negative consequences.

Cover stories support plausible denial with distortions, misdirection, and lies—all mixed with false, selective, and misleading "evidence."

***

Human cruelty and destructiveness are not aberrant. Nor are compassion, altruism, and self-sacrifice. All of these qualities are human, normal, "ordinary."

It turns out that "inhumanity" is characteristically *human*.

The real lesson of Milgram's work is that a strong general inhibition against causing great pain is overridden by a strong, almost hypnotic instinct of Obedience to Authority. No one foresaw these results, which are surprising and shocking.

Each of us humans is capable of acting heroically, of rising to the moment and doing what is needed or might help, even at risk to our own well-being.

In other circumstances, each of us is also capable of turning our eyes away from a serious problem where we could be of some help, but instead we let that moment pass.

Every one of us, without any exception, has done that and is doing that in some ways.

And, every one of us can change and do better, at least in a crisis—no matter how we've lived our lives until that moment.

We all make mistakes, and we all take gambles that put others' lives at risk (for example, driving a car). Catastrophes, however, are *failed gambles* on a larger scale. They are made by people like us who are within—and at the head of—powerful organizations, bureaucracies, and nations.

**

"Collateral damage" describes impacts and casualties that were not intended or desired. If you didn't intend it, then it doesn't "count" morally, and you are not culpable for it.

State-sponsored killing, even mass killing of innocents, is not defined as a "crime." It is an "option," which may or may not be seen as an "error."

**

Do not delegate conscience unquestioningly, unconditionally. Consider telling the truth when vital principles are at stake, or when you may save lives by doing so.

Silence is complicity, as are secrets and concealed crimes, when others' lives are endangered by your silence. This is so even if you "promised" it, "owe" it, or are ordered or coerced to remain silent.

An unauthorized disclosure can be a patriotic act and a service to the country, helping to save lives and preserve core principles of democracy.

My old career is no longer available to me.

For an Insider, going public against the war and the President is not a good career move.

Do I prefer my new lifestyle? No, *not at all.*

(See my dreams of my old life.)

Socrates was given a choice: flee into exile, or take poison to end his life. He chose the poison.

**

Advice to myself: at speeches, and everywhere I go:

Make people's lives lighter. Make them feel appreciated.

Don't just inform, worry, and condemn.

Don't evoke rage and hatred in an effort to use these as motivators—even against outrageous, awful behaviors and institutions.

Don't take out your negative feelings (rage, anger, frustration, hurt, or bitterness) on people who haven't provoked them.

Do say and do things that will make others feel good, and that make you feel good that you said and did them.

***

Our imprint on other humans and species extends far beyond our present-time personal horizon of concern. We must now evolve, using our species' unique capacity for group cultural change, and drawing upon our long-range concern for future generations of humans and all life.

From *The Russell-Einstein Manifesto*: "Recall your (our) (common) humanity, and forget the rest."[78]

***

I am proud to be an American—to bear the obligations, responsibility, and accountability that are associated with freedom.

There is another America out there, waiting to be born.

Look at our nation with the same daring shown by the Founding Fathers, who "invented" free speech.

Dick Falk[79] says that the "politics of the impossible" need not be trapped by the conventional wisdom as to what is "possible" at any given time.

"Don't be hypnotized by reality," he says. "Question it. The challenge is not just to *understand* reality, but to *change* it."

I have no confidence that good will prevail, nor that the odds are in favor of Good and Humanity. Yet, I fight.

Think anew. It is in our power to change the world.

2003

I am an American by birth, a Midwesterner, and a Jew.

I am a Person of Hope.

I am a Patriot by conviction of what this country can be—and, for the most part, wants to be.

We can do better than this.

We can *be* better than this.

***

Am I "relieved," as others suppose, at last night's news that my meningioma [brain tumor] is harmless? Or am I disappointed that I don't face a short deadline, forcing me to write and publish, and relieving me of other obligations?

***

On the Impossibility of Heuristic Biography:

Many people have sought to understand me as a whistleblower. This has given me an unusual basis from which to evaluate the limits of people's ability to understand or predict another person's behavior.

Each person is unique not only in their fingerprints, iris, and DNA, but also in the Gestalt of their thoughts, feelings, and experiences. No one can truly understand another person's motives, feelings, beliefs, meanings, expectations, and actions.

Nor is a memoir the full and true story, due to processes of Selective Memory, Concealment, and Self-deception.

***

Humans tend to ignore or reject the likelihood that an act of vengeance will lead to further reciprocation and a cycle of violence.

To feel justified in seeking revenge, one needs to feel that the "enemy's" act was "unprovoked." However, "You all started it" may be a smokescreen, a form of self-deception that overlooks the role of one's own side in sparking and maintaining the conflict.

In humans, violence is married to technology. Technology-aided violence is so easy that humans are led to commit violence for a wide range of motives.

How much killing in history has occurred without a tool, with only the use of bare hands? Today, this rarely happens.

***

Humans' reluctance to cause suffering or to refuse succor is much less than "we" imagine.

The seeds of violent conflict are sown in despair and injustice.

Someone who deployed to Iraq told me that no soldier he knew felt good about what they did there.

***

We need to be skeptical of what we think God tells us to do, or permits.[80]

***

Exemplary disobedience challenges habits of obedience, passivity, and silence.

Cooperation in wrongdoing is more widespread than people realize. Part of it, an essential part, is simply keeping silent. This silence—by failure to protest, discuss, debate, and challenge wrongdoing—keeps it a non-issue, off the political agenda.

We have both the responsibility and the power to act. We can choose to withdraw our cooperation and end our complicity, our failure to perceive and act morally on what we have seen.

Gandhi says to consider many courses of action against a social wrong—not violence, but nonviolent actions such as non-cooperation, withholding, obstructing, disobeying, and challenging authority.

"I won't let you. I will use all my weight and influence and strength not to hurt or punish you, but to stop you."

It is Thursday night, the day the war began. I'm about to join a rally, and I expect to be arrested tonight. This seems like a good night for a patriotic American who opposes this war to be in jail.

I'm proud to join so many others around the world who have seen through this illegal and unjustified war, and who are protesting it with their voices and their bodies.

***

You do not increase your own security by lowering the security of a powerful rival.

***

Fritjov Capra's definition of spirituality: a deep awareness of connection to the rest of the Earth, the Universe—of being part of, one with, all life.[81]

Also, Earth as a living organism, an entity: Gaia.

Someone told me that I sound like a "secular humanist."

I'm certainly not a "humanist."

How can our species awaken to Gaia?

***

"In this amazingly beautiful world, there is such beauty that it brings tears to your eyes . . . and there is so much misery in the world that it brings tears to your eyes." —Matthew Fox[82]

***

The Four Noble Truths of Buddhism are seriously misleading. There are very different degrees of, and intentions of, *dukkha* (suffering). Not all are morally equivalent, nor are all "evil."

See Huston Smith's[83] comparison of a dropped ice cream to the Holocaust.

Someone said, "If I lived in a hamlet in Vietnam and a helicopter dropped napalm on me and my family, would my suffering be caused *only* by my 'greed, ignorance, and aversion'?"

NOTES FROM JOHN SEED'S TALK[84]

The through-line of life on Earth is nearly 4 billion years. The through-line of the Universe is nearly 14 billion years.

Brian Swimme says that 60,000 years ago, there were only a couple of thousand humans. We could easily have gone extinct.

Arne Næss says that we need an *ecological identity*.[85]

What past karma led to the extinction of 99.9% of Earth's species?

What will "bad" humans, as well as "good" ones, be reincarnated as?

It doesn't take long to heal the illusion of separateness from Nature. But how do "we" ecological beings *change* destructive processes and power "realities" such as war, debt enslavement, capitalism, ecological destruction, and empire?

We need to release and express feelings such as fear, rage, and concern for what is happening to the world, to free our intelligence to take protective action.

Spirituality is a sense that life is a *mystery*. We do not know how it emerges, and we will *never* know.

∗∗∗

I don't have time now for rage, terror, despair, shame, guilt, depression, or recrimination.

Drew Dellinger[86] says we are in a period of "new emergences and emergencies."

Among the emergencies we face are the ecological crisis, creeping fascism (not creeping . . . galloping!), and the 500-year crisis of white supremacy.

Among the emergences: a growing sense of our profound interdependence.

This is wisdom: to love life, to have a passion for living, to defend life.

Life is mysterious and fragile. Don't be confident that we can't destroy it.

"Positive peace" is the presence of justice and Beloved Community.

We have to learn how to speak to people with whom we do not agree. As Martin Luther King Jr. said, "You have no ability to influence the minds of people who can feel your contempt."

Civil disobedience is not the whole answer. We also need elections, lobbying, legislation, citizen initiatives, and global actions.

For me, civil disobedience is community, ritual, and retreat.

What are people responding to, when they admire or thank me?

I believe that their response reflects that I am a source of encouragement, a basis for hope for them.

* * *

Joanna Macy[87] was asked, "How do you keep cheerful, happy, joyful?"

Her reply: "I look at where I want us to get in 50–100 years; then, from that, where in 10–20 years; then, next year; then, today.

"I *am* attached to the results of my actions—don't talk non-attachment to me! But don't let your actions be *dependent* on being assured of a particular result."

Notes taken during Matthew Fox's talk:

Q: How do you find joy in terrible times?
A: *Be ready* to find it.
Do things that in your experience bring you joy.
Find joyful people to be with.
Pay attention to beauty and hunt for goodness.
Fall in love with the world, in spite of History.
There's a lot more than human folly going on in the world and the Cosmos.

2004

I have a lifelong interest in catastrophes: how they come about and how to avert them. Through my Critical Incident Studies [study of past crises], I have learned about how catastrophes happen, how to foresee them, and what warning signs to look for.

***

When I was 15, I *experienced* a catastrophe. My hypothesis is that to avert overwhelming feelings of loss, sadness, meaninglessness, and guilt about the Accident, I developed a two-part "cover story."

First, I told myself that the meaning of the Accident was that Mother's death was necessary to free me from a piano career. (Not Gloria's death; she was "collateral damage.") However, this repressed the fact that I had already abandoned my piano career months earlier. Although not a crisis for me, this surely contributed to Mother's depression, which may have played a role in her death.

The second part of my cover story was that my life was expendable, and in fact, I "owed a life." Preferably this was to be through heroic sacrifice. It wasn't about fame or appreciation; only I had to know about it. It would be nice if one survivor knew, but no need to tell others. The prospect of this relieved me of feelings of guilt for being alive and happy.

At Wellfleet: A survivor's concern is finding *meaning* in the event, so that one's remaining life can have meaning.

For me, "meaning" was liberation. But as part of the "Devil's bargain," I "owed a life" (to Gloria). I also owed vigilance to Dad, as well as the obligation to warn.

"The dead must not have died in vain." A survivor seeks the *meaning* in the deaths, questions the *cause*, and resolves to warn and awaken others.

***

A fundamental American myth: "It is God's wish that America take over the world."

We must give up "illegitimate means and infeasible goals" in Iraq.

In some efforts and some wars, there is no good substitute for accepting failure, changing course, and redefining priorities.

As in Vietnam, we are not *on* the wrong side; we *are* the wrong side. Bombing the Iraqi people will not win hearts and minds.

Overthrowing Saddam Hussein did not give us the right to rule Iraq, nor the ability to do it peacefully.

Pacification means getting people to accept rule by foreigners peacefully, without violent resistance. That is not going to happen in Iraq.

Are we going to continue fighting endless wars for empire? Or could we give up our aspirations to be a super-empire, and simply live within our means?

***

To tell secrets is to break a promise, vow, or oath.

What is one to do when oaths conflict with one's loyalties or obligations?

***

A soldier at the My Lai massacre said, "No, I wasn't ordered—but I felt like I was ordered."

***

There are not enough leaks of the kind that democracy needs—the kind that strengthen our national security by exposing policies that weaken it.

Can a democracy be healthy if it operates with Executive secrecy, covert action, and lying? Can such a "democracy" survive?

Officials act as if democracy were a dangerous luxury, a privilege—not a right, a fundamental value, a protector of other values.

They discuss leaks as if *only* unauthorized disclosures pose ethical issues and risk damage to national security and welfare.

In a democracy that wants to remain a democracy and continue to enjoy its benefits, the risks of secrecy must be weighed against the risks of disclosure, with a presumption in favor of openness—even with all of its inherent dangers, debates, frictions, and controversies.

I want to write a book on "The Pathologies of Secrecy, Obedience, Loyalty, and Promise-keeping."

***

Question conscience, just as we are to question authority. Conscience can often be manipulated and distorted, ill-guided and ill-founded.

Always consider the human consequences, especially to life and limb.

Do not trust your conscience if it says to kill, lie, or harm humans or other living things.

Conscience is often an untrustworthy guide. It overvalues, or puts absolute priority on: loyalty to the group; obedience to authority and rules; revenge of others or the group; the interests of family, tribe, group, or nation; and the values of one's own group or of people in authority.

***

In retrospect, I realize that I need not have revealed myself as the source of the Pentagon Papers leak. I *did* have a choice, and I was wrong to think I did not.

Also, I need not have told Carol or involved Robert and Mary.[88]

***

HA! I see, now, the feelings I arouse in the National Security community, which I left, betrayed, and created suspicions about in their clients and masters.

It is the same feeling that I had about former pupils of my teacher who had left the piano:
They had quit.
They were the Renegades—*like the astronaut who cuts the cord.*

***

There are two ways of responding to the Holocaust: One is, "Never again should this happen to Jews." The other: "Never again should this happen to *anyone*."

Must one abandon one's Jewish identity to support Palestinian rights?

***

To forgive is not to imply that the offending party is not culpable, or did not have a choice, or was not acting from ignorance, fear, or misunderstanding.

Something can be inexcusable, yet not unforgivable.

Unforeseen consequences opposite to one's initial expectations are common.

Why is there a concept of "blessings-in-disguise," but not one of "disasters-in-disguise," which must be at least as common?

***

Someone said that if religion were a quest, it would be fine. However, a religion is the *end* of a quest. Religions have the answers, which their adherents then seek to impose on others.

My religion: do not order, obey, conceal, or carry out the deliberate killing or reckless endangerment of noncombatants, broadly defined as women, children, old and sick people.

Can we divest mysticism from its ties to mainstream religion, especially religious beliefs and doctrines?

I don't believe in a God that listens to us, responds to us, or protects us (as in war). One can, however, for calm and reassurance, profitably consult with and attune to spiritual energies such as Love, Beauty, Consciousness, and Unity.

Norman Mailer spoke of how we all have within us a center of stillness, surrounded by silence. It is like the quiet eye of a hurricane.

We're all in the storm at every moment ... and at every moment we can be the *eye* of the storm. Contemplative life is living in that quiet eye, continually moving in harmony with the hurricane's movement to remain in the storm's calm center.

***

At Wellfleet: Climate change has removed the uncertainty about Apocalypse, as human agency brings this brief benign period of climate to an end.

The reports of the IPCC,[89] derived from political compromise, are very conservative. Actually, it's all happening much, *much* faster. There is *no precedent* for such rapid change.

Climate change is irreversible, as heat-trapping CO_2 stays in the atmosphere for about 200 years. We know what will happen, quickly. Yet we seem curiously paralyzed.

It will take a heroic effort to limit the warming to two degrees Centigrade. If we do nothing, five degrees Centigrade of warming is predicted by the end of the century.

We must act globally and cooperatively. Yet here is little sign of humans' ability to do this.

Will human society as we know it continue to exist in the face of massive extinctions, violent storms, and decades-long droughts?

***

Civil disobedience is like being a whistleblower. Both are a form of truth-telling. Both involve stepping over the line and separating yourself from what your organization or government is doing, identifying it as *wrong*.

I'll go down speaking truth, opposing violence, and supporting alternatives.

2005

For my Morality Book:

My moral obsession is: *How does mass killing of civilians happen, and how can it be averted?*

This includes the planned and prepared use of nuclear weapons.

The word "evil" may not be helpful, but I aspire to consensus-based extreme condemnation of genocide, massacre through bombing of civilians, nuclear war, torture, assassination, apartheid, and massive detention or relocation.

Most physical harm/intimidation/endangerment is done by the coordinated behavior of people in groups, usually groups that are hierarchically organized and directed. Alternatively, it is done by individuals acting as members of a group that condones or directs such behavior.

The average group members who perpetuate, conceal, or tolerate such harm are not more prone to commit such acts on their own, one-to-one, when they are not representing the group or pursuing the group's aims and directions.

You can get most anyone to do most anything by making the wrongful harming of others a condition of remaining a respected member in a valued group, or of maintaining or attaining a valued status or role within a group.

The "good enough" reasons to kill or endanger other humans do not include "I was ordered to do it by a competent authority," or "others were doing it," or "I was warned that if I didn't do it, I would be punished and ostracized."

***

A more complete paraphrase of *"the end justifies the means"* would be:

In retrospect, if and when victory is achieved or a state is secured, the public will approve of—will find worthy or justified—*any* means used. The public will not condemn, investigate, or criticize if "success" or "victory" is achieved. No consideration will be given to what the costs and crimes may have been to achieve it, nor to what new problems or dangers may have been created in the process.

This approach assumes that in the eyes of the public, success justifies itself retrospectively. So, you can forget international law; instead, win "by any means necessary." Then keep the resulting abuses secret, or at least deny them until victory is achieved.

What the public will *not* forgive is failure—even if, or especially if, it is seen as the result of restraint, of observing the rules.

***

The Curse of Cassandra is that she was given the gift of foresight—*without documents.*

Avoiding the use of nuclear weapons has been my focus for 47 years. At this point I see no reversal of direction toward Abolition.

I no longer seriously hope to see the world spared "nuclear next use" via nuclear terrorism, nuclear first use, or "accidental" nuclear war.

***

"The greatest danger to humans is from other humans." This is said to be "human nature."

Well, hope and inspiration come from other humans, too. Are these not also "human nature"?

Pat says we shouldn't think that people who *should* know better actually *do* know better. Smart, educated people can believe and do crazy things.

People with more information don't always make better, wise, or not-insane decisions.

If a policy looks crazy, it may very well be.

At Dr. Helen Caldicott's book talk:

Helen holds up her book and says, "We have 20 years at most, before we destroy life on Earth." She also says: "I would be lying if I said I were certain that there is *no hope* and no basis for hope. No one can know the future."[90]

My friend Joe Rotblat was the sole scientist to leave the Manhattan Project[91] 60 years ago on grounds of conscience. Until his death this year, he worked toward the abolition of nuclear weapons—a goal that I have come to share.

To those who find this goal Utopian, Joe's attitude was that it was Utopian to imagine a human future otherwise.

***

Peter Ustinov said, "War is the terrorism of the rich and powerful. What they call 'terrorism' is war of the poor and powerless."

On the first anniversary of the 9/11 attacks, George Galloway said, "The monstrosities in New York, which seemed to emerge from a clear blue sky, really flew out of a swamp of hatred and bitterness that has been drenched in blood by the West."

The children murdered by sanctions in Iraq died before they even knew they were Iraqis. They died for no other reason than that they were Iraqis, born at that particular time and place.

***

Hurricane Katrina has strengthened the case for the European social model: capitalism with a high minimum of social welfare.

"Disasters seek out the poor, like heat-seeking missiles. This is partly because poor people have had to live in places where disasters are more likely to happen." —Kai Erikson[92]

***

Someone said, "When you boil it down, empire consists of going into other people's countries and stealing their things."

***

There is little data, but [Erik] Erikson and [Robert Jay] Lifton have a growing suspicion that traumas have a more long-lasting effect on the lives and psychology of victims of the disaster than is commonly thought.

***

What changes in human behavior, attitudes, and aims could reduce human danger and suffering and improve all-around human welfare?

***

When fascism (Christian authoritarianism) emerges in the U.S.—as it will, suddenly, I believe—it will be said wrongly, "No one foresaw this or could have foreseen this. It is inexplicable." But *everything* could have been foreseen—and was (by me and others), given certain all-too-likely conditions.

***

Jesus said, "Resist not evil, turn the other cheek, love your enemies, and do good to those who persecute you."

Do good to those who harm you? to those *who harm others?*

No condemnation? Keep their secrets?

As an alternative to "love your enemies," how about *"respect them" as fellow humans much like yourself*, for good and bad?

Be open to talk with them ... to understand them ... to negotiate with them.

***

I was electrified by a poem I read this year, in an essay that was written in prison by an American veteran of Iraq, Camilo Mejía. He was imprisoned for refusing to return to what he viewed as a criminal war.

The poem is by Albrecht Haushofer, a German diplomat, poet, playwright, and professor of geography. He was imprisoned in 1944 for his long participation in the anti-Nazi resistance, and he was killed on April 23rd, 1945, two weeks before the Germans' surrender.

When Haushofer's frozen body was found in a field next to the prison, inside his coat were 90 sonnets he had written in solitary confinement. One of these was entitled "Schuld" ("Guilt"):
I am guilty,
But not in the way you think.
I should have earlier recognized my duty;
I should have more sharply called evil evil;
I reined in my judgment too long.
I did warn,
But not enough, and not clearly enough;
And today I know what I was guilty of.

***

Morality and Politics: There is a moral dimension to poverty, war, the environment, and telling the truth. Reframe these issues in the context of morality and values.

The foundation of morality is wisdom, compassion, self-sacrificing altruism, empathy, and a sense of responsibility for one's direct and indirect effects on others.

"The world is longing for a connection between the hunger for spirituality and the passion for social justice." —Jim Wallis

***

Species Awareness: it is wise to know oneself—one's group, government, nation, species. What are our limitations, capabilities, inclinations, talents, faults? What is hard (impossible?) for us to do ... to want ... to think? Such awareness brings wiser choices and a capacity to foresee problems.

This species has not shown it can organize itself and act effectively to address the long-run, species-wide dangers of nuclear weapons and global warming.

What is needed is not to feel guilty, nor to punish ourselves or others, but to *change* ourselves and our lives.

It is time for us to tell the truth to each other. We must act together to change our world and its future.

***

The Catastrophist: Humanity is the cause of the Sixth Great Extinction.

The last extinction, 65 million years ago, was a cosmic event, caused by an asteroid. Now *we* are the catastrophe.

I am not a "person of faith"; I am a "person of hope"—and conscience.

I have hope that progress is possible, *and* that catastrophe may be postponed or averted. My basis for hope is the *uncertainty* of impossibility, as well as the possibility of historical surprises: "miracles."

I don't have confidence that "things will turn out well" for humanity and its contemporary species. I lack faith in "progress." I don't think the odds for humanity in the long run are tilted favorably toward us.

But I also think it is possible to *postpone catastrophe*, or at least its worst forms and effects.

"When your gift meets the pressing need of the world, that's your vocation." —Frederick Buechner

"Hope is acting in spite of the evidence, and watching the evidence change." —Jim Wallis

Might we hope for more time, for us and for humanity? Might we hope for more promising behavior, more kindness and concern? Yes, we can—drawing on our human creativity and intelligence, and *some* of our so-far-neglected characteristics and capacities, such as our love of children and life and the beauty of nature.

We can cultivate compassion, friendliness, cooperation, and trust, extending beyond our own group, tribe, organization, or nation.

We still have each other. That's a gift.

2006

I think of myself, unreservedly, as a Jew. I am more at home among Jews, other than very orthodox Jews, than among most other groups.

I have been obsessed with Hitler since 1942, when I was 10 years old. My mother was not educated, but she was intelligent and sensitive. She knew right away that no one had ever been as bad for the Jews as Hitler. She went to a school every day where Jews were called "sheenie" and "Christ-killer."

***

Evil is the use of power for bad purposes.

There is no limit to what most people can do or support, tolerate, or at least refrain from resisting or exposing.

An individual or group that has been labeled an "enemy" is someone against whom anything may be done to exterminate them, punish them, and stamp them as "bad" or "evil"—and by doing so, deter others.

Norman Mailer says that there is a touch of evil incarnate in each of us, which is amplified in a group.

***

An inconvenient truth is that U.S. nuclear weapons policies are *evil*.

What else is one to conclude when successive U.S. governments have prepared and threatened genocide—even omnicide—to preserve the careers, power, prestige, and profits of a few?

This embrace of the nuclear threat has institutionalized and internationalized what Hannah Arendt has called "the banality of evil."

We have long pretended to be a country ready to launch nuclear weapons (again) when our President thinks it is in our interests. We have been prepared to gamble that our "superiority" will protect us.

We are what we pretend to be.

We have had the bomb on our minds since 1945—first weaponry, then diplomacy, and now our economy.

All of this has kept us from seeing, ever, that our highest human priority has been to transcend this danger and prevent any use of nuclear weapons from ever happening again.

How could we suppose that something so monstrously powerful would not, after many years, come to compose our identity? Its logic, its faith, and its vision are now part of our culture: our "bomb culture."

Nuclear war is total evil . . . a "rain of ruin" . . . a "jog to oblivion" . . . "reaping the whirlwind."

***

What would happen if nuclear winter met global warming?

What would the carbon dioxide released by burning cities and forests do to global warming?

What effects would the lower temperature bring, as a result of the increased cloud cover? Would this just slow the warming for a year?

After the discovery of the probabilities of nuclear winter, there should have been an abrupt and radical drawing back from nuclear threats and production. But there was none.

Nor, although the number of U.S. and Soviet nuclear weapons has declined, have *any* of the dangers that contribute to the possibility of nuclear winter changed significantly for the better. These include: large alert forces, hair-trigger alert, delegation/"Dead Hand,"[93] secrecy, vulnerable command and control systems, tactical nuclear weapons for ignition, nuclear weapons back on ships, nuclear threats, and first use policy.

Humanity is being held hostage—and that is not metaphorical.

***

What 9/11 had in common with Pearl Harbor and Vietnam: the U.S.'s sense of invincibility and invulnerability was shattered.

Did King George III fear the Domino Effect from the loss of the American colonies?

***

Clearances convey prestige among those who are of equal or higher position. To hold a clearance signals that you are trusted, valued, superior in knowledge and foresight, and able to influence.

***

Why don't people blow the whistle on a planned action *in time*, before it happens? In part, this is because it may not be certain and clear to the Whistleblower that the plan will actually be carried out.

President Ulysses S. Grant said, "If I were a stronger person, I would have resigned my commission over the Mexican War." Not having done so was his greatest regret.

I was willing to go to prison for a *small* chance of affecting others and the war.

It is easy for a Whistleblower to wonder if it's worth it. "If I do come out with this, it probably won't effect change—but my life and career and friends and marriage will be hell."

***

Bertolt Brecht said that a soldier can do many things: he can endure, he can kill. But he has one defect: *he can think.*

The greatest decision a soldier faces is *whether* and *when to think.*

An Army officer asks, "How can I order other men to die for something I believe is wrong?"

Does an order to participate in an illegal war constitute an order that you need not obey? A protected right of disobedience can't be prosecuted or convicted.

Or is such an order one that you *must not* obey, yet one for which you can be prosecuted for obeying, directing, or conspiring? (like the generals at Nuremburg!)

***

I'm not a lawyer; I'm a defendant. But I did have an extensive education in certain aspects of the law, as the first American after Nathan Hale to be tried for giving secrets to other Americans.

I am not more ethical overall. But I have thought deeply about certain ethical problems I encountered in my experience, and I have acted on my conclusions.

What explains my willingness to risk long captivity?

Hypothesis: maybe it *was* "the Accident," and the negligence of my love and trusted father and mother, that made me hypervigilant about the failings of Authority and fueled my determination to tell truths that might save lives and preserve democracy.

***

To break a taboo, a norm, you don't need a reason. You just need a superior's order—along with the expectation that you will not be held accountable or sanctioned, that your "excuse" of your obedience will exonerate you.

We need more acts of courage.

Yet to feel "I would never do *that*" (i.e., carry out an act of resistance) is understandable in a situation with incentives of orders, conformity, promises, and threats of ostracism, with no models of resistance.

If you have failed tests of courage so far, know that *it's not too late.*

***

In Vietnam at an Awards Ceremony:

This is a great honor. It is the first award I have ever received from a government, except for my indictment with 12 felony counts, which I received from my government in 1971.

To be back here now, seeing young people on motorbikes and women in rice fields without fear of bombs, is to realize that my hopes of 35 years ago have been partly achieved.

Someone recently showed me a copy of the Pentagon Papers that I had inscribed to his young daughter, "For Peace and Truth, and in hopes that this history will never be repeated." It is almost unbearable for an American to reread these words now. Tragically, horribly, and criminally, my country is again raining rockets down on a country that had not attacked us and was no threat to us.

***

Reflections at Wellfleet Gathering: Do I want to be a "saint," even an imperfect one? *No.*

Saints have a drive toward obedience to God or to an order. Their lives are centered around worship, adoration, submission, austerity.

Perhaps I am more of a "prophet"?

Like Cassandra, I am a "doomsayer"—not to be believed, to be thought mad, extreme.

Did Cassandra hear—or overhear—the future?

Was she a whistleblower?

As for me, I want to *change* the future—not only foresee and warn.

For the foreseeable future I will continue to work urgently to educate the American public through writing, lecturing, and activism.

***

This is a time for ordinary people to do extraordinary things.

It is time to defend the American Revolution.

2007

I have a tendency to procrastinate over writing for publication, whether blurb, statement, press release, essay, or book. It is equivalent in strength to an addiction. Could a 12-Step program help?

I am as likely to die with my major messages unpublished as some people are to die of obesity, cirrhosis, or a drug overdose.

I now acknowledge: "I do not have control over my proclivity to procrastinate writing for publication."

I experience this trait as a moral failing, a "sin."

Have I "reached bottom" on this?

(A paradox is that I write very well, and quite fast, when I do write.)

To tell all the truth, to expose all the lies, ensures a very lonely, isolated life.

Truth is antithetical to intellectual community. It is not what most intellectuals do—or even aspire to.

Yet when truth must be kept silent, one can become intellectually sterile . . . unfruitful . . . forgotten . . . lost.

***

Now, either I must increase my dosage of antidepressants or reduce my dosage of daily news.

***

"Vital interests": what leaders will send others of us to kill or protect.

Nothing is more human than "inhumanity." We are the only animal that kills other adults of our own species—the only species that makes war on, kills, and tortures our own kind. We are the only species that hates, punishes, and takes revenge.

***

"Moral" has a bad ring to many activists due to the abuses they have experienced from religion and religious leaders who claim authority using the language of morality.

***

What would we do to alter or escape global warming if it were being engineered by the Soviets or the Chinese against us?

We must stop comparing *our* theoretical best (ideological or religious) to "*their*" historical worst.

***

You are not to commit an evil act unless you *must* do it to avert imminent, otherwise unavoidable greater harm/evil to others.

Dream: I am to give a speech—not with answers, but to wake people up to the multiple crises, as well as to the human and group flaws that can and must be transcended, "mastered," by other existing human potentialities.

***

We need a new, much better civilization and culture (more than one!) vs. modern Western industrialized culture.

The more you identify with—feel one with—inorganic forms such as stars, other planets, rocks, waves—the easier it is to be optimistic.

　Likewise for oneness with bacteria, viruses, and cockroaches.

　The more you care about humans and other mammals, the harder it is not to feel the pain of prospective near-total or total extinction over the next century or two.

We need to work together in new ways. Are humans capable of the needed cooperation at a global scale?

2008

A friend told me, "In my California school, I grew up with many Japanese friends. I didn't know until college that *all* of their parents had gone to camps in Utah and had lost everything."

***

There are great inequities with pain and power.
    Those who have power are too comfortable to feel the pain.
    Those who feel the pain have no power.

A professor rushes past a homeless student lying in the street as he hurries not to be late to the lecture he is giving on the Parable of the Good Samaritan.
    "We're all in a hurry. We don't want to notice. It is so hard to notice."

***

I was a Cold Warrior, a Deterrer, and a Humane Imperialist "protecting Vietnam's sovereignty."
    My focus now is not on avoiding American failures, but on avoiding or ending American crises or disasters.

There is a difference between the U.S.'s *declared* values and priorities and its *actual* operating policies and values.

The real secret is what is *really* secret.

Be very skeptical of all arguments to go to war, or to torture, massacre, or mass-imprison—even if, or *especially* if, for "humanitarian" reasons.

Above all, be very skeptical if you are asked to go to war for *freedom*, *democracy*, or *regime change*.

"Humane imperialism" assumes it is preferable to run a country through our dictators than to have it become a Communist slave state.

But a neo-colony is still a slave state.

For the non-Communist regions that were at risk of becoming Communist, that would have been better—both for them and for us—than seeking to maintain anti-Communist dictatorships.

All Empires do evil, but not all to the same extent or at the same time.

Moral equivalence is meaningless and irrelevant.

Be skeptical/wary of overall, definitive comparisons. You are probably being kept ignorant of the crises of your own Empire.

"There is no flag large enough to cover the shame of killing innocent people." —Howard Zinn[94]

***

We have seen, in my lifetime, surprising and remarkable changes—faster and bigger than the Civil Rights movement in the South and the movements for women's rights, labor unions, and gay rights. These dramatic changes included the Berlin Wall falling, Eastern Europe, the Soviet Union, the Cold War, and the transformation of South Africa.

With this came a conversion of military budgets and cooperative security, bases, and wars.

***

As someone said, we're missing out on the story of the decade: the slow death of the planet. It is not defined as *news*; there is just a page a week on the environment.

Are humans among the endangered species of our time? Does humanity have a chance of avoiding the fate of, as of now, a third of all mammals? For how long? For centuries? For longer?

It is time for mutiny. Without radical, comprehensive, fast change, we face the collapse of human civilization and the world economic order, not just Western economic empire.

Are our efforts probably hopeless?

Is our only real option to go down fighting?

***

Questions for My Twilight Years:

What do you wish for?

What are the best things you've done?

What are the worst, most shameful things you've done?

What were your best years yet?

What were your worst years yet?

What were your wasted years?

What mistakes have you made?

How do you wish you were different?

What is the difference between the way things are and the way they ought to be?

What is the difference between what you ought to do and what you probably will do?

What has to happen to bring change?

Do you believe in an afterlife? God? Spirituality?

What would you like to pass on?

If you had $10 million and exactly 1 (healthy) year to live, how would you live?

What if it was 2 to 5 years?

What if it was one month? One week?

What would you like to know, to understand? From whom?

How would you like to see the world change?

2009

Certain human traits that have been adaptive evolutionarily—traits that underlie war and threats and risk-taking—have become, in the era of the H-bomb and global warming, massively maladaptive for the human species and most others.

It is a delusion to think that wars will be ended by a weapon that makes them too terrible.

"War is the unfolding of miscalculations." —Barbara Tuchman

We are the wrong species to avert the catastrophes that we have prepared.

***

It is extremely difficult to oppose a war once it is under way.

To pursue an immoral, criminal, or insanely reckless policy and protect it from effective challenges, it is necessary and sufficient to keep it secret from the public and outside experts for as long as possible—ideally, until it has succeeded, or failed.

This prevents, or effectively discounts, any leaks about internal considerations and dissent until the policy emerges to public awareness as a *fait accompli*. It is then described to the public as "essential to national security," backed up by the unanimous judgment of his advisors.

"Find out what the President wants to do, and recommend it. If you don't know what he wants, try several proposals and see when he leaves."

Hence, there can be a failure to incorporate prudent, useful internal feedback that might identify a possible choice as an error.

Reliance on internal-only feedback to assess realistic prospects invites error and is inadequate to prevent disaster.

External feedback is also prevented or switched off in order to make certain policies "feasible" by keeping them secret, private, and unacknowledged.

***

Do people mainly mis-learn from history as it is written?

There are no "definitive lessons" of history. Ambiguity, incompletions, distortions, and different concerns and problems are brought to bear in interpreting history to others or oneself.

A useful lesson to learn: the impossibility of having a definitive account of a decision-making process and its aims or wins. The account will reflect the written and verbal lies of both that time and later.

"Official" lessons, born of general consensus, are drawn from incomplete, distorted, or outright dishonest accounts. Such lessons are usually little more than loosely inferred myths.

***

"The Truth" can be self-deception.[95]

***

Some of our "sacred beliefs" that define us as "good people" are actually false beliefs about us and about humanity.

When people are indirectly, passively, unknowingly complicit in evil, usually ignorance, unawareness, or false belief are present and factor into their culpability.

In political conflicts, religion is hijacked.

You want to win; you want power on your side. Well, what greater power is there than having God "on our side"?

Religion may also give license to do "whatever is necessary" to win a "holy war against evil."

Karma: at every moment you are planting the seeds for happiness or unhappiness in your future life.

But what about the present or future unhappiness of others?

Denial of harm to others is an easy and effective way to protect *your own* happiness.

***

Secrecy is always convenient. For some policies, it is essential.

In a crisis, secrecy is a constraint on correction, feedback mechanisms, and accountability.

Secrecy corrupts. It should never be absolute or unmonitored.

***

We need *rapid evolution*.

Our species is likely to decimate itself if we don't evolve culturally—rapidly and radically.

Let's try, *as if* we can do it—with all deliberate calm and desperate haste.

***

"The Twilight Years."

Are we in the Twilight of Humanity?

Consider what it would be like to be among the surviving remnants of a species that had done *this* . . .

Questioner, to Kurt Vonnegut: "You seem to have a grim view of humanity, as if there is no hope."

His reply: "That's right—but I've met some wonderful people."

2010

"A better world is possible." However, a much, much worse world is probable—and soon.

Can the human species and civilization—as well as most other species—survive humans' dangerous proclivities?

We are a very flawed species, dangerously so. We are dangerous to ourselves in the short and long run, and we are the enemy that threatens the long-run survival of most other species.

Seeing humanity's flaws, depression sets in. I am ashamed of my species, and I am sad for us and other species.

***

How to deal with my fear of being seen as hopeless, as spreading despair and apathy? What do you tell people to do if nothing specific you can say seems to have any promise of moving the big problems and policies in the necessary ways, *now*?

My current understanding of politics does not indicate a feasible "way out" of future ecological catastrophe and nuclear attacks. Still, we can adopt a "proceed as if" approach.

Someone said, "I fear there's not enough time, and it's too late to achieve enough change in enough people to shift things."

My response: "We cannot be sure of that. It *may* be too late; that day is coming before long. But no one can know reliably if it has passed."

A long-term plan amounts to a promise to ourselves that we *will* have time.

***

Trying to think out a blueprint or strategy can be paralyzing. Instead, imagine a goal—then imagine/reverse-engineer how you got there.

From Joanna Macy's workshop:

"As if from 2210: 'Looking back' to 2010–2015 and The Great Turning, *how did you do it?* How did you start, and how did you keep going despite failures along the way?"

In a similar vein, Elise Boulding[96] says to imagine a world without weapons. How does it work, and what did we do to get there?

Joanna said to me, "People already know. The voice they need to hear is not yours, or mine; it's their own."

She says that we are constantly changing, like a whirlpool whose shape is formed by its changing flow.

***

Joanna Macy's Gratitude Exercise:

QUESTIONS TO ASK ONESELF:

—A magic place in childhood was . . .
—A warm memory in childhood was . . .
—Someone who made me believe in myself was . . .
—Someone who influenced me and helped shape my life was . . .
—Some classic books and movies that helped shape my life are . . .
—Some public figures who helped shape my life are . . .

QUESTIONS TO ASK ANOTHER PERSON:

—How did you two get together? How did you fall in love?
—What were some high points in your childhood? in your later life?
—What do you secretly appreciate in yourself?
—What do you love to do?
—What do you love?
—What kind of movie would your life be? What would the storyline be?
—To the extent that anything does, what gives you hope?

***

Organize. Resist. Tell the truth.

Do not passively accept.

I fear there's not enough time, and it's too late to achieve enough change in enough people. But I'm not going to give up.

If we do go down, we'll go down fighting, helping each other.

2011

Hypocrisy is the human condition, and double standards are the only kind there are.

***

To see others as "less than human" is to see them as undeserving of humane treatment. People labeled as "Other" may be referred to as animals—not good, "cute" animals like pets or horses, but the "bad" kind such as "rats," "lice," "snakes," "vermin," or "pests." This sets them up to be targets of what would otherwise be viewed as "evil" treatment.

Rev. David Beckmann, the President of Bread for the World, told me, "You can't have *real religion* unless you work for justice for hungry and poor people."

I replied, "I don't think you can have much humanity, either."

***

Reasons for hopelessness and despair:

- —the strength and power of the voices who sustain the current disastrous course
- —the short time available to avert disaster
- —the mass unawareness of, and resistance to, nonviolent resistance
- —the extent of public acceptance of U.S. empire, fossil fuels, and related ideologies

—the ease with which Congress, the media, the courts, Democrats, unions, and universities are manipulated—i.e., the breadth and depth of the military-industrial complex
—the lack of a youth movement
—the seeming "remoteness" of the evils we face: wars, global warming, empire, and global inequality
—widely shared feelings (realistic ones!) of impotence and hopelessness

***

Can humans, in the larger sense—including nation-states—develop an all-inclusive "we-ness" for *all* humans in all circumstances, with empathy, concern, compassion, and a lack of enmity? We don't know if that is possible.

Nor do we know that it *isn't* possible.

Satyagraha: "truth force," "clinging to the truth with one's entire weight."[97]

Gandhi's truth was not only the truth of Oneness, but also the truth of injustice, disrespect, and cruelty—by one's own people as well as by others.

Nonviolent non-cooperation is assertive and constructive. One discovers a power in refusing to do the will of another person who is calling for wickedness, cruelty, lying, harm, or lack of respect.

***

"And did you get what you wanted from this life, even so?
I did.
And what did you want?
To call myself beloved,
to feel myself beloved on the earth." —Raymond Carver, "Late Fragment"

2012

I have faith in humans' potential for being better. I also see humans' boundless potential for destructiveness, cruelty, and indifference to others. The latter, combined with modern technologies and use of fossil fuels, threatens the survival of most complex life on earth, including us.

Why don't we learn from our failures? Because we don't learn from history—especially other people's failures. ("They're not us. *We* can do anything.")

Some lessons are hard to hold onto, especially for the next generation.
   Also, certain beliefs are hard to kill. They come back—like zombies.

***

"The time is out of joint; O cursed spite!
   That ever I was born to set it right!" —from *Hamlet*, by William Shakespeare

2013

No human is wholly transparent to another—even to a mother, lover, spouse, or sibling.

***

Did I do too much, too soon, for "too little"?

***

One of the reasons I went into psychoanalysis was to understand my semi-suicidal behavior at Rach Kien.[98]

***

Comments at Wellfleet on the struggle to save humanity from itself:

"Climate change is the great human rights challenge of our time. For too long we have spoken about it from the head, not the heart. Yet cooler heads have not prevailed."

"We need to be more emotionally honest with ourselves, while still having our wits about us."

2014

Jesus said, "Resist not evil. Turn the other cheek. Go the second mile."
But *doesn't this facilitate evil*?
What if the evildoer goes on to hurt or threaten or coerce someone else because you did not stop him?

***

The *Operational* Code of Ethics overrides internal messages that say "Do not harm." Instead:

—If someone frustrates you: *be angry.*
—If someone harms you: *harm someone.*
—If someone humiliates you: *harm someone violently; kill someone.*

Thus, demonstrate to yourself and others that you are *not* harmless, and that you have the capability and the will to inflict harm on someone who has harmed or threatened to harm you.
You can be dangerous if you choose to be.

An Alternate Code of Ethics:

—Do not resist evil violently.
—Don't let evil turn you into an evildoer.

—Don't make evildoing something that becomes "banal": ordinary, non-problematic, to be expected, not giving rise to guilt or shame.

***

Not all unauthorized disclosures are good, on balance or even at all.

Not all unauthorized disclosures are whistleblowing.

Not all secrets are bad or wrongful.

Not all whistleblowing is good.

Even good whistleblowing can have bad effects.

Most leaks in violation of classification rules are authorized by an agency or the White House. Some of these are very bad. Many are informative, yet incomplete and misleading—a form of disinformation.

***

There is no "worst case." It is always realistically possible to get worse than we are currently considering, or than we can even imagine.

The worst we can currently imagine with the climate is the most likely outcome.

Is it too late, then?

On Artificial Intelligence:

We do not need an explosion of intelligence or technology at the service of humans as we are. Such intelligence will almost surely be put to work creating better weapons and surveillance, increasing power and control, and supporting victory in war.

Already, we have too much intelligence in the service of too little compassion and concern for others.

What is needed: *an exponential increase of wisdom.*

2015

Responsible officials who are potentially blameworthy rarely think only of what's good for them, both personally and for their families. Usually, they are *also* thinking of what is good for the country, the Administration, their party, or their legislative program.

They believe that losing their position would be bad for the country. They act as if this would be worth almost any risk to avoid.

To avoid blame or reprisal—especially for failure or catastrophe and its consequences—decision-makers regularly keep secrets. They lie or mislead about the information available to them, the advice received, the alternatives considered, the considerations and concerns weighed, and the aims and interests bearing on a decision.

They are aided by cover-up, scapegoating, lack of cooperation with investigators, or active efforts to denigrate or derail the investigation.

All of this hinders or distorts learning from history and our experience of error and failure—especially recent experience, where the officials involved are still alive and active. Such learning is essential to correcting course and reconsidering our aims and strategies.

***

We have "pre-traumatic stress syndrome."

Humans can't stand too much reality.

"No matter how cynical you get, it's never enough to keep up." —Lily Tomlin in Jane Wagner's *The Search for Intelligent Life in the Universe*

***

Climate change has been added to the *Bulletin of Atomic Scientists'* Doomsday Clock. We are at about 5 minutes to midnight.[99]

Any nuclear plan is a plan for madness.
  I am living in a society that is preparing a catastrophe.
  I taste ashes in the wind.

***

"Beware that, when fighting monsters, you yourself do not become a monster . . . for when you gaze long into the abyss, the abyss gazes also into you." —Nietzsche

"One looks into the abyss in order to look beyond it." —Robert Jay Lifton

***

What to do when you question your aims? Your values?
  Rilke says, "You must change your life."

Moral courage is when you have little or no chance of being rewarded, and a big chance of punishment, yet it is the right thing to do.

I do vigils and civil disobedience to encourage others to go through this life-changing experience.

2016

I was seen as a "fanatic" because my loyalty to my country and to moral principles was greater than my loyalty to the President.

***

Growing up as a white, male, middle class American, I am aware that I am incredibly privileged in the world.

As someone who was highly educated and a good test-taker, I lived in a world of privilege at Harvard, rubbing shoulders with the 1%.

Then I was co-opted to become one of those who make the government work for the 1%, which was a path to living comfortably and raising my children safely.

Many people in the world, especially poor people, face daily hardships and indignities and a struggle to survive. They might as well be living on a different planet.

2017

Trump's destruction of facts, evidence, and truth does not *newly* prevent us from knowing the reasons for our policies; these were always lied about. The difference now is that the purveyors of denials, assertions, and cover stories no longer bother to appear "plausible" or "moral," nor do they hesitate to embrace racism and misogyny.

***

Don't believe that anyone is, or should be, exactly like you.

Don't believe that anyone is entirely different from you.

Don't believe that you can entirely know what is in another person's mind, or even in your own mind.

Don't believe it when you are told how different, inferior, or dangerous "they"—"the Other"—are.

Know that any Authority can be wrong, including you.

2019

We need *rapid evolution*!

If people knew we risked omnicide, would they care enough to overcome corporate resistance?

Have we hit the iceberg? Maybe not yet, with climate. But we are heading full speed ahead, in the dark of the moon, toward iceberg waters.

Yet there is still time for mutiny.

We need to shout "FIRE!" in this burning theater!

***

War may be caused, or facilitated, by the preparations to prevent or survive it.

***

I don't blame or condone "officials," or "us," as much as I would have earlier, because my expectations for most Americans and most humans, as well as their nations and empires, are much lower than they used to be.

Officials are acting in what are normal, ordinary, "banal," everyday, near universal ways.

***

All institutions resist being understood realistically or studied productively. "Anti-learning" mechanisms prevent them from gaining insight from their mistakes.

***

If we can't stop climate change, we can't survive.

Will democracy survive anywhere?

Will the fossil fuel industry permit a president and Congress that will take adequate action over the next 10 to 30 years to reverse climate change?

Is U.S. democracy up to this? Are other nations?

***

I want us to be more like who we *think* we are.

***

This life, this civilization, this species, this Earth are the only game in town.

"Play it as it lays."

Play the hand you're dealt.

2020

I felt that I "owed a life" so as not to feel guilty for enjoying my freedom, as well as for my lack of mourning and sorrow after the Accident that killed my mother and sister.

***

I've often written about "us," about my complicity.

How much was my staying at the Department of Defense based on my enjoyment of being close to power, "in the know," near decision-making? Especially from March to June of 1965, I was near decision-making as much as anyone.

Like fame, it was not a happy time. My happiest time was from 1961 through 1963.

***

Hypothesis: Every human is capable of being deluded, conned, self-deluded, persuaded, and tempted by self-interest into engaging in group wrongdoing.

All mass harm or killing is done for reasons—usually not all bad, invalid, or selfish—that are not enough to justify it.

The risks of unintended, undesired war are wildly underestimated.

***

My research of the last 62 years deserves attention. My beliefs and predictions (not in my books) and the questions I raise have never been more relevant.

***

Does humanity have standing to bring a "species-action" suit against fossil fuel interests, to argue for the right to survive?

Strikes are a fundamental instrument of nonviolent resistance, as are other forms of withdrawing support, work, obedience, deference, "loyalty," membership, and secrecy.

Put concern for humanity—identification with, loyalty to, regard for, obligation to protect and preserve—above all else.
    Be wary of obedience.
    Challenge, confront, and master the fear of being ostracized.
    Extend your human capacity for compassion and courage.

***

Has the *Titanic* already scraped the iceberg?
    When did its doom become inevitable?
    What iceberg warnings were received and ignored?
    Did the pressure to set a speed record take down the *Titanic*?
    When did other ships stop or change course?

We are making our "appointment in Samarra."[100]
    I see many terrible consequences of the U.S.'s killing of Soleimani, the Iranian military commander.
    My feeling state is similar to what I felt after RFK's assassination: "There is no way for us to change."
    I *strongly, passionately* hope that I am wrong.

2021

For officials, publicly opposing the policy of a President for whom they work is not an *option* that they reject; it is literally *unthinkable*.

It is as if the "promise to obey" or keep secrets relieves a "man of honor" from any responsibility for his actions and their effects.

***

Humans can easily be led to regard any harmful, evil act as a "necessary" or "lesser" evil—or as "convenient" or "cost-effective."

There is "normal," "ordinary" human madness and evil; then there are climate change and nuclear weapons: extraordinary and unprecedented madness and evil.

Still, even these things are done by ordinary people—which again shows the banality of evildoers and evil-doing.

***

The firebombing of civilians was considered to be of no importance. It was not even promoted as "necessary"—only, falsely, as "expedient."

It is easy to con young men into killing and dying for things that are not real, or for things that are not worth—and do not justify—killing or dying.

We were wrong in Vietnam. It was murder. It was evil. It is less important that it was dumb, an "error."

***

My past work that is unknown, relevant, and timely: my dissertation, *Risk, Ambiguity and Decision* (published by Routledge, 2001), my paper "Revolutionary Judo" (July 24, 1970), and my writing on the Desperate Proposal Pattern, Crises, Faits Malaccomplis, RAND, Ambiguity, and the Cuban Missile Crisis.

***

Questions:

What will survive climate change? What won't?

What temperature increase is now near-inevitable? (1.5 degrees? 2 degrees?)

What temperature increase is more likely than not? (2.5 degrees? 3 degrees?)

This is a moral, cultural, political, and technical failure. We are a self-estranged, failed, bankrupt species.

Suffering will greatly increase for 95% to 99% of the global population (less so for the 1% or 5%). With growing pressures of rising emissions, migration, military spending, and the climate emergency, democracy will decline and fascism will increase.

Increased migration caused by climate change is already contributing to rising fascism in the West.

***

We are asked to imagine that we have only one month to live . . . or that we are awakening from coma.

What do I debrief on? Why?

What were happy moments? Years? Decades?

What were good choices? Regrets?

We must aim to do better than protecting or restoring known values and practices. *We must create something new.*

***

The generation that saw us get out of the Depression and defeat fascism—my generation—is dying out.

***

To reject imperial morality will take a moral, nonviolent revolution, a revolution in morality and practice.

We need a moral revolution of caring about the distant future, even if we can't get there in the end.

What can we expect?

Prepare to step into the moment when sudden surprise opportunities for change arise. (Look at the example of Gorbachev, or the tragedy of George Floyd.)

Knock on doors, many doors, not knowing which may open.

Be ready to drive through.

PART III

Essays on Morality

Against Terrorism

October 2001

All my life I've absolutely opposed all terrorism by anyone under any circumstances. I define terrorism as the deliberate killing of noncombatants, war on civilians. That includes the bombing of populated areas and all nuclear threats and attacks and the support of death-squad states or movements, whether right or left.

I propose this as a moral/political absolute: to regard all such killing and threats of all such killing as forbidden, to be absolutely and unconditionally condemned, to be regarded as something that under no matter what circumstances one must not participate in or conceal, to be exposed and denounced and obstructed and resisted, individually and through all formal structures.

Terrorism by my definition does not encompass all mass killing, whether justified or not. It does not encompass all evil, all reckless or deliberate endangerment of civilians or others. For example, it doesn't cover deaths caused by tobacco and other toxic products, or global warming. To my mind, this is true "collateral damage," unsought but inadequately prevented by one's chosen policies. Or slow mass death by inadequate food or health policies, by poverty.[1] Terror bombings have pretended the damage they caused was collateral, but in reality the civilian deaths were the goal.

My proposal is to see all such killing as murder: mass murder. Whether done by the aggressor or the defender. Whether done by a revolutionary movement or state or a counterrevolutionary movement or state, First, Second, or Third World. It is not to be accepted as a Lesser Evil, whatever the alternatives. Just Evil: not to be done.

But not an Evil that requires or justifies combating by any means necessary against it—there are no examples that fit this criterion. Not an Evil that justifies further Evil in combating it or seeking to eliminate it, or those who performed it.

Evil is not justified as retaliation, or punishment, or reprisal, or deterrent, or revenge, although it is usually done in that spirit or guise, and justified in the eyes of the perpetrator in such terms. These terms are widely accepted as justifications, in principle, though they should not be. Terrorism, and other evils and wrongs as well, generally provoke such responses, and often specifically evoke terrorism in return. Such responses are predictable and "understandable," but not justifiable.

Terrorism cannot be defeated by terrorism. It will almost surely be enhanced, multiplied, reinforced, and legitimized by counterterrorism. One who fights terrorists must take care that in the process he does not become a terrorist himself.[2] And does not create more terrorists, which he will, if he becomes one. Terrorism is a cancer, self-reproducing, a chain reaction, unless there are "absorbers," neutralizers, as in a reactor. "We have looked into an (nuclear) abyss for half a century, and the abyss has looked into us."

We're likely to create regimes throughout the Middle East and the Muslim world that actively harbor and support terrorism, even nuclear terrorism, if we execute terrorist acts. Or if we show as little regard for the lives of noncombatants as terrorists do as we begin to inflict "collateral damage." Even when attacking what would be acceptable military targets near densely populated areas. Revenge generates revenge; terrorism generates terrorism.

I don't, as an absolute matter, reject violence. I do reject collateral damage that is wantonly disproportionate to the human stakes, the values or lives we seek to protect by our violence.

In effect, I am calling for the restoration of the moral/legal/political/military barrier against noncombatant killing.

Note an important distinction: I'm calling the *practices* "evil," not the perpetrators, or their supporters, who are legion. The point is not to punish regimes, but to stop their practice and endorsement of terrorism.

Defining terrorism is difficult only when you are trying to exclude from the definition all activities by your own government or your allies or those you support. If you have any success in that, you end up with a definition that will not be accepted by political adversaries.

It's hard to find someone who truly condemns this activity no matter who perpetrates it, who regards it as "murder" under all circumstances, as taboo, as morally wrong. The exception is pacifists, who regard all killing as "murder" and wrong under all circumstances and deem "terrorism" not particularly worse than other forms of killing.

The pacifists' arguments against war, and against all violence, apply more compellingly, I believe, to terrorism in its broad sense. As I still see it, not all deliberate killing is murder. But a great deal of killing, even in war or in violent political or religious struggle, is.

And even more than the view that "violence begets violence," terrorist mass murder begets more such mass murder. The deliberate, indiscriminate killing of civilians, of unarmed people—this form of "asymmetric warfare"—evokes indiscriminate revenge against the population of the perpetrating force.

We need to recognize, acknowledge, and change our own involvement—through our government and its allies—in mass murder. We must do this with the same urgency with which we move to protect ourselves from further mass murder being inflicted on us. We must stop those acts and policies that are especially provocative of terrorism against us, that are seen either as persisting in terrorism ourselves or being oblivious to our past provocations.

I wish to encourage whistleblowing in our own government about (1) our own terrorism and support to terrorists, and (2) responses being planned that will provoke greater terrorism and are terroristic in themselves.

This situation is too grave to allow for a lot of "counterproductive" experiments or rote, misguided reflexes.

A general denunciation and actual renunciation of all forms of terrorism—in revulsion against this particular instance on 9/11, and in rejection of response in kind—would be a rainbow after long storms, an actual benefit from this tragedy. The death of the people in the World Trade Center would not have been in vain.

Massacre and Humanity

November 3, 2001

It is time for us to face something about ourselves, we humans. In truth, it is well past time; it is very late in the day. But perhaps not yet too late. It is certainly not too soon.

It's this: As a species, we are much less inhibited about slaughtering one another than we tell ourselves, or imagine. We are almost unique among species in this respect. And we remain almost entirely oblivious to this as a species-wide characteristic, and to its being nearly unique among animals.

I address us in our broadest sense of species, as individuals and collectively. Nearly every one of us reacts with shock to concrete descriptions of a new instance of the massacre of humans. That is, with a combination, first, of horror and revulsion, and second, of surprise and incomprehension. The first part is appropriate (after the World Trade Center, as after every such mass murder); the second is not. It reflects willful ignorance, long participation in deliberate denial, not just about our own "civilization" but about our species.

We ask: "How could anyone—any human—do such things?"

Who do we think has been perpetrating these massacres, every one of them? Animals? That is, other forms of animal?

That's what we imply by the way we describe the perpetrators. The generic term for such behavior is "inhuman." "Animalistic." Monsters, brutes. Brutal, brutish. But which species of brute are we talking about? What other animal species behaves to other members of its own species like this? Or more generally—toward other species, except to eat them, which is simply to survive.

We are, after all, almost the lone species that kills other animals for reasons other than to eat them. We are joined in this by a few strains of ants; and of chimpanzees, our closest cousins genetically. And we are almost the only species that regularly kills others of our own species at all—never, or almost never, to eat them.

There is among humans, as among other species, an inhibition, a taboo, that is genuinely effective: We do not eat members of our own species. We don't eat humans. And by that, we demonstrate that we recognize that those other people we are killing and torturing, no matter what we say about them—"subhuman, a lower race of animals"—are really part of our own species.

But unlike other species, we do not have an instinctual inhibition against killing our own. Nor do we have a social taboo against killing humans remotely comparable in effectiveness to the taboo against cannibalism. There is, of course, a taboo against "murder" in virtually all human societies, but murder has a very flexible definition; there is occasion for argument and subjective application in almost every case of homicide. Obviously, this taboo fails to prevent a very large number of murders. More significantly, the very concept of murder is regarded as inapplicable to the vast majority of homicides, which take place in wars and other social conflicts.[3]

But are not the humans who act this way—the perpetrators of massacre—different from "us," in our conception of civilization? Their behavior is commonly described as "savage," "primitive," "uncivilized," "barbarian."

So we thought of the Germans in World War II. Indeed, the Nazis self-identified with these kinds of terms, such as "blond brutes." They appealed to German citizens' deep impatience with the restraints of civilization, the supposed weakening, unmanning bonds of law and civility. They appealed to Germans to raise this barbaric, tribal energy. But how much of this was just rhetoric or propaganda, like the theatrical costumes that Hitler designed for the SS, or the avenues of tall banners designed by Albert Speer for the Nuremberg rallies?

Germany, barbaric? What culture in Europe by the late nineteenth century was more advanced in technology, in music, in philosophy and poetry, more educated and literate, more acculturated to orderly life? If Germans could do such things—we Americans might have asked ourselves, but rarely did—who couldn't?

Well, I felt that Americans weren't capable. So I thought, as much as my friends and neighbors, growing up in World War II, watching newsreels of bombs falling on Coventry and London—the destruction of housing and apartment buildings filled with families and children. I recall my horror at the notion that Germans used magnesium bombs on civilian targets, bombs that burn through flesh with a fire that cannot be put out with water. Yet we later proceeded to drop between ten and a hundred tons of bombs for every ton by the Germans—many of them incendiaries—on families in Hamburg, Cologne, Dresden, and Tokyo.

It is not that we humans often behave "like animals"—like other animals. *We* are the animals who behave like this. And we are the only ones who do it on the scale we do, and with organization and planning. We are the ones who do it, very often, with deliberate cruelty. Killing is not the whole of it: there is torture, imprisonment, and enslavement, all unique to our species.

In pointing these truths out, am I a self-hating human? Actually, no, not at all. As I know, we are also the species more capable than any other of empathy, compassion, self-sacrifice, altruism, love, and creativity. I can say patriotically: I love humanity. I am proud to be a human. I love America, and I'm happy to be American—although I am intimately familiar with the atrocities this country is capable of.

That "tolerance," that sense of we-ness, does not mean, for me, indifference to the evil that we do, or that we condone. Nor does it mean that I forgive it in the sense of wiping it off the books and putting it out of mind, as if I knew nothing of it.

My own experience and reflection have convinced me that terrorism, massacre, and slaughter of noncombatants is never justified, necessary, or appropriate, for any reason or under any circumstances, by anyone. Nor is it an appropriate or justified response to terrorist massacre, as revenge or retaliation or deterrence, revolutionary or counterrevolutionary.

Osama Bin Laden's ideology is crazy, and in service to it, he is culpable of mass murder. He and his followers deserve to be condemned and must be resisted and stopped. But all these statements apply just as well to leaders of some of the "friends" of the United States, who were just as crazily ruthless before they became our enemies, like Saddam Hussein. There was a time when Bin Laden himself "aided" the U.S. government. Similarly, there are leaders of regimes toward which we have been alternatively hostile and supportive—like the Pol Pot regime, and now the Taliban—and client regimes we have instituted or supported in terroristic programs in Guatemala, Iran, Indonesia, El Salvador, and Chile in both wars and internal campaigns of repression.

In fact, these characterizations apply to some of our own leaders: not only in their backing for "death squad" regimes in Central and Latin America and Indonesia; not only for our murderous strategic bombing of Axis-controlled cities in World War II;[4] but also for our past and present reliance on the threat of first-use nuclear weapons. The U.S. government's first-use nuclear threat can be described as terroristic in a variety of ways. This current American policy is a present justification and incitement for other nuclear nations like India and Pakistan to make comparable threats toward each other, a game of chicken that could turn parts of South Asia into a radioactive graveyard.

The ubiquity of such moral and social insanity makes the problem of eliminating terrorism broader and harder. But not less urgent.

In a world in which the advance of technology has made nuclear weapons, radioactive materials, and weaponized biological agents available to both state and non-state terrorists, we cannot afford to "live with" terrorism any longer, to legitimize it ever, or to accept it as an ineradicable human institution. That means, among other things, that we Americans have got to stop practicing our form of terrorism, and stop our leaders from threatening terrorism covertly through proxies.

I think we could afford to drop the notion of "war" on terrorism. Aside from the fact that a "war on terrorism" would put us at war with ourselves and some of our allies, "war" has in the last century become a justification for terrorism.

To say that eliminating terrorism is difficult, and even unlikely, is simply to be realistic. To say it is impossible would be, in this technological era, to give up on our survival—certainly our survival in large urban areas. And it is to say more than we can know.

Humans can change, themselves and society, on a very much faster timeline than biological evolution. That is one of the wonderful things about our species.

The innocent lives lost and families disrupted on September 11 cannot be restored; but the occasion of their tragedy would be a source of untold human benefit if it could shock humans—Americans and others—to begin a serious worldwide effort to try to eradicate massacre from human behavior and tradition: a species change of evolutionary proportions.

Let us take this recent, spectacular instance of cruel human evildoing—even while we take effective steps to protect our own families and country—as an occasion to look clearly at human massacre in general: who does it, how and why it comes about, and what might possibly reduce the inclination and circumstances that precipitate it. Let's stop before we slaughter a lot more people—perhaps nearly all of us—with nuclear or biological weapons.

No truly effective steps in that direction can occur while we continue, in oh-so-human ways, to blind ourselves to a fundamental reality of human character and experience. The readiness and propensity to slaughter humans is not confined to some subset, however broad, of "other" humans.

Murder Mystery
April 17, 1989

For thirty years I have been investigating a crime that has not yet been committed.

The crime in question—the execution of existing U.S. and Soviet nuclear war plans—would involve mass homicide so vast that it has never been committed, and could not have physically been accomplished until about thirty years ago. Furthermore, it could not be carried out more than once in human history, perhaps twice—the second time, after a long interval, in the Southern Hemisphere.

It is thus a crime of mass murder. "Crime" and "murder" because the implementation of these existing plans, using existing nuclear arsenals, would necessarily violate fundamental moral codes and international law ratified in treaties forbidding homicide—even in wartime. Execution of these plans would be grotesquely disproportionate to legitimate ends, would disregard the rights and survival of neutrals and noncombatants, and would permanently destroy the environment.

Or perhaps these legalistic categories—conceived prior to the nuclear era, though still relevant and binding—seem inadequate, unnecessary, and euphemistic in this context. There may be no need to justify or explain the use of the term "crime" in connection with decisions that set in motion the destruction of most life in the Northern Hemisphere.

At the same time, these decisions would almost surely be taken in good conscience, with no awareness of criminal intent or culpability, in the minds of the perpetrators, who would include the most prestigious governmental elites. They would have in mind justifications of national security, of "supreme emergency," that would seem to them at the time to overshadow all legal and moral considerations.

They would be mistaken in these beliefs, as would be evident to any survivors (say, in the Southern Hemisphere). Just how they could so delude themselves is one of the things that needs investigating, preferably before the event. What "real" motives could generate such a delusional system and trigger such murderous, suicidal, catastrophic responses in intelligent, successful men of affairs?

My purpose in investigating this crime is not to condemn, convict, or punish anyone for past or future actions. It is to avert a new crime: to warn potential victims, potential bystanders, potential facilitators, and potential perpetrators.

Nuclear Holocaust and Evil
May 20, 2009

In the spring of 1961, and to this day, I regarded SIOP-62—in the light of the Joint Chiefs of Staff's own estimate that it would kill 500 to 600 million people—as the most evil plan that had ever existed in the history of humanity.

Twenty years after the end of the Cold War, the completed preparations for nuclear war—including the operational readiness to implement them within minutes and the official consideration of even the most murderous of these capabilities as a legitimate option—continue to be as evil as ever.

Every aspect of the process that culminated in this operational readiness to exterminate half a billion humans—which in reality would kill between one and six billion via nuclear winter—represented a moral catastrophe.

For the fifty years the plan has existed, each incremental step in it leads us closer to the complete extermination of humans.

***

Look at the modern history of bombing. First its roots in World War II city bombing: the German Blitz, followed quickly by UK terror bombing, USAAF [the United States Army Air Forces] pseudo-"precision" bombing leading to participation in indiscriminate city bombing and the firestorm in Dresden, USAAF firebombing of Tokyo and 67 other cities, and finally Hiroshima and Nagasaki.

Then came postwar planning, in which A-bombs were targeted on Soviet cities. This was followed by the development and testing of the H-bomb and the substitution of H-bombs for A-bombs.

Each step seemed, to its proponents, reasonable and legitimate. But each step since the Blitz was kept effectively secret, lest it arouse controversy and moral unease in at least a minority of the public. Even if, in the atmosphere of the World War and later the Cold War, it would have had majority support.

Inside these governments, there were intense qualms among some doubters at various points[5]—including scientists before the Trinity test and the crash development and testing of the H-bomb. Yet in no case did the dissenters take their warnings or their ethical struggle to the public.

In February 1942, a moral threshold was crossed secretly by the UK,[6] followed by an incremental progression by the USAAF over 1943–44 that culminated in the five-month firebombing campaign against Japanese cities: by any standards, a horribly immoral and illegal project and one of the great war crimes of the twentieth century. The latter was a precedent that made the A-bomb decisions morally unproblematic for U.S. decision-makers and, unchallenged, made postwar nuclear planning almost inevitable, with its species threatening implications.

My own feelings when I looked at the plans and concrete preparations for carrying them out in 1961—and really ever since—were that they represented a human project, by Americans, as evil as the completed "final solution" of the Nazis. Or rather, even more evil, by a vast proportion, in light of its scope. The projected body count promised a hundred Holocausts. I didn't know then of the possibility of nuclear winter and the consequent likelihood of extinction or near-extinction.

Surely the planning and preparation of our first-strike nuclear plan was worse than the planning and preparation for the Holocaust—even though the latter was "unconditional," meant to be carried out "no matter what."

How does one compare the morality of a deterrent threat to do unprecedented harm that may well be carried out under foreseen or unforeseen conditions, to the morality of a decision to do large but very much less harm unconditionally that is actually carried out? I know of no general ethical analysis of such comparisons.

But I was moved at the time, and I still am, subjectively—in the light of the absolutely staggering difference in the unprecedented destruction proposed by the SIOP compared to all historical experience—to conclude that not only were we like the Germans at their worst, but also what our leaders had directed and their subordinates carried out was worse than what the Germans, or anyone else, had ever done.

It was and remains, I believed and still believe, the most evil human project in history, even compared to massacres that have actually been carried out. To conceive of doing *this*—to decide to make it possible to carry out, to threaten it and to be ready operationally and psychologically to do so under circumstances that had a significant probability of occurring (much higher, in retrospect, than most are aware of to this day): such human intentionality and effort does not bear favorable comparison to any policymaking that has ever existed, from the earliest empires and barbarian invasions to the worst of modern times. Merely as risk-taking it has been an unbearably reckless, evil gamble.

It may be imprudent, in terms of the public acceptance and influence of my argument, to present this particular judgment in my book.[7] Even Tom Reifer was resistant to it when I first suggested it to him: that the planning, policy, and posture themselves were worse than the Holocaust. Not that our planners and decision-makers were more evil than the Nazis, but that what they have done and maintained is worse—in its implications and actual consequences for humanity—than what the Nazis accomplished. That's what I feel. It doesn't mean to me that Americans are worse than the Germans who went along with what the Nazis were doing. It does mean that we are no different, no better. I believe that.

Others have been thinking the same thing, of course, over the last six years, with reference to our actions in Iraq, compared to Hitler's aggressions, rather than to the Holocaust specifically. That comparison is exact, and inescapable to any knowledgeable about both. Some years ago, the *New Yorker* quoted the child of German immigrants to America as saying that she had, like others, always condemned her parents' generation of Germans for their passivity, for their failure to resist the Nazis effectively or at all. Now she realized, she said, "how helpless they must have felt."

That still leaves the Holocaust without precedent in American experience in recent history, at least since the extermination of the Native Americans. The 1.7 million civilians killed by bombing in World War II—800,000 Japanese before Hiroshima, 600,000 Germans, 300,000 in Hiroshima and Nagasaki—and the more than one million Iraqi civilians killed so far are in the range of, say, Auschwitz. Few Americans are aware of any of these except for Hiroshima and Nagasaki.

But the secret planning of which I became aware in 1959–61 exceeded any of these earlier massacres in its projected death toll to an almost unimaginable degree. It exceeded every massacre in known history put together, including those of Stalin, Mao, Pol Pot, Suharto, Tamerlane, Genghis Khan, the Romans, and the Assyrians, and in Armenia, Rwanda, and the former Yugoslavia. *All the massacres of innocents in human experience put together.*

My thinking here followed directly from a related comparison, likewise unknown to most Americans. The first test of a single thermonuclear bomb, the American Mike test in 1954, *released more explosive power than that in all the wars in human history.* The power of fifteen million tons of high explosive was unleashed. This is compared, for example, to the two million tons dropped by the United States in World War II.

SIOP-62 scheduled the dropping of *thousands* of thermonuclear weapons on the "Sino-Soviet Bloc," including virtually every city in the Soviet Union and China. Most were not of the yield of the Mike test or larger—perhaps only a few dozen of those—but very many, perhaps most, had the explosive power of half a World War II, equivalent to a little over a million tons of explosive.

When I first read these plans in 1960–61, I was already more knowledgeable than nearly anyone else about ways they could be triggered by accident, either by unauthorized action or by delegated authority far below the level of the president. I knew of our commitment to execute them in case of a serious blockade or takeover of Berlin or a major incursion into West Germany. This NATO plan, in which all our European partners participated, was itself, I already thought, the most reckless, irresponsible plan in history. But not until I realized in 1961 how conscious the Joint Chiefs of Staff and Eisenhower were of the potential scale of our "response" did it appear to be unequivocally condemnable as evil.

So: tentatively, I gave up comparing the evil of SIOP-62/NATO planning to the Holocaust, American officials and the public to the Nazis and Germans.[8]

The bottom line is that I regarded the planning as greatly evil. And the shock of that realization revealed to me something more than the simple conclusion that our side had done something bad. It bore on what people like us would do in the future. I could have said, and one could say now, "might" do, even "might well" do. But my reaction was stronger than that. I had the dark epiphany that the people who had made these plans, formed these intentions, and carried out these preparations could not be trusted not to destroy civilization in the not-distant future.

More than that: people like that, people like ourselves, *would* execute these plans eventually. Before very long. Recall, this was early 1961. I still believed, not entirely, in the full missile gap—thanks to Andy Marshall[9] in 1960—but in a sizable Soviet missile force, larger than ours. I assumed that the balance of terror was delicate, à la Wohlstetter, with two large and vulnerable forces tempting each other to false alarms or preemption. The Berlin crisis was at hand. I had never set up a TIAA/CREF[10] retirement account at RAND, as I had believed—since 1959—that there was a very small chance that I would live to enjoy it.

In short: I felt I had learned how the world, our world, would end. When I held the JSCP in my hands—one of the only civilians ever to do so—I was reading the death warrant for civilization.

I continue to believe that what I learned about humans that day—in light of the JCS's conscious and unashamed awareness of what they had wrought and Eisenhower had approved, however reluctantly—demonstrated what I have said since: This is not a species to trust with thermonuclear weapons. We are a species of unprecedented, unique danger to ourselves and all other advanced species.

My Anguishing Secret
January 26, 1984

The anguishing secret that I hold to myself, that isolates me, that I feel I must disclose to the public yet which I fear to express, is that with regard to planning for nuclear war that would kill hundreds of millions of people instantly and result—via nuclear winter—in billions dead, "We are like the Nazis. We are doing something worse than the Nazis."

The answer to this is: "All right, yes, the scale is worse. But it's entirely different: because the intent is different. What we are doing is for the best of reasons, or at least acceptable reasons, though mistakes are made and there are excesses, along with blindness, shortsightedness, distraction, inertia. And the Russians are doing the same, and there *is* reason to be fearful of them—weren't you just as fearful once, and were you entirely foolish? All in all, our leaders have no real *choice* . . ."

But there is an answer. Why be fearful of saying it? Because it is very bad news; it is agonizingly painful to hear, and say, and believe. It does not make one more happy or hopeful. Quite the contrary. Times are hard enough for everyone without this. And it is—for patriots like me—very hard to believe, very out of key from everything we learn from authorities we have trusted, and from the news. So to say it is to evoke, at best, skepticism, a loss or crisis of credibility. Above all: to insist that there really *is* an analogy with the Nazis, or with Stalinist Russia, is taken by Americans to be so out of touch with reality, so obsessed with hatred for America, so wildly insulting and wrong, that merely to utter this thought is to discredit oneself.

For the fact is that our leaders do have choices and they frequently exercise that freedom of choice in a direction that seems—to me, though not to Reagan, who believes he has made the world safer—to enlarge the probability of extinction.

Our leaders do not do this with the intent to exterminate any group unconditionally. But they are conscious—more than they let on—that the effect and *intent* of their choices is more credibly to threaten extermination under some circumstances, "precisely in order to deter, to avert those circumstances arising." For this reason, they continue to invent, design, produce, and deploy new technologies of destruction and extermination, to demonstrate their own commitment to carry out these threats and preparations "if necessary."

The increased risk of actual extermination resulting from all this does indeed reflect that the Soviets are doing it too. But if extermination does come about, it will not be wholly unplanned, unintended, or unavoidable—in the sense of an earthquake, a meteor, an increase in sunspots—as it will be linked directly to human policy.

It will reflect the efficient, obedient, self-adjusting implementation of national plans called for and approved, in secret, by our national leaders (along with the Soviets), consciously designed and intended to exterminate humans and destroy cities. It will occur under the very contingencies we have long foreseen as possible, though never certain or desired. The result will be what our leaders foresaw and "accepted," at least as a risk—though it will be worse than they imagined.

And they are making these choices for reasons that they do not dare to tell us: not because they are "evil" or wholly self-serving reasons, though an observer can perceive more influence of ego in their motives than they themselves may realize, but because they know that these reasons would seem grossly disproportionate and inadequate to the risks being accepted.

They explain this discrepancy to themselves by judging that much of the public overestimates the dangers and fails to appreciate the stakes involved. So they don't tell us.

Those who think of themselves as sophisticated and subtle analysts of complexity tend to have an overly simple moral conception: Good people don't do *very* bad things. Therefore when they hear my account of what our leaders are actually planning and doing, with considerable awareness and intentions that they conceal and lie about, these analysts react as do uncritical members of the public. Either:

1. I am wrong, these plans and threats were never made.
2. I must be saying that the leaders are monsters, evil men, since that is simply implausible, unbelievable.
3. The short-run intent must be entirely different from what I describe. Since good men could not be *that* "corrupt," there must be considerations I am ignoring. They must be responding to pressures or acting inadvertently on the basis of bad info . . .

The connecting thread: the leaders could not be responsible to the degree my analysis implies. "They must feel they have no choice."

Well, in fact I have come to realize that it is true that the leaders commonly feel that "they have no choice." This feeling allows them not to feel responsible—hence guilty—even if things go wrong and worse does come to worst. But their basis for feeling that way is less compelling to other observers than it is to them. And they are aware enough of this possibility that they take care to conceal facts and alternatives and estimates that might suggest to others their real intentions or the existence of a degree of freedom and responsibility. Not because they have a guilty conscience or feel culpable, reckless, or irresponsible, but because they suspect some others would find them to be so.

Indeed, this conscious risk they take of being regarded as criminals, gamblers, or wrongdoers is part of their sense of pride, of courage and loyalty and patriotism, a basis for their self-esteem and *good* conscience: like that of the patriotic spy, the volunteer fall guy, the Grand Inquisitor—*Beau Geste, The Four Feathers*[11]—or the Watergate team.

What has to be understood, explained—and shared with audiences—is that good men, decent men and women, can not only act to evil effect but also can do so with a great deal of awareness and purposiveness. They can keep a secret and tell lies about it, all without any intent to add to the evil in the world.

Part of the explanation: their obedience, desire to belong to a team, an organization, a nation, to be loyal and patriotic, to be appreciated and meaningful and useful. Another part, related to this: their desire and ability to believe—what may seem incredible or unrealistic to others—that they are working to avert or reduce a "greater evil," otherwise inevitable; that they are working with the "cruelty" of *surgeons*, for the good of the community. Such beliefs are not always unjustified.

Without this realistic understanding of intent, we can neither appreciate the degree or nature of our real, existential risk, nor act skillfully to change it and ourselves.

The point is that—in addition to all the risks of accident, Soviet attack, Soviet first use, third-party use of nuclear weapons, proliferation, madmen, false alarms, unauthorized action, all of which are real and growing—we live with a real risk that a president we have elected will, in some future crisis or limited war or confrontation, decide to initiate what he hopes will remain a limited nuclear attack with tactical nuclear weapons. And that the response of the Soviets or others to this will lead to an escalating, two-sided nuclear war, with a strong possibility that one or the other side will initiate an all-out strategic preemptive attack.

The president's decision, as deliberate and calculated as is humanly possible in the conditions of intense crisis, will be shaped in this direction by the existence of plans, weapons, trained operators, and deployment capacities designed precisely to carry out such an initiative by a U.S. president. Recent decisions, like past ones, on design, production, and deployment, as well as operational planning, have markedly increased the chance that a president will so decide. No other risk to our security and survival is greater than this one.

Yet these preparations have not been made by any president because he *wanted* to initiate nuclear war, on any level. Some presidents whose preparations were crucial—Kennedy, Johnson, Carter, perhaps Truman after Hiroshima and Nagasaki—have abhorred nuclear weapons and been determined never to initiate their use under any circumstances. But even these examples were persuaded—in the context of major political pressures—that they should not reduce the credibility of U.S. threat-commitments, or the presidential capability to make credible threats.

Their hope was never to have to carry out such threats. Their best chance of avoiding that, they were persuaded, *was to act precisely as if they desired and intended to carry out those threats under specific circumstances.* So that is what they did: taking the same preparations as other presidents who may have been much less reluctant to initiate nuclear war "if necessary," at least at the lowest end of the scale.

Various short-run, political, or diplomatic advantages to these particular humans and their administrations can also be seen influencing their choices in these budget decisions or crisis moves. These actions, along with Soviet reactions or parallel moves, uninhibited by negotiated or tacit agreements halting the process, have almost surely increased the risk of nuclear war for the whole species. But these influences are almost surely underestimated by the high-level participants, in comparison with benefits to the nation and the strategic world—perceptible mainly to themselves.

The moral: Do not give decent, well-intentioned humans at the apex of large, hierarchical organizations instruments of mass destruction that may be wielded as solutions to narrow, parochial, egotistical, short-run problems, which challenge their perceived success or position of control. These men are all too likely to discover, in such circumstances of duress, that the long-run strategic interests of their nation and humanity demand and compel their use of all instruments at their command. When their job or the core of their self-esteem is threatened, or, acting under orders, they are told that the survival of the system they serve is at stake, humans are easily persuaded that the destructive consequences of using what may be an "effective" instrument constitute a "lesser evil," whatever those consequences are.

"Even an unloaded gun will go off eventually." —Russian proverb

If God did not want nuclear wars to occur among humans, he should not have arranged there to be an element that emits two neutrons when fissioned by one neutron.[12]

For almost forty years, American presidents—and many of the scientists, servicemen, and political analysts who work for them—have been pursued by the nagging thought that unlimited destructive power must be transmutable into political power. They have searched steadily for ways to do this, with some success, though the Philosopher's Stone of influence commensurate with the destructive capability has been maddeningly elusive.

The Implications of the Twentieth Century for Theology

February 21, 2002

In April 1968, Tom Hayden said at Princeton: "The Vietnam War holds a mirror up to American society." Not quite: the country didn't have enough documentation, like the Pentagon Papers, to be able to judge convincingly the character, the values and priorities, the motivations and justifications, of those who were conducting the war. Now we do, though still without having fully compelling answers to the question that Patricia asked me this morning: "Why were we doing this?"

The overall facts of the wars and genocides of the twentieth century are enough to reach certain conclusions, and raise some fundamental questions, about not only our own society but also the human species, and the existence and nature of God, if there is One.

The century seems to me to establish one thing convincingly: Humans are a species with the physical, psychological, emotional, and organizational capability to exterminate their own species entirely—and with greater likelihood and nearness, most of the species or, say, a third—along with most or many other species. Indeed, that capability, starting with the physical and organizational means, is in physical existence right now, and has been without any diminution for the last forty years.

Has that ever been true of any other species? Perhaps others—I don't know, but it seems possible—have acted, unwittingly, to destroy the conditions for their own survival. But other species' destruction of the conditions for their own survival did not come about by destructive activity directed at other members of their own species. If we do that, will it not be a first? Is not even the "possibility" that we will entirely exterminate our own species, along with many others, the very "capability"—psychological and physical—unprecedented?

It could be said to have been a potential in the human species from the beginning; or it could have become a potential from some later development, like industry or science, or industrialized warfare.

But the physical capability can be dated no later than the development of atomic weapons; or its almost inevitable product, thermonuclear weapons. And the physical capability has been in place and ready, on a scale capable of producing nuclear winter, since 1960 in the U.S.

What does this say about the process, or the God (or Goddess, or gods), that "created" us or led us to this situation?

First: Is there free will, choice, responsibility, among humans, or in the universe? Has everything come into existence and every event happened as it had to, inevitably? Or has there been some contingency, some randomness? And has there been, is there, some room for individual or societal human choice, or freedom of action?

If the answer to the last two questions is yes, we can conclude that some events, and some human choices, made a difference and helped bring us to this moment. Thus, those who made those choices—and the will of any God or Being that allowed those to be possibilities—bear some responsibility for subsequent events.

If the killings of the twentieth century, and the capabilities for killing that have been created, and the propensities for using them that have been exhibited, are the products of human choice, or real free will (and human character as it exists), then I would conclude that the benefits of free will to humanity and other species are greatly outweighed by the ills. There are wonderful things about humanity, but I know of no plausible argument that these virtues and rewards "require" the propensities and capabilities for killing and torturing other humans that exist alongside them. Nor that the former justify or adequately compensate for the latter.

Certain repressive dictatorships appear to have been better to live under than the chaotic genocidal warfare that succeeded them: as in the former Yugoslavia, where the reign of Tito looks better than it did at the time. By the same token: What should we think about a God that chose free will for humans, along with their other propensities and limitations, in a world where God also chose to have U-235 emit extra neutrons in the process of fissioning? And thus the consequences we have seen in the last century?

Just what benefits in the "free choice of obeying and praising God, freely" outweigh the ills for both the victims and the perpetrators of vast human enslavement and destruction, and the current readiness for omnicide?

In creating other species, God—if monotheism is realistic—built in a species inhibition against killing other members of the other species, especially en masse. Humans share the same inhibition as other species when it comes to eating others of our own species. But we don't share the inhibition, at all, against killing each other, either individually or in indefinitely large numbers.

Such a God—and if there is one, and only one, that is certainly the kind we have—would be highly blameworthy, not admirable. At best they would be foolish and negligent, certainly not omniscient and omnipotent and all-loving.

Conceivably, they might be malevolent—the gnostic view of the demiurge in control of this earth. Another possibility is that the situation on earth is the product of a group of gods, competing and warring in a way that is consistent with what we experience. But Monotheism confronts the challenge, in this century and the last, that the single god is no refuge, and is not to be trusted with human welfare. Indeed, such a god is part of our problem, perhaps all of it—unless his/her foolish "gift" of free will gives some of us some of the blame.

I don't find the arguments for the existence of a single god compelling; and I find the thought of it, in the light of experience, painful and conducive to hopelessness. So I don't choose to "believe" in it. On the other hand, the thought that our condition could be the result even of benevolent deities that are multiple and competitive is productive of useful thinking about human and societal interaction. But this is not necessary or compelling to me.

Whatever made us what we are in this world, we are capable of acting with the destructiveness we have prepared. We are capable of doing so without the intention of true, lasting malevolence—but instead out of a sense of being threatened or merely potentially threatened, or from emotional impulses of revenge or anger at humiliation.

That capability—and its past expressions—it seems to me rules out the plausibility of a single, overseeing, wise, and compassionate deity, either causing every event in action and in thought, or having chosen to endow humans with the capability, overall, of freedom in action and thought.

We must all face the question that many Jews have faced since the Holocaust: Are we a "chosen" species, in the image and likeness of God? If so: God help us! And who will cure God?

Indeed, if the Jews ever *were* chosen by a single God, what did they do to deserve what has happened to them over the last two thousand years? Refuse to recognize the Messiah? Were they adequately warned of the stakes? Were they ever told what would happen to them, in God's favor and human retribution, if they failed to accept a true Messiah when he arrived? And what does such punishment say of the loving God of the Christians? Who was it, then, who created a species that required the reality and prospect of Hell to cause them to do right? What does that say of such a Creator?

It does seem to me that a Jew who continues to accept monotheism should consider, at least, the likelihood that God is to be condemned and resisted—understood, perhaps, as being no better than the rest of us. As a being, indeed, "in the image and likeness of man," but definitely not to be relied upon, trusted, admired, emulated, or obeyed unquestioningly.

That's not my problem; I am not a Jew who accepts monotheism. That doesn't rule out interest for me in other "spiritual" questions. But they are not among my obsessions, as moral and ethical issues are, along with a quest for understanding and for social change, especially relating to warfare and other forms of violence.

Human morality, as it exists, is certainly part of the problem too. It is not, as it has commonly existed, the solution, or perhaps even part of it. If the existing machinery for our complete extermination is set in motion, it will be done by people directing it and obeying directions all in good conscience, doing not only what their individual morality and the morality of their societies permits, but also what their consciences and the morals of their societies obliges them to do. Any hesitation in executing this plan would open them to societal threats and social ostracism, as well as feelings of guilt.

Either a God created this situation too, or there is no one God. Or there is no possibility of changing the situation, no real contingency or freedom in human thought and action. Or we have a chance; and it is our problem, our challenge, to change ourselves and human society and our future.

Dark Wisdom

November 25, 2004

How do we understand the participation of ordinary humans in Abu Ghraib, My Lai, and nuclear planning?

(A) People will do anything to stay in a valued group.
(B) Staying in a group requires retaining the respect of the group, and maintaining reliable acceptance by the group—in particular, by its key members who determine inclusion in or expulsion from the group. One must be treated as a full member, with all rights, and be included in all group activities and rites.

All of this requires:

1. Obeying the orders of constituted authority within the group.
2. Keeping promises to other members of the group: especially those made as a condition of membership.
3. In particular, obeying the specific orders to keep certain things secret, even from other members of the group. This may require not only silence but also lying to these other members, as well as to outsiders.

4. Keeping all secrets of the group from outsiders, an action that requires silence and lying when necessary, even to outside authorities.
5. Obeying group decisions and the laws and regulations of the group. Conforming to group behavior, values, and key beliefs.

All of these practices must be followed at the expense of the preferences or interests of oneself and/or the general public. One must demonstrate the readiness and ability to observe these requirements even against one's personal interests, even if this is painful or effortful, and preferably without complaint or hesitation. This expectation is demanded even against the interests of other groups to which one belongs, at the expense of other loyalties, even to family members or fellow countrymen. This includes the expectation of keeping secrets from loved ones, the general public, and from courts of law or Congress—anyone not included in the group.

Obeying these orders could mean being prepared to kill, torture, imprison, enslave, or massacre.

But can this be done in good conscience, maintaining self-respect? Yes.

(C) Self-respect is based largely on fulfilling the conditions necessary to be accepted within the group.

The first group in which these conditions are learned is the group of two: primary caregiver and infant. Even in conditions that are not externally threatening or exigent, this is a condition of total vulnerability and dependence for the human infant, for a length of time almost without parallel among species. The relation of the mother or caretaker to the infant is that of a god. This is a god with total power and autonomy, inscrutable and unpredictable (unless crying invariably gets a quick and thoroughly satisfying response), total ability to nurture or withhold, with power of life, death, torture, bliss. A breach with the mother or caregiver could mean expulsion to outer darkness and overwhelming anxiety.

The infant's ability to crawl and then walk, the ability to talk, understand, request, and say "no": all these are conducive to relative autonomy. Up to a point. But childhood dependence, like infancy, is almost uniquely prolonged in humans. "Getting along" with the caregiver's power and authority—on whom your welfare and existence depend—is the basic requirement of human existence. This starts with being acceptable, or better yet, pleasing and interesting to mother, and somewhat later, to father.[13] And going along, as the condition for getting along, is learned very early and continuously throughout life.

This may be the genesis of "conscience." I suggest that the function of this internalized voice of authority is primarily and usually to guide your behavior in ways that will maintain self-respect by earning the respect of others. It also keeps you exhibiting the characteristics that fit you for acceptance and respect as a member of human groups in general.

Conscience, I hypothesize, is a social organ, formed in infancy and childhood (and to some little-known extent by instinct), subject to learning and modification later. Its purpose is to make you an acceptable group member and thus enable you as a human to survive and prosper, and to avoid ostracism, which can be fatal.

The resulting readiness and ability to cooperate, organize, and obey orders—in company with other human characteristics—has benefits for human groups that allow achievements unparalleled by other species. But the combination of these human capabilities with the capacity for group activity—and the power to use energy sources beyond our bodies—have dark consequences that may lead to the extinction of humans and many other species with them (probably before long, as things are going).

In particular, these combined characteristics have made wars, slavery, tyrannous oppression, torture, and massacre commonplace for at least the last five thousand years—5 to 10 percent of the life span of current humans. Humans behave atrociously to other humans in ways virtually unknown to other species.

Along with these attributes, to be sure, humans exhibit compassion for other humans and even other species, and self-sacrifice in the interests of groups, in ways and in degrees uncommon—except between mothers and nursing infants—in other species. But this compassion rarely outweighs hierarchical orders within their group for organized killing. This difference has—throughout recorded history and long before it—made humans available to leaders who use and direct them to threaten, torture, enslave, or kill other humans.

What is new, with the unleashing of nuclear energy and with new chemical-industrial-biological processes, is that ordinary humans—carrying out in good conscience their regular promises to obey authority and to keep secrets—have brought the world to a brink where apocalyptic prophecies of the destruction of whole civilizations can now be accomplished within hours of the flick of a switch sending out an electronic signal.

The switches are in the hands of thousands of ordinary humans ready to obey, without hesitation or question, orders to flip the switch they are monitoring.

Ultimately, the orders will come from other fairly ordinary humans—unusual only in the degree of their desire and effort to achieve and keep the highest status and power in their societies—who believe that the moment has come to carry out these long-planned preparations for apocalyptic destruction. These are not persons without conscience, any more than any of their subordinates or citizens. They will give the orders in good conscience because they believe it is necessary, decisively better than their alternatives.

What makes the survival of our species problematic over the next several generations—given the destructive capabilities currently in place at the disposal of national leaders and many others—is this: men in power[14] will do anything, and risk everything, to maintain their positions of power. That includes risking catastrophe to avoid what they see as an otherwise certain setback that would jeopardize their prestige and job.

(D) "Where are the consciences of people who direct or carry out such actions? Are they without conscience? How can their consciences permit them to do such things?"

These questions, which always seem to arise when news of more atrocities surfaces, seem to reflect a common delusion about the nature and function of conscience: in effect, a basic misunderstanding of ourselves as humans.

What human conscience does not do—ordinarily, or for most humans—is to prevent or effectively inhibit them from killing, torturing, enslaving, or massacring other humans. Or from planning, preparing, and readying themselves and others to carry out the prompt annihilation of hundreds of millions of humans, when these activities are ordered by the authorities of a group one values. On the contrary, the demand of conscience is generally to obey those orders, by "legitimate authority;" and if they are designated as secret, to keep them secret.

What of the commandment "Thou shalt not kill"? Is this not the most fundamental Judeo-Christian—and more broadly cross-cultural—proscription? No. There is no such commandment in the Bible, as I learned late in life. That proposition is a common mistranslation—from Aramaic, Hebrew, or Greek—of "Thou shalt not murder." In other words, one must not "kill"—a different word from the commandment, in all those languages—in circumstances when killing is not legitimized or prescribed by society or by God. Exodus itself is one of many books of the Bible that describe wars and massacres ordered and monitored by God, along with detailed rules for capital punishment.

The human need for having moral rules or laws covering the conditions for killing other humans reflects the fact that we humans lack the instinctual inhibition that prevents most animals from killing another member of their own species. That is a price we pay for having the flexibility that goes with a lack of such instinctual constraints. It is an aspect of our "free will"—which may not, at this point in social/technical evolution, serve us well in terms of survival.[15]

Even so, we obviously do have considerable inhibition—both instinctive and socially trained—against killing another human face-to-face, especially the "innocent," one who neither threatens us or our loved ones nor has evoked our rage, jealousy, or desire for revenge. It takes a good deal of training—the nature of which has been well understood and practiced for thousands of years—to reduce this inhibition among soldiers. Even then, it is hard at first for most to do it face-to-face. Distance makes it much easier. For airmen, bombing through clouds, there is virtually no problem, no more than for staff planners in distant capitals.

When it is not done face-to-face, killing on command does not evoke the guilt or shame of individual murder of the innocent. Conscience is not merely silent in this context: it generally demands obedience to authority, in the pursuit of national security and honor. At the same time, prudence counsels conformity to the practices of others and the avoidance of punishment. In other words, ordinary conscience serves, and may even be essential to, the carrying out of massively destructive pursuits of war, including planned atrocities, as in the massacres in Rwanda and Bosnia, torture in Abu Ghraib and other secret CIA facilities, suicide bombings, and the bombing of cities.

If humans are to survive much longer—if the long-prepared nuclear apocalypse is to be postponed—it is urgent to raise these particular characteristics and proclivities of humanity to social consciousness, to recognize that they are just exactly as "human" and universal as our most valued characteristics. Indeed, they are in many contexts our most valued characteristics, in the guise of "loyalty, honor, trustworthiness, fidelity, respectability, reliability, bravery, courage, self-sacrifice." These are all exhibited paradigmatically in the process of killing other humans on orders of group authority, presumptively in the interests of the group.

Our rightly valued human capacity for compassion is, in practice, highly selective and socially shaped. It can change from one day to the next as our authorities designate new "enemies" among recent allies. Our ability to care about those who belong to none of our valued groups—let alone those designated as enemies—is very limited, even negligible. Few humans seem to be aware that we don't much care what happens to most of the victims we read about, or don't read about, except when advocates for particular victims bring it to our attention by loudly deploring the lack of prevention or concern. Then it tends to be surprising, over and over. "How can this genocide, this famine, this slaughter, have been allowed to happen—again!—by society? Didn't we all say 'Never again'?"

Yes, "we" did say that, repeatedly. But when will we notice that no one has ever done much about it? The simple historical truth is that almost no single instance of any of these atrocities has ever been prevented or stopped by the action of any outsiders or international organization, whether before or after the Holocaust. A strong rule of thumb: Other nations will not intervene to stop genocide or massacre. If there are exceptions to this—India intervening in Bangladesh, Vietnam invading Cambodia belatedly, NATO in Kosovo to suggest themselves—special interests beyond simple humanitarian concern are not hard to find.

Human societies, and most humans within societies, simply don't act as if they care very much about the slaughter or mass death of those beyond their borders. Obviously, many individuals and some organizations do act otherwise, but they are exceptional. But, I hypothesize sadly, it may be mostly because we humans generally simply don't care. At least not enough to make much effort, or to risk our standing in any valued groups.

It is time we recognize this very unpleasant reality, and adapt to it in ways conducive to our collective survival.

43 Seconds

March 14, 2000

A dream this morning: in it, I know that we will use nuclear weapons to destroy a city tomorrow. I'm walking with someone; I'm crying, choking. I say, "I always felt—I always *knew*—this would happen again in my lifetime."

I say, "I would give my life to delay it by a day—an hour."

***

On waking, I think: By a minute? Could this be worthwhile? Yes: to give a hundred thousand people another minute of life.

I recall my epiphany during my visit to Hiroshima on August 6, 1995.

A hot day, almost unbearably hot in the sun. I thought: This is what it was like *that day*. This is Hiroshima; this is ground zero. It was this time of year, this time of day, this weather. The heat of the day in 1945 amplified the heat of the fires ignited by the bomb and the smoke; it added to the deaths from dehydration—I imagine the universal cries for water.

Waiting for the speakers, I saw children, surprisingly obstreperous, playful, beautiful, joyful, but naughty, unmindful of their parents' commands. I was surprised they were so playfully rebellious: "Is this a new, postwar generation?" I ask.

No, I'm told, Japanese children have always been like this; they are allowed to run free up to a certain point, till they go to school; then the roof falls in and playtime is over, for good. "They say, 'Japan is heaven for little children, hell for everyone else.'"

I thought: So this is what the children looked like, *that day*. Today, fifty years ago.

Then, this minute. Doves are released at 8:15 A.M. There is one minute of silence, in the huge crowd, in the city. But that morning, in a book I bought at the museum, I've learned two facts that explain a puzzle.

Histories usually record the time of the explosion as 8:15. And they mention that clocks and watches stopped at the time of the explosion all over the city, from the pressure and the heat. But the museum displays a number of these watches and clocks, and most of them show hands fixed not at 8:15 but somewhat after that, 8:16.

What I learn in the book, and later in others, is that the bomb left the *Enola Gay* at 8:15:30. It was on a parachute so as to slow its descent and allow the plane to escape from the blast. The device was set to explode at a certain altitude above the city in order to maximize the area of damage, of damage to humans. It took 43 seconds to descend from the plane to that altitude. So the explosion was at 8:16:13. The moment of silence on the Day of Commemoration should have been 43 seconds long, not 60.

That is still longer than people think it is. I've asked some audiences—the first one, that evening, at a temple in Hiroshima where pilgrim-activists were gathered in a circle to share thoughts—to close their eyes for 43 seconds, which I measure on my watch. It was the length of time of a Third Period, a transition phase, between Before and After. It was a time of no return, a time past the point when human agency could have delayed or altered what was to come.

But during this transition period, while the bomb fell, life continued, still possible, underneath it in Hiroshima, as the parachute floated down: for 43 seconds. I ask the audience to spend that period of time, eyes closed, thinking of what was happening during that interval.

It was breakfast time. Some people were already at work. Children were on their way to school. Many people were eating. Some couples were making love. Some were looking at flowers. The *Enola Gay*, wheeling and flying away, was too high for them to see, though they might have heard it. Some were about to go blind.

Forty-three seconds is a long time. I know that many with their eyes closed can't believe it's not up yet, they think I'm extending the time. Try it yourself. A lot can happen in that time.

And then the clocks stopped. Human history had been cut in two. Or three: allowing for the period when the explosion could not be stopped by human choice but hadn't happened yet. That will happen again, that three-way split, the third part taking place after the next explosion, or the next nuclear war.

Which phase of this next division are we in now? The earlier, where human choice—individual and organized effort—can still make a difference, can bring the bombs back from the brink, even dismantle them? Or the middle part, where it is too late, where the course toward detonation is irreversible, inevitable? There's no way to know.

The bombs are still in human hands. But are they still "really" under human control, subject to free choice? Were they ever? Can the process still be stopped, short of explosion? Will we say, afterward—if the nuclear exchange is limited enough so that there is a human afterward, a "we" to draw lessons—that "there was a chance: if only . . ."? Or will we conclude that it was too late, that we had set things in motion that couldn't be undone?

My memory of my visit to Hiroshima answered the question posed by my dream: Could it be worthwhile to give your life, to delay a nuclear explosion by an hour, or a minute? Could it be worthwhile to give a hundred thousand people an extra 43 seconds of life? Yes.

An hour: ninety periods of 45 seconds, end to end. Each one precious, marvelous, miraculous, wonderful. (Not, perhaps, for every one of the hundred thousand, some of whom might already be in terrible pain, and many of them anxious, distracted, oblivious, asleep. But still, for very many of them.)

A day? Time enough for something to happen that would give them all much more time, give the world time enough to head this off for now, to move in another direction.

On November 1, 1968, thanks to the belated ending of the bombing—just five days before the election—polls were moving in Humphrey's direction. This slowed sharply when Thieu, at Nixon's secret urging, announced on November 3 that he wouldn't go to Paris. Yet it continued in Humphrey's favor. A pollster concluded that if the voting had taken place eight hours later, or a day later, Humphrey would have won, instead of losing by seven tenths of one percent.

Not certainly, but probably, the war would have ended seven years earlier than it did; hundreds of thousands of Vietnamese (and more than twenty thousand Americans) would have lived instead of dying violently. A day's difference—in ending the bombing earlier, in delaying Thieu's announcement, in the White House revealing Nixon's machinations before the election—would have made a big difference in the life or death of many thousands.

Given the preciousness of life, it is worth one's own life, or career, to affect everyone else's, every minute.

ACKNOWLEDGMENTS

This book is the fruit of fortuitous circumstances.

First, it would not exist without the involvement of the Special Collections & University Archives (SCUA) at the University of Massachusetts Amherst, where Dan's papers are housed. In the process of organizing his 600+ boxes of papers for the archive, a vast trove of unpublished writing revealed itself, which became the primary source for this book.

It was meaningful to Dan that his papers landed at UMass Amherst, with its rich social justice roots including housing W. E. B. Du Bois's papers. We are grateful to SCUA team members Jeremy Smith, the Daniel Ellsberg Archivist, and to Aaron Rubinstein, the Head of SCUA, for their role in securing Dan's papers for posterity. Special appreciation to Robert Cox, the former longtime SCUA Head of blessed memory, who set things in place for the archive to be housed there. Rob's guidance and unfailing warmth brought grace to the early stages of a daunting archive project.

Professor and Vietnam specialist Christian Appy organized a special UMass course that immersed students in the newly arriving archive materials, along with Dan and other speakers from the Pentagon Papers era. Dan loved the interactivity of the class; the students' insightful questions seemed to fuel his interest in exploring his own papers as they emerged from the boxes. Dr. Appy now heads up The Ellsberg Initiative for Peace and Democracy at UMass Amherst, continuing to center issues that were among Dan's vital concerns: foreign intervention, the threat of nuclear annihilation, the defense of democracy through truth telling, and nonviolent civil resistance.

UMass Amherst turned out to be the perfect landing spot for Dan's archive, as well as an intellectual home in his last years, when he became a Distinguished Research Fellow at The Political Economy Research Institute (PERI). This institutional connection was significant for Dan in linking him to economics, his original field of study. We are grateful to PERI's cofounder, Professor Robert Pollin, who had learned earlier of Dan's overstuffed basement of boxes and helped facilitate the university's obtaining his papers.

Now we turn to those who were in the editorial trenches with us, helping this book to shine. First and foremost is Robert Ellsberg, Dan's son. His editorial input, endnote contributions, and overall feel for the material deepened the book at every turn. Robert's foreword is a doorway for people to understand more about Dan's unusual background, which brought him to the life that he led.

In addition to his efforts with our book, we remain grateful for the close work that Robert did with his father on *The Doomsday Machine* (Bloomsbury, 2017). Dan carried that book in his heart for over forty years. It was an enormous relief to him in his last days to have completed it, thanks to Robert's devoted editorial efforts.

The other close-in ally of this book is Dr. Thomas Reifer, professor of sociology at the University of San Diego. Tom was Dan's research associate, intellectual companion, and close friend of many years. Not only was he an early reader and editorial eye for the book; he also proved to be an encyclopedic resource about Dan's life and thinking, and he contributed substantially to the endnotes. Most of all, Tom's moral support was constant and unfailing.

We are grateful to Nancy Miller and the Bloomsbury team for sharing our vision for this book and helping us to make it real. A massive shout-out to Evan Hansen-Bundy and Janet McDonald for their fantastic editing and support. Thank you also to Andy Ross for connecting Dan to Bloomsbury originally.

We extend special thanks to Peter Touchard, Dan's other assistant, who teamed with Jan to sort through all of Dan's 500-plus boxes of papers from his sixty-year career. Peter's resourceful problem solving, tech support, and good humor helped us navigate every roadblock.

We are grateful to Norman Solomon, a longtime friend and colleague of Dan's, who was an early reader and cheerleader for the book. The organization that he cofounded and directs, Roots Action, provided financial support for the book just as its contours were beginning to take shape.

Dan's friend Mark Graham provided a scanner that facilitated the book preparation process at a critical phase. Earlier, Brewster Kahle and Misha Steier jump-started the organizing of Dan's papers.

Special thanks to Mary Ellsberg, Dan's daughter, and his grandchildren and great-grandchildren. Dan sometimes found hope hard to come by in his life; he found it most with the people he loved, especially his family, who meant so much to him.

Finally, Patricia Ellsberg, Dan's loving wife of fifty-three years and Michael's mother, was an enthusiastic supporter throughout this project. She took great delight in reading and giving feedback about Dan's reflections that had been hidden in his notebooks all those years. Her input was enormously helpful and clarifying, and led to a better book. Thank you, Patricia!

NOTES

PART ONE: PERSONAL ESSAYS

1. Thomas Reifer, PhD, is professor of sociology at the University of San Diego and an associate of the Transnational Institute. Tom was DE's longtime research associate, colleague, and friend.

2. Owen Smith, "The World's Most Famous Filing Cabinet," *Smithsonian* (October 2012), smithsonianmag.com/history/the-worlds-most-famous-filing-cabinet-36568830/.

3. Daniel Ellsberg (DE) note: I didn't steal the Pentagon Papers, though most people assumed I had, and even though several counts of my indictment, threatening several decades in prison, were for conversion, or theft. This was a bum rap, but I never made a point of it since almost nobody understands the law on this, and it isn't a high priority for me to explain it.

4. See DE's account in *Secrets* of sobbing uncontrollably for an hour on the floor of a men's room stall at Haverford College on August 28, 1969, after hearing draft resister Randy Kehler speaking of his impending imprisonment. This was a turning point at which DE asked himself "What could I do, what should I be doing, to help end the war now that I was willing to go to prison for it?" Daniel Ellsberg, *Secrets: A Memoir of Vietnam and the Pentagon Papers* (Viking, 2002), chapter 17.

5. DE note: As I write this, I recall my extremely hostile reaction to the movie *The Deer Hunter* (1978) because of its theme of Russian roulette, either forced or as a gambling sport. In the movie, the Vietcong force their captives, on pain

of death, to play Russian roulette with each other. Later, Saigon civilians are shown betting on Americans and Vietnamese who play Russian roulette in front of them.

When I saw the movie that had these scenes—which had no basis in Vietnamese reality, either in Communist prisons or gambling habits in Vietnam (the plot had been lifted from a purely fictional script set in the Bahamas)—I felt that these were vicious slanders on Vietnamese character. No real culture in the world actually imposed or enjoyed literal Russian roulette as either a sport, a gamble, or a torture. The conservative, pro-war moviemakers were slanderously presenting Vietnamese, both South and North, as excited by the spectacle of seeing someone risk blowing his brains out in front of them.

It is interesting that my reaction to it when I saw the film was that it was one of the worst charges you could make against people, to show them as capable of forcing others to gamble with their lives as torture or for the entertainment of an audience. Perhaps the idea of being forced to play Russian roulette—especially doing it as a performance for an audience, some of whom were betting on you—was not all that new to me.

I recall three instances of the notion of Russian roulette, or ultimate risk-taking, appearing in my life. My honors thesis at Harvard was on the subject of decision-making under uncertainty, and my PhD dissertation was entitled "Risk, Ambiguity and Decision." Both of these conceptualized all risk-taking, from personal and business decisions to matters of war and peace, as forms of gambling behavior.

My PhD dissertation included as an appendix a paper I had given at the Econometric Society meetings, "Winning at Russian Roulette." It argued that certain formal decision criteria could imply that a player choosing an "optimal" strategy might, under varying conditions, put one, two, or three or more bullets in the chamber before spinning it. (This was presented ironically, as a tacit critique of the realism of these particular decision-making criteria.)

Finally, in a fiction writing course as a sophomore at Harvard, as a self-imposed exercise I wrote a series of very short stories, each a page or a page and a half long. One of these was about a man who gets up alone in a single room, grooms himself carefully, and then, as a ritual performed every morning for a generation, before he goes out, spins the chamber on a service revolver, puts it to his head, and pulls the trigger. Once more, it fails to go off, and he wraps it up, puts it away, and leaves for the day.

The story mentions his realization that since the revolver has never fired in thousands of tries, the chances are very strong that the firing pin is broken or the bullets have become inert. But he has never checked this, so the ritual still works for him.

Nothing is said about what this does for him. Does his self-esteem or equilibrium depend on: confirming his invulnerability, his immortality? On winning a bet, being destiny's tot? On redeeming, by a gamble with death, the sins of the day before, or the day to come, or a lifetime, or a particular crime of the past? Assuaging guilt feelings about any of these? Proving undiminished daring, masculinity? There could be so many good reasons for what he does; no wonder I didn't try to pin it down.

6. DE note: I started to cry as I wrote that sentence. Maybe there's something to it.

7. DE's father was chief structural engineer on what was the largest engineering project in the world that year: the buildup of the atomic energy installations at Hanford, Washington. DE tells this story in *The Doomsday Machine*, chapter 18.

8. DE note: I vaguely remember my father telling me that my mother wanted only a Christian Science practitioner in attendance at my birth, but that the state required a doctor's name on the birth certificate. Since they had to hire a doctor anyway, she decided to have the birth in a hospital—the Edgewater Hospital in Chicago. It occurred to me that this was the last time I was allowed to be in a hospital till the day she died.

9. DE note: In my late teens, after Mother died, I came across a book in the Detroit Public Library titled *Mrs. Baker Purloins from Hegel*, by Walter Haushalter. This book showed that Eddy had plagiarized whole passages of *Science and Health* from a book called *Philosophic Nuggets*, which presented quotations and summaries of the views of German philosophers, in particular Hegel.

Her other source of many unattributed passages was another manuscript found in her private library, *The Metaphysical Religion of Hegel*, attributed to an academic philosopher named Francis Lieber. Of the many arguments I brought up against Christian Science in my late teens, the founding plagiarisms demonstrated in this book, which I got my father to read, gave him the most pause. A central Christian Science tenet is that *Science and Health* is essentially revealed truth, "inspired writings" solely "channeled" through Mary Baker Eddy.

But he recovered quickly, as I had learned to expect. (Though he did not, to my surprise, simply forget what he had read; he occasionally referred to this book years later.) It didn't matter to him through what channel God had revealed these truths to Mary Baker Eddy; the important thing was that it was the truth. How did one know it was the truth? Because it worked. (An American answer: in the spirit of James and Dewey!)

10. DE note: I didn't raise my hand with my forefinger extended to mark the points and hypnotize the hearer—as my father did. Still, there was the same intensity, the fixed gaze, the lack of interest in dialogue or interruption, and above all the endlessness. The sense that I conveyed, and actually felt, was that I had knowledge to impart to the listeners that they lacked and desperately needed, whether they knew it or not—knowledge for their salvation in some sense, or even for the salvation of the country or the world.

No one would have said they were really interested in hearing my father on his subject, so the feeling of being preached at and taken hostage would set in from the first moment. But I know this happened with me, too, for people (like my wife) who had heard me on my topics before. I had become my father—and at not a very great age. The differences in the subject matter and, it seemed to me, its immediate relevance for my hearers had long concealed that from me. But my father, after all, had had the same feelings about the importance of what he was saying for his listeners.

11. DE note: My father had been a highway engineer in Nebraska. He said that highway walls should never have been flush with the road like that. Later, laws tended to ban it. This wall took off the side of the car where my mother and Gloria were sitting, Gloria looking forward and my mother facing left with her back to the right side of the car.

12. DE note: I described this once to a psychiatrist, a specialist in post-traumatic stress. I had always assumed that amnesia was a natural consequence of the trauma, especially the concussion that put me in a coma for thirty-six hours. But he said no, amnesia was common for the moments before the trauma and

perhaps for hours or a few days afterward, but not for thirty days. That was unusual.

13. The *New York Times Magazine* profile, "After the Pentagon Papers: A Month in the New Life of Daniel Ellsberg," by J. Anthony Lukas (December 12, 1971), quotes DE saying the following to Lukas: "When I was 15, my family was in a car crash driving back from the Fourth of July. My mother and sister were killed outright. My father, who was driving and apparently fell asleep at the wheel, had just minor injuries and I broke my knee. I can remember standing in the wreckage, looking down at my mother and thinking, 'Now I don't have to be a pianist any more.'"

    Over the years, countless inaccuracies and untruths have been printed about DE, as happens to many public figures. Generally, he was unperturbed by these. However, this fabricated scene of him standing over his dead mother—which never happened, as he was immediately knocked into a coma—got under his skin.

    In addition, according to DE's writing herein, he never said the words "Now I don't have to be a pianist" to Lukas. According to DE's writing above, Lukas got it through the friend to whom DE had confided the story. If that's the case, then—aside from fabricating the part about him standing over his mother's corpse, Lukas also fabricated that he received that quote directly from DE.

14. DE was likely listening to *David Helfgott Plays Rachmaninov Piano Concerto No. 3*, Sony Classical, 1996, recorded live in Copenhagen in 1995 with the Copenhagen Philharmonic Orchestra.

15. In the previous essay, "The Piano," DE describes an episode in 1960 during a therapy session, in which he started sobbing uncontrollably when he "became conscious that [he] had worked very hard for a decade to earn Mother's love, at frequent peril of losing it." The sobbing, it seems, was grief for his own lost childhood and the need to practice relentlessly to earn his mother's love.

PART TWO: SELECTIONS FROM THE ELLSBERG NOTEBOOKS, 1971–2021

1. In late January 1968, North Vietnamese and communist Vietcong forces launched what became known as the Tet Offensive, a coordinated attack against targets in South Vietnam. U.S. and South Vietnamese militaries

suffered heavy losses before finally turning back the assault. Afterward, Walter Cronkite, the most well-known and trusted news anchor of his time, famously stated: "To say that we are closer to victory today is to believe, in the face of evidence, the optimists who have been wrong in the past. To suggest that we are on the edge of defeat is to yield to unreasonable pessimism. To say that we are mired in stalemate seems the only realistic, yet unsatisfactory, conclusion." (From Fred R. Shapiro, ed., *The New Yale Book of Quotations* [Yale University Press, 2021], 190).

As DE explained in *Secrets*, there was a reason the Tet Offensive was so startling to the public. General Westmoreland, the commander of U.S. and allied forces in South Vietnam, famously asserted—in his upbeat November 21, 1967, address to the National Press Club—that the U.S. had reached a "point where the end begins to come into view." As DE (198) stated in chapter 13, "The Power of Truth," "the immense impact of Tet on public consciousness and the attitude of Congress can be understood only against the background of the intense public lying over the preceding six months."

Subsequently, DE published an award-winning essay, "The Quagmire Myth and the Stalemate Machine," *Public Policy* 19, no. 2 (Spring 1971): 217–74, which was the first to draw publicly on the Pentagon Papers to explain these phenomena and critique the "quagmire myth." A revised version of this essay later became part of DE's *Papers on the War* (Simon and Schuster, 1972).

2. In 1961, on his thirtieth birthday, DE finished the first draft of the Basic National Security Policy for the Kennedy administration, helping to shape the Single Integrated Operational Plan (SIOP) for thermonuclear war. This revised war plan provided the president with nuclear options short of all-out nuclear war against the Soviet Union, the Warsaw Pact, and China—which was what the Eisenhower Plan called for.

At a time when it was still believed that the Soviets had overwhelming military superiority, DE saw the need for presidential options that were less destructive. He later realized this had been an illusory goal. Nevertheless, his guidance, subsequently revised, exercised a "critical influence" on nuclear war planning.

See Daniel Ellsberg, *The Doomsday Machine: Confessions of a Nuclear War Planner* (Bloomsbury, 2017), chapter 8, "'My' War Plan," 118–28. For a description of the Eisenhower planning, see the original Netflix series featuring DE,

Turning Points: The Bomb and the Cold War, beginning with the end of episode 2, and especially episode 3, "Institutional Insanity."

3. Quoted in Stanley A. Blumberg and Gwinn Owens, *Energy and Conflict: The Life and Times of Edward Teller* (G. P. Putnam's Sons, 1976).

4. Janaki Tschannerl (d. 2024) was an Indian who grew up in the Gandhian movement. DE's meeting with her in 1968 was one of the transformative influences in his life, introducing him to the philosophy and practice of nonviolence. She was instrumental in his attending the War Resisters' International conference at Haverford College in 1969, where he also met Randy Kehler. The young draft resister's impending imprisonment prompted DE to ask himself, "What could I do to help end this war if I were willing to go to jail?"

5. In "Responsibility of Officials in a Criminal War," in *Papers on the War*, 301, DE mentions the "need not to know," in Vietnam, in government more generally, and in the world. As the essay continues, DE eventually relates this most powerfully to Hitler's architect and Minister of Armaments in World War II, noting that in an interview, Albert Speer "sums up the moral burden of the need not to know" (as quoted in Robert Ellsberg's foreword herein, p. ix).

6. Albert Speer (d. 1981) was a high-ranking official in Hitler's government—unusual among the Nuremberg defendants for accepting his own culpability for the crimes of the Nazis. After serving his prison term he published *Inside the Third Reich*. On the basis of his own complicity in a criminal war, DE felt deep identification with Speer, a topic he explored in a lecture in May 1971, "The Responsibility of Officials in a Criminal War," reprinted in *Papers on the War*.

7. "I came from a culture in which the concept of enemy was central, seemingly indispensable—the culture of RAND, the U.S. Marine Corps, the Defense and State departments, international and domestic politics, game theory and bargaining theory. Identifying enemies, understanding them and predicting them so as to fight and control them better, analyzing the relations of abstract enemies: All that had been for years my daily bread and butter, part of the air I breathed." Ellsberg, *Secrets*, 211.

8. Per retired Pentagon security officer William G. Florence, in testimony before Congressman William Moorhead's Foreign Operations and Government

Information Subcommittee, quoted in Arthur Schlesinger Jr., "The Secrecy Dilemma," *New York Times*, February 6, 1972, www.nytimes.com/1972/02/06/archives/the-secrecy-dilemma-you-cant-run-the-government-if-every-important.html.

9. In copying the Pentagon Papers in October 1969, DE's original intention was to deliver them to Congress. Through 1970 he made efforts to persuade Sen. William Fulbright (D-AR), Chairman of the Senate Foreign Relations Committee, and other members of Congress to accept the papers as the basis for hearings on the war. By 1971, when none of them was willing to accept classified documents, he turned to the *New York Times*.

10. In August 1969, DE learned from his friend Morton Halperin, a member of the National Security Council (under Kissinger) that, contrary to Nixon's stated plan to end the war, "Nixon's staying in; he's not getting out." The strategy was to pursue victory through escalation, ranging from expanded bombing to nuclear threats. This knowledge, combined with DE's reading the Pentagon Papers and meeting draft resisters at the War Resisters' International conference, prompted his plan to copy and leak the Pentagon Papers. His hope was that in revealing this history of presidential lies, it would provoke Congress to preempt the Administration's clandestine plans.

11. DE mentions climate change in an August 1973 notebook entry, long before most people outside of academic climate science were aware of the issue. Fifteen years later, in June 1988, NASA scientist James Hansen broke through to the broader public when he testified to the U.S. Senate that the climate was changing.

12. DE was shocked when several former RAND colleagues testified falsely in his trial.

13. RAND was arguably one of the most powerful think tanks during the Cold War—and after, given how many people who worked or consulted there went on to play prominent roles in U.S. foreign policy and the National Security State right up to the present. Many RAND people became part of Secretary of Defense Robert McNamara's "Whiz Kids" at the Pentagon, working on issues such as nuclear planning and the escalation of the war in Vietnam. See

Fred Kaplan, *The Wizards of Armageddon*, with a new foreword by Martin J. Sherwin (Stanford University Press, 1991). Also see Alex Abella, *Soldiers of Reason: The RAND Corporation and the Rise of the American Empire* (Mariner Books, 2009).

14. A paraphrase of the famous line from George Orwell's *1984* (1949).

15. As explained in *Secrets*, in 1963, DE conceived—and was, in 1964, the sole researcher on—a study of "patterns in high-level decision-making in crises, with unprecedented access to data and studies on past episodes such as the missile crisis, Suez, the Skybolt decision, Berlin, and the U-2 incident." It was in this context that McNamara's assistant, John McNaughton, convinced DE to work as his assistant in the Pentagon, telling him that he really wouldn't be able to understand crises unless he had the experience of being an insider. For as McNaughton put it, "Vietnam . . . it's one long crisis." See Ellsberg, *Secrets*, 34–37.

16. Since DE wrote this, new evidence suggests that FDR opposed France's continued control over Indochina, and that this policy changed only with the advent of the Truman administration. See Stein Tønnesson, *The Vietnamese Revolution of 1945: Roosevelt, Ho Chi Minh and de Gaulle in a World at War* (Sage Publications, 1991), and his "The August Revolution of 1945," in Edward Miller, ed., *The Cambridge History of the Vietnam War*, vol. 1: *Origins* (Cambridge University Press, 2024), 106–26. DE strongly believed that in various circumstances, it could and did make a difference who was president, on matters of war, peace, and foreign policy. See Frank Costigliola, *Roosevelt's Lost Alliances: How Personal Politics Helped Start the Cold War* (Princeton University Press, 2013).

17. The identity between means and ends was an axiom of Gandhian philosophy: "The Means are the End in progress."

18. BNSP refers to "Basic National Security Policy," a document guiding U.S. nuclear war plans.

19. This is from the inscription at a grave for British soldiers who died in the battles of Lexington and Concord:

"They came three thousand miles, and died, / To keep the Past upon its throne; / Unheard, beyond the ocean tide, Their English mother made her moan."

20. Reference to Stanley Milgram's *Obedience to Authority: An Experimental View* (Harper and Row, 1974), which described a controversial series of experiments at Yale designed to test obedience to authority. DE was deeply fascinated by this work and its implications.

21. In 1960, while on a government mission in Japan, DE happened in a beerhall in Kyoto to meet the Beat poet (and Zen practitioner) Gary Snyder, who was familiar to DE as the inspiration for a character in Jack Kerouac's *The Dharma Bums* (1958). Though at the time they represented radically different worlds, the memory of this encounter haunted DE, and he later sought Snyder out and began a long friendship. In the meantime, he had grown closer to Snyder's views on nonviolence and ecology. This story is recounted in Daniel Ellsberg, "The First Two Times We Met," in John Halper, ed., *Gary Snyder: Dimensions of a Life*, section on "Culture and Politics" (Sierra Club Books, 1991), 331–40.

22. Dave Dellinger was a legendary activist, and one of the famous Chicago Eight put on trial for a supposed conspiracy to protest the Vietnam War at the Chicago Democratic National Convention in 1968, which turned into what has been accurately called "a police riot." An advocate of revolutionary nonviolence, Dellinger wrote a powerful memoir, *From Yale to Jail: The Life Story of a Moral Dissenter* (Pantheon, 1993), which is still available as part of the *Catholic Worker* reprint series.

23. Robert Ellsberg (RE) note: I was at this time a sophomore at Harvard, struggling over the draft, and moving to the decision to take a leave from college to pursue antiwar activities.

24. Regarding Satyagraha, this concept of nonviolent "truth force" or "truth telling" was an integral part of Gandhi's campaigns of nonviolent resistance to racial oppression, discrimination, and colonialism, from his campaigns in South Africa in 1906 to famous efforts to resist British colonial rule in India. "Satyagraha largely appears to the public as Civil Disobedience or Civil Resistance. It is civil in the sense that it is not criminal . . . [The civil resister] considers certain laws so unjust as to render obedience to them a dishonor. He

then openly and civilly breaks them and quietly suffers the penalty for their breach." *Young India*, January 14, 1920, quoted in Shapiro, *New Yale Book of Quotations*, 313.

25. Daniel Berrigan was a Jesuit priest and prominent figure in the antiwar movement. He was arrested in 1968 for destroying draft files as part of the Catonsville 9. At this time DE's son Robert was working with Dorothy Day at the *Catholic Worker*.

26. The Church Report, produced by a Select Senate Committee under Sen. Frank Church (D-ID), was released in 1976. It disclosed details of wide-ranging misconduct by the Intelligence agencies, both domestically and through cover operations abroad, including assassination attempts and support for military coups in Chile and elsewhere.

27. A karass is a concept from Kurt Vonnegut's 1963 novel *Cat's Cradle*, where it represents a group of people who are cosmically connected to fulfill a shared purpose, though they may be unaware of their connection or what that purpose might be. The connections can be supportive or antagonistic. According to the fictional religion of Bokononism in the novel, members of a karass are bound together by fate across time and space to carry out God's will, often discovering their interconnectedness only through seemingly chance encounters and coincidences.

   DE loved the concept of the karass, and frequently referred to various people in his life as part of his karass, particularly his activist friends with whom he repeatedly got arrested in civil disobedience.

   Most interestingly, in what was surely one of the stranger traveling acts in history, DE and G. Gordon Liddy, the head of the Plumbers, made a few stops together on the college lecture circuit in 1981. DE says that at one of these events, he said on stage that "Gordon Liddy and I were part of a karass to end the Vietnam War." We are not sure how Liddy responded, but surely he did not appreciate that sentiment.

28. In "The Accident," DE mentions that, after the accident, the thought "I owe a life" would pop into his mind at random times. The line "my boldness in Vietnam in driving the roads" refers to a period in the fall of 1965 when he spent weeks driving on militarily dangerous roads to provincial outposts

around Saigon, initially with civilian adviser John Paul Vann. He narrates this period in detail in *Secrets*, chapter 8, "Travels with Vann."

29. In 1978 DE took part in a yearlong campaign by the Rocky Flats Truth Force, blocking railroad tracks into the Rocky Flats Nuclear Weapons Plant, which manufactured the plutonium triggers for all U.S. thermonuclear bombs. For these acts of civil disobedience, he and other members of the campaign were repeatedly arrested. DE's son Robert joined him for one of the arrests. DE contributed text to a photo documentary of these protests, *A Year of Disobedience* (Story Arts Media, 2013 and 2021).

30. In "The Monkey's Paw," a 1902 short story by W. W. Jacobs, a mummified monkey's paw bestows three wishes. But in each case the wish is fulfilled in a terrible way.

31. Michael Nagler is a scholar of Gandhian nonviolence, an author, and a peace activist. He is cofounder of the Metta Center for Nonviolence as well as the Peace and Conflict Studies program at University of California, Berkeley.

32. In landmark articles and his senior honors thesis (later turned into a dissertation and eventually published as a book, *Risk, Ambiguity and Decision*, Routledge, 2001), DE had a significant impact on the field of decision-making under uncertainty. Noted decision theorists Daniel Kahneman and Amos Tversky were influenced by DE's work on decision-making and risk-taking under uncertainty, and their work in turn influenced DE. All of them, in different but complementary ways, challenged the reigning belief in decision-making about how people make decisions, as well as existing assumptions about human rationality in decision-making. Yet so strong were the assumptions of classical decision theory that the famous Ellsberg experiments, looking at how people made decisions when faced with uncertainty, led to a voluminous literature on the so-called Ellsberg Paradox.

33. From William James, *The Moral Equivalent of War*, first published 1910, from a speech given at Stanford University in 1906.

34. Herman Kahn was a friend and colleague of DE's at the RAND Corporation; one of the inventors of the concept of the Doomsday Machine; a brilliant,

albeit macabre, strategic analyst, focused especially on nuclear weapons; and the author of important books including *Thinking About the Unthinkable* (1962) and *On Thermonuclear War* (1960). See Sharon Ghamari-Tabrizi, *The Worlds of Herman Kahn: The Intuitive Science of Thermonuclear War* (Harvard University Press, 2005).

35. This quotation is from the 1964 Time Incorporated edition, p. 411.

36. See Heinrich Zimmer, *Philosophies of India*, ed. Joseph Campbell (Princeton Classics, 2020).

37. Written when in jail, June 20–July 4, 1983, for civil disobedience at Lawrence Livermore National Laboratory in Livermore, California, where nuclear weapons have been designed.

38. DE and Patricia Marx began dating in 1965, while he was working at the Pentagon. At that time Patricia had her own nationally syndicated radio program. Later that year, she visited DE in Vietnam and was appalled by what she learned about the war. She challenged him, "How can you be part of this?" He felt she didn't understand that he was trying to stop the bombing; it was difficult to share about his work because it was Top Secret. After this, their relationship went on hold until their reunion in 1969. They married the following year, and she helped him put out the Pentagon Papers to the press in their first year of marriage.

39. Albert Wohlstetter and his wife, Roberta, were two legendary strategic analysts with whom DE worked at the RAND Corporation. They and their protégés have played critical roles in U.S. foreign and strategic policy right up to the present day. See Ron Robin, *The Cold World They Made: The Strategic Legacy of Roberta and Albert Wohlstetter* (Harvard University Press, 2016).

40. During the 1980s, nonviolent activists carried on a campaign to bring attention to the White Trains that transported nuclear weapons across the country. DE testified at one of their trials.

41. Almost forty years later (2023), as he was dying, Daniel proposed this same epitaph.

42. Toward the end of his life, DE estimated that he had been arrested around ninety times as part of civil disobedience actions, most of them in protest of nuclear weapons and U.S. intervention.

43. This quote from Henry David Thoreau's 1849 essay "On the Duty of Civil Disobedience," particularly resonated with DE.

44. DE draws a connection between his original field of study—decision-making under conditions of uncertainty—and the foundational event of his early life.

45. In 1974, Roger Morris, a former Kissinger aide, revealed that Nixon had planned for massive escalation, including possible use of nuclear attacks on North Vietnam, for October–November 1969. Nixon himself, in his memoirs, admitted that his planned escalation was deferred in light of the massive antiwar demonstrations of October and November—the National Moratorium. Those who took part in these demonstrations had no idea of their effectiveness (Ellsberg, *Doomsday Machine*, 312–14).

46. DE's early research revealed that in situations of uncertainty, when people face a prospect of a loss, they will act to prevent it in ways that contradict the assumptions of classical decision theory. DE's findings on decision-making and risk-taking under uncertainty revolutionized the way people conceptualized uncertainty.

47. Treya Wilber was married to the author and philosopher Ken Wilber until her death from cancer in 2007. Their journey in her last years is the subject of an impactful memoir. See Ken Wilber, *Grace and Grit: Spirituality and Healing in the Life and Death of Treya Killam Wilber* (Shambhala, 1991).

48. Barbara Marx Hubbard, Patricia Ellsberg's sister, was a noted futurist and visionary.

49. DE note: See The Accident, World War I, World War II, the Holocaust, strategic bombing, Hiroshima, nuclear planning, Pol Pot, torture, and death squads.

50. Until the end of his life, DE remembered his time at the RAND Corporation with nostalgia. He was working with fellow intellectuals on problems that seemed of ultimate significance, while being provided space and resources to think, debate, and seek understanding.

51. At the War Resisters' International conference in 1969, DE joined participants in protesting outside the courtroom in Philadelphia where draft resister Bob Eaton was being sentenced. Randy Kehler's willingness to go to jail for draft resistance was a crucial catalyst in DE's own transformation.

52. Ned was DE's uncle Edward Ellsberg, an acclaimed Navy admiral and author.

53. DE worked on General Edward Lansdale's staff in Vietnam, traveling throughout the country to evaluate the success of "pacification efforts."

54. DE begins *The Doomsday Machine* by recounting this story: the day "I was shown how our world would end" (1–3).

55. This refers to the revelation that General Westmoreland, Commander of U.S. forces in Vietnam, had requested 206,000 troops *after* the Tet Offensive. DE was not responsible for this revelation, but it alerted him to the fact that there could be public outcry, and he came to realize that the lying and secrecy that stealthily got the U.S. involved in Vietnam, as if it were a covert operation, were key aspects of the Americanization of the Vietnam War. At that point, DE sought to prevent this escalation, and there are indications that his secret revelations to the press—unattributed for many years—may have been one among many factors in Johnson's inability to grant Westmoreland's request, which he lamented at the time. See Ellsberg, *Secrets*, chapter 13, "The Power of Truth," especially 199–209.

56. DE is referring to his decision to resign from the RAND Corporation in November 1969 after copying the Pentagon Papers, hoping to spare his colleagues further difficulties that might arise from their association with him.

57. After photocopying the Pentagon Papers, DE cut off the "Top Secret" markings. This offered a level of increased security when transporting them, and it made it possible to produce fresh copies from commercial copiers.

58. See Helen Fein, "A Formula for Genocide: Comparison of the Turkish Genocide (1915) and the German Holocaust (1939–1945)," *Comparative Studies in Sociology* 1 (1978), 271–94.

59. Evidence for this insight comes from Herbert C. Kelman and V. Lee Hamilton, *Crimes of Obedience* (Yale University Press, 1990).

60. The classic book on this subject, which helped coin the term in relationship to U.S. decision-making on Vietnam, is David Halberstam, *The Best and the Brightest*, with a foreword by Senator John McCain (Modern Library, 2001), first published 1972.

61. In an interview after the first explosion of the atomic weapon in the Trinity test of July 16, 1945, Oppenheimer, who led the successful effort to build and test the atomic bomb, recalled the words from the *Bhagavad Gita* that came to his mind: "I have become death, the destroyer of worlds." For DE as well, these quotes evoked nuclear explosions.

62. DE's wife, Patricia, gave a peace lecture at a transpersonal psychology conference, following one by the anthropologist Angeles Arrien. In her lecture, Arrien said, "There are four basic human taboos, universal to all known cultures: lying, stealing, murder, and incest." In Patricia's subsequent talk, she said, "With the exception of incest, these basic human taboos are what we call 'foreign policy.'" DE quoted this often.

63. Cathy Caruth, whom DE knew in part from the gatherings at Wellfleet, is Class of 1916 Professor of English at Cornell University and has published extensively on this topic. Among her books is *Listening to Trauma*, interviews and photography by Cathy Caruth (Johns Hopkins University Press, 2014).

64. DE was a friend of psychiatrist Robert Jay Lifton, who wrote *Death in Life: Survivors of Hiroshima* (Random House, 1968). Later, Lifton wrote about "psychic numbing" as a response to the threat of nuclear war.

65. The quote here is from Kai Erikson, *A New Species of Trouble: Explorations in Disaster, Trauma, and Community* (W. W. Norton, 1994), 214, 223–24. The full quote is "What if there is a leak into the biosphere at any moment in the ten millennia the repository is required by law to remain secure? In posing a question like that, one is asking something very special of the social science imagination. On the old DOE calendar, the period of years we are being asked to think about stretches from 1998 to 11,998; on the more recent calendar, from 2010 until 12,010. Now if one were to write the numbers 11,998 on every blackboard in America, how many people would guess that they referred to dates? . . . Thus the time may have come to abandon the cool, measured language of technical reports—all that talk of 'pertubations' and 'surprises,'

and 'unanticipated events'—and simply blurt out: 'Holy shit! Ten thousand years! That's incredible.'"

66. JSCP refers to Joint Strategic Capabilities Plan, the main document used by the Chairman of the Joint Chiefs of Staff to plan joint military operations.

67. Thich Nhat Hanh (familiar name "Thay") was a Vietnamese Buddhist monk, writer, peace activist, and global spiritual leader. He is known as the father of Engaged Buddhism.

68. Though he had no regrets about his decision to copy and later release the Pentagon Papers, DE regretted the fallout this caused for associates, including former Secretary of Defense Robert McNamara (who commissioned the Study), Leslie Gelb (who oversaw and invited DE to contribute to the Study, and who later authorized him to receive a copy), and Harry Rowan, President of RAND (who lost his job following the release of the Papers).

69. *A Report on the Banality of Evil* is the subtitle of Hannah Arendt's classic study of the trial of Nazi criminal Adolf Eichmann, *Eichmann in Jerusalem* (Viking, 1963). DE reflected deeply on the fact that "monstrous deeds" can be implemented by people who are not clearly "insane" or "monsters."

70. See Robert Ellsberg's foreword in this volume, as well as his book, *All Saints: Daily Reflections on Saints, Prophets, and Witnesses for Our Time* (Crossroad Publishing, 1997).

71. Rabbi Abraham Heschel was a progressive Polish American rabbi, a theologian, and an activist who advocated for Civil Rights and protested the Vietnam War.

72. John Paul Vann was DE's best friend in Vietnam. Vann's extraordinary story, including his friendship with DE, is used as a lens to examine the Vietnam War in Neil Sheehans' book, *A Bright Shining Lie: John Paul Vann and America in Vietnam* (Vintage Books, 1988).

73. DE attended the annual Wellfleet gatherings frequently over a thirty-year period, from 1982 to 2013. About the Wellfleet gatherings: Robert Jay Lifton was a well-known psychiatrist and historian who hosted an annual gathering of scholars and activists at his Wellfleet home for 50 years. This politically minded group, known as the Wellfleet Psychohistory Group, focused on the

psychological motivations behind events like war and genocide. They were instrumental in establishing psychohistory as a distinct field of study, receiving sponsorship from the American Academy of Arts and Sciences in 1965. The group's research was compiled into a collection of papers published in 1975, titled *Explorations in Psychohistory: The Wellfleet Papers*. Notable attendees at these gatherings included Erik Erikson, Kenneth Keniston, and others. Lifton himself downplayed the idea of a purely "shrink gathering," emphasizing that Wellfleet was also home to a diverse group of artists, writers, and intellectuals.

74. See Robert Levine's paper, "The Devil and Daniel Ellsberg" (January 5, 1971), dn790008.ca.archive.org/0/items/TheDevilAndDanielEllsberg/ELS027-098.pdf.

75. DE memorized this passage from Shakespeare's *Henri V*: "But if the cause be not good, the king himself hath a heavy reckoning to make, when all those legs and arms and heads, chopped off in battle, shall join together at the latter day and cry all 'We died at such a place;' some swearing, some crying for a surgeon, some upon their wives left poor behind them, some upon the debts they owe, some upon their children rawly left. I am afeard there are few die well that die in a battle; for how can they charitably dispose of anything, when blood is their argument? Now, if these men do not die well, it will be a black matter for the king that led them to it; whom to disobey were against all proportion of subjection" (act IV, scene 1).

76. DE is referring to his release of the Pentagon Papers.

77. During the Iraq War in 2004, Senator Zell Miller (D-AR) gave a speech excoriating Presidential candidate John Kerry and other Democratic critics of the war. Sen. Miller commented, "No one should dare to even think about being the Commander in Chief of this country if he doesn't believe with all his heart that our soldiers are liberators abroad and defenders of freedom at home."

78. The original quote from the manifesto reads "Remember your humanity and forget the rest." The context preceding the Manifesto was the Lucky Dragon incident, in which a Japanese fishing boat was showered in radioactive ash after the March 1, 1954, Castle Bravo thermonuclear test in the Bikini Atoll of the Marshall Islands, with these hydrogen bombs some thousand times more powerful than

the earlier atomic bombs, their force expressed in megatons versus kilotons. The test was supposed to be seven megatons, or seven million tons, of TNT, but it turned out to be fifteen megatons, and it helped to bring to the consciousness of the world the realities of the thermonuclear era. The last wish of the fishermen who were killed as a result of this exposure was "Let me be the last person killed by this awful weapon." This test gave rise to the modern-day antinuclear movement, inspired by the motto "Nuclear weapons and human beings cannot coexist." Some 670 million people signed the Vienna appeal against nuclear weapons and nuclear tests, and 1955 saw the Bertrand Russell–Albert Einstein Manifesto calling for the elimination of these weapons, helping to lead to the Partial Test Ban Treaty in 1963 prohibiting atmospheric testing.

79. Richard Falk is a renowned expert on international law, a promotor of human rights, and professor emeritus of international law at Princeton University. He and DE first crossed paths as graduate students at Harvard; their friendship emerged later through their common opposition to the Vietnam War, nuclear weapons, and other U.S. military interventions.

80. DE often invoked biblical references as examples of the dangers of unquestioned obedience to authority—such as God's command to Abraham in the Book of Genesis that he sacrifice his only son, Isaac.

81. Fritjov Capra, an Austrian physicist and ecologist, is the author of *The Tao of Physics*.

82. Matthew Fox is a theologian, an Episcopal priest, an author, and founder of the contemporary Creation Spirituality movement.

83. Huston Smith was a prominent interreligious scholar and author of the 1958 classic religious studies book *The World's Religions*.

84. John Seed is an ecophilosopher, founder of the Rainforest Information Centre, and a leading force in the Australian Deep Ecology movement. He is coauthor (with Joanna Macy, Pat Fleming, and Arne Næss) of *Thinking Like a Mountain: Towards a Council of All Beings* (New Catalyst Books, 1988).

85. Brian Swimme is an evolutionary cosmologist who, with Thomas Berry, has called for humans to understand our place within the wider "Universe Story." Arne Næss is a Norwegian philosopher who coined the term "deep ecology."

86. Drew Dellinger is a poet, writer, and teacher whose work is at the nexus of social justice, ecology, and cosmology.

87. Joanna Macy, a friend of DE's, was a noted Buddhist scholar, an author, and an environmental activist. She was the root teacher for The Work That Reconnects, a framework for turning despair into meaningful action to address ecological and social crises. She also cofounded the Nuclear Guardianship Project to address the safeguarding of radioactive materials to protect future generations.

88. DE invited his children Robert, 13, and Mary, 10, to play a small symbolic role in copying the Pentagon Papers. He said he wanted them to see, in the event that he was imprisoned, that there were times when one might need to take a risk for a higher good. Their mother, Carol Cummings, was deeply upset to learn this.

89. The Intergovernmental Panel on Climate Change (IPCC) is a UN body, established in 1988 by the World Meteorological Organization and the United Nations Environment Program (UNEP) to monitor and report on the changing global climate.

90. A noted Australian physician and author-activist, for over forty years Dr. Helen Caldicott has sounded the alarm on the risks of nuclear weapons and nuclear power.

91. The Manhattan Project was a top-secret U.S. research and development program formed during World War II, tasked with developing the world's first atomic bomb.

92. Professor Kai Erikson's research has focused on the effects of disasters on human communities. See Erikson, *New Species of Trouble*.

93. "Dead Hand" refers to an automated or semiautomated nuclear weapons control system, the purpose of which is to ensure a nation's capacity to respond even if its entire armed forces are eliminated.

94. Howard Zinn was a noted historian, an author, a professor, and an activist. His magnum opus, *A People's History of the United States: 1492 to Present* (Harper and Row, 1980), presents American history through the lens of ordinary people, especially marginalized groups.

95. Richard Ned Lebow has explored the phenomenon of self-deception in international relations: holding false beliefs while suppressing or downplaying evidence that would contradict those beliefs. Self-deception is often at the root of poor decision-making by leaders and governments. (This notebook entry by DE was written nine years before the publication of Lebow's *Self-Deception in Politics*, Cambridge University Press, 2018.)

96. Sociologist Elise Boulding was an influential twentieth-century peace scholar, writer, and activist, focused on building cultures of peace. Known as the "matriarch of peace studies," she contributed significantly to Peace and Conflict Studies' emergence as an academic field of study.

97. Satyagraha is the strategy of nonviolent resistance that was employed by Gandhi's movement for Indian independence.

98. From *Secrets*, page 158: "They thought that they were shooting at trespassers, foreign occupiers, that they had a right to be there and we didn't. This would have been a good moment for me to ask myself if they were really wrong about that and whether we had a good enough reason to be over there in their backyard to be fired at. But I don't think I faced that question squarely till I left Vietnam. When you're under fire, and armed, you don't think twice about firing back. The question of whether you had a right to be there to be shot at doesn't occur till later, if it hasn't occurred before then." For more, see the full chapter "Rach Kien" in Ellsberg, *Secrets*, 143–68.

99. The Doomsday Clock of the *Bulletin of Atomic Scientists* represents how close we are to global catastrophe, with "midnight" symbolizing the point of destruction. As of January 28, 2025, the Doomsday Clock is set at 89 seconds to midnight.

100. The moral of the folktale "Appointment in Samarra" is that death and fate are inescapable.

PART THREE: ESSAYS ON MORALITY

1. DE note: My definition could be expanded to include torture of prisoners. What about bombing of soldiers in their barracks or off duty, in restaurants or bars or on the street? That is not terrorism by my definition, even though

the U.S. government takes it as the archetype of terrorism, if done against our troops. What of civilian officials, either leaders or cadre? I would include it, even though these could be argued to be "combatants." That's how we saw the Vietcong cadre, though we were really looking at a political movement, or even an administration.

2. This line, and the one at the bottom of this paragraph, are adaptations of Nietzsche's aphorism 146 in *Beyond Good and Evil* (1886): "He who fights monsters should see to it that he does not become a monster himself; and when you gaze long into an abyss, the abyss also gazes into you." This was one of DE's favorite quotations.

3. "Homicide a Bigger Killer Than Armed Conflict and Terrorism Combined," The United Nations Office at Geneva, December 8, 2023, news.un.org/en/story/2023/12/1144392.

4. DE note: I make that judgment—which covers not only Hiroshima but also the firestorms and attempted firestorms that preceded it—on the basis of long and careful study of the history of that program, in ignorance of which the American public at large has accepted the greatest acts of terrorism in history as "necessary" and justified.

5. DE note: From the record, the fewest qualms came during one of the most consequential decisions in moral/legal terms, the project of firebombing Japanese cities.

6. The reference is to the change in strategy of British Bomber Command to deliberately target urban populations as the *principal* way of fighting a war. This is discussed in the chapter "Bombing Cities" in Ellsberg, *Doomsday Machine*, 243–45.

7. At this time, DE was in the early stages of drafting, writing, and planning what came to be *The Doomsday Machine*.

8. ME note: This is the only time I've ever seen my father contemplate self-censoring an intellectual point, for fear of how provocative it would be. On numerous occasions, I heard him express to me that he had refrained from telling audiences how truly hopeless he felt about the situation he was talking

about. In these cases, his restraint on that matter seemed to stem from not wanting to depress or demoralize others, particularly young people.

9. Andrew Marshall (d. 2019), at the time a colleague at RAND, disclosed to DE that there was in fact no "missile gap" between the USSR and the U.S. This was not confirmed until later. The missile gap was an axiom of nuclear planning, and JFK had campaigned on the issue. See Ellsberg, *Doomsday Machine*, 158.

10. The Teachers Insurance and Annuity Association and the College Retirement Equities Fund (now known as TIAA), provides retirement and insurance benefits to academics and researchers.

11. These are novels that contain plot points about a "fall guy."

12. Leo Szilard described a fateful moment of discovery: "[On March 3, 1939] everything was ready and all we had to do was to turn a switch, lean back, and watch the screen of a television tube. If flashes of light appeared on the screen, that would mean that neutrons were emitted in the fission process of uranium and this in turn would mean that the large-scale liberation of atomic energy was just around the corner. We turned the switch and we saw the flashes. We watched them for a little while and then we switched everything off and went home. That night there was very little doubt in my mind that the world was headed for grief." Leo Szilard, *Leo Szilard: His Version of the Facts*, ed. Gertrud Weiss Szilard and Spencer H. Weart (MIT Press, 1980), 55.

13. ME note: It's highly likely that my father's relationship with his mother was in his mind when he wrote this. The issue is explored further in the chapter "The Piano."

14. DE note: National leaders, and subordinates with control over nuclear weapons, are still almost all men. I believe that gender characteristics do play a dangerous role here. But women who achieve this status in the current patriarchal societies tend almost necessarily to exhibit the same dangerous characteristics, more "like men" in these ways than representative women. See the familiar examples of Margaret Thatcher, Golda Meir, and Indira Gandhi.

15. See DE's critique of "free will" theodicies in the chapter "The Implications of the Twentieth Century for Theology."

INDEX

Note: The abbreviation DE refers to Daniel Ellsberg.

Abu Ghraib, 309, 314
"The Accident" (DE)
    DE's account of, x–xi, 29–42
    DE's amnesia and, 35, 39
    DE's division of life around, xiv
    DE's recovery and, 35–37, 39
    DE's survivor's guilt and, xi, 36–37, 38, 39
Adams, Samuel, 188
Afghanistan, 209
Africa, 137. *See also* South Africa
"Against Terrorism" (DE), xxii, 279–82
All Saints (Robert Ellsberg), xvii–xviii, 189
American Mike test, 294
American Revolution, 52, 80–81, 239
Arendt, Hannah, xiii, 189, 193, 236
Armenians, 294
artificial intelligence, 262
Assyrians, 294
atomic bomb
    Ellsberg Notebooks on, 95, 96, 102, 120, 128, 184, 193
    history of, 291–92, 304, 317–19

Bach, Johann Sebastian, 16
Basic National Security Policy (BNSP), 80, 183
Bay of Pigs, 80
Beau Geste (Wren), 62, 300
Beckmann, David, 255
Beethoven, Ludwig van, 15–17
Bell, Derrick, 155
Bellow, Saul, 194
Berlin, Isaiah, 178
Berlin Wall, fall of, xviii, 244
Berrigan, Daniel, 95, 130
Bin Laden, Osama, 286
Bondurant, Joan, 167
Bouilly, Jean-Nicolas, 93
Boulding, Elise, 252
Brazil, 97
Brecht, Bertolt, 237
Bruce, Lenny, 92
Buber, Martin, 52
Buchanan, Pat, 145
Buddhism, 146, 219
Buechner, Frederick, 234
Bundy, McGeorge, 69

Caldicott, Helen, 231
Cambodia, 135
Camus, Albert, xviii
Capra, Fritjov, 219
Carter, Jimmy, 144, 179, 301
Caruth, Cathy, 177
Carver, Raymond, 256
Challenger, 144
Chile, 97
China, xiii, xxiii, 208, 242, 294
Chomsky, Noam, 110, 132
Chopin, Frédéric, 5, 16
"Christian Jews" (DE), 21–27
Christian Science, xvi, 5, 21–27, 30–32, 92, 192, 204
Church Report, 97
Clamshell Alliance, xxxi
Cold War, 150, 205, 244, 291, 292
conscientious disobedience, x
Contras, 158–59, 208
Cuba, 97
Cuban Missile Crisis, 47, 82, 117

"Dark Wisdom" (DE), 309–15
de Klerk, Frederik Willem, 180
Dellinger, Dave, 84, 167
Dellinger, Drew, 220
Deming, W. Edwards, 167
Detroit Institute of Musical Art, 5–6
Doomsday Clock, 264
The Doomsday Machine (DE), viii, xv, xxi, xxvi, xxvii
Dostoevsky, Fyodor, 62
Dr. Strangelove (film), xiii
Dumas, Alexandre, 62
Durant, Will, 75

Eastern Europe, 180, 244
Eaton, Bob, 50, 154

Eddy, Mary Baker, 5, 26
Eichmann, Adolph, 189
Einstein, Albert, xi–xii, 211, 216
Eisenhower, Dwight, 144, 295–96
Ellsberg, Adele (mother)
    the Accident and, x–xi, 29, 30–32, 35, 37, 96, 120, 147, 148–49, 183, 203, 223, 271
    Bertha as sister of, 33
    Christian Science and, xvi, 5, 21–22, 24, 25, 31, 32
    Clara as sister of, 4, 6, 12, 16, 30–31, 35
    DE as concert pianist and, xi, xxvii, 3–10, 11, 12–13, 17–19, 24, 32, 37–38, 39, 40, 41–42, 79–80, 101–2, 149
    death of, 5, 10, 19, 35, 38, 39, 40, 42, 68, 80, 148, 187, 202–3
    DE's fear of losing love of, xi, xxvii, 13–15, 19, 37–38, 41, 79, 89, 147
    DE's relationship with, 41–42, 68, 79, 89, 90, 101, 109, 116, 148–49, 187, 191
    on Adolf Hitler, 235
    husband's relationship with, 32–34, 42, 79–80, 90, 120
    lack of desire for children, 11–12
    Lou as brother of, 4, 12, 16, 30–31, 33, 37, 147, 183
    as pianist, 4–5, 19, 40
Ellsberg, Carol (wife), 3–4, 10–11, 36, 225
Ellsberg, Daniel. *See also* Ellsberg Notebooks; *and specific works*
    antinuclear movement and, xxxii

appreciation for beauty, vii
assigned destiny as concert
  pianist and, xi, xxvii, 3–10,
  11, 12–13, 17–19, 24, 32,
  37–38, 39, 40, 41–42, 79,
  101–2, 149, 191, 203, 223
on bureaucratic morality,
  ix, xxxiv
on capacity for empathy with
  outsiders, viii
childhood headaches of, 22–23
childhood of, xxvii, 3–12, 4, 16,
  22–25, 37, 79–80
childhood reading of, 7–9, 11
civil disobedience of, viii
on courage, xix
as decision theorist, xxiii, 47, 76,
  116, 148
as defense analyst for RAND
  Corporation, xii, xiii, xvii, 72,
  76, 97, 115, 135–36, 185, 197,
  204, 295
on deterrence, xii, 107, 138, 164,
  184, 286
dreams of, xxiii, 154, 184, 185,
  242, 317, 319
essays of, xxviii–xxix
on evil, xiii, xv, xvi, xxi–xxiii,
  xxxiv, 280, 281, 285, 287,
  291–96, 300
on evolution of human
  consciousness, xii
Lewis Fielding as psychiatrist of,
  xxvii–xxviii
on first-use nuclear threat, 286
on group membership, viii,
  309–10
handwriting of, xxix, xxxii, xxxiii
on hope, xvii, xviii, xx

on humanity, viii, x, xi–xii, xxiii,
  xxv, 52, 283–87, 303–4
on human nature, viii, xii,
  47–48, 49
on human survival, viii, xi, xii,
  xviii, 50, 84, 287, 303–4
MacArthur Foundation grant of,
  xxvi–xxvii
memoir of, viii
on moral evolution, xii, xvii, 275
morality-related themes of, xiv,
  xxxiii, xxxiv
on moral/political absolute
  against mass noncombatant
  killing, xxii
on moral stupidity, ix
note taking of, viii, x, xvii,
  xix–xx, xxiii–xxiv, xxv, xxvi,
  xxviii, xxix
on nuclear annihilation, vii–viii
on nuclear war planning, viii,
  xii–xiii, 76, 117, 175, 289–90,
  292–96, 297, 298–302
on obedience to authority, viii,
  ix–x, xi, xii, 47, 55, 62, 73,
  82, 83
on organizational behavior,
  122–23
pancreatic cancer diagnosis
  of, xvii
as parent, xxiv–xxv
perfectionism of, xxvii
piano lessons of, 5–7, 14–19, 18,
  37–39, 92, 147
piano practice of, 3–8, 10–11,
  13–14, 17–19, 22, 36, 39–40,
  89, 101, 105, 115–16, 169, 191
piano recitals of, 8–10, 14, 15, 17,
  89, 101, 105

Ellsberg, Daniel. (cont'd)
  "proto-drafts" of, xxix
  psychoanalysts and, 41–42
  publishing block of, xxvi–xxviii,
    105–6, 241
  on responsibility to raise alarm, xi
  on revealed preference, xxiii
  role as prophet, xvi
  on sanctity of human life, 62
  self-definition of, 101
  spiritual beliefs of, xvi–xvii
  on subordination of individual
    ethics to organizational
    ethics, viii–ix, xi
  on thinking, viii
  on trapped stage of
    conversation, 26–27
  University of Massachusetts
    Amherst archive of, xxv, xxxii
  unpublished writings of, xxviii,
    xxix–xxx, xxxiii
  as whistleblower, xi, 125, 161–62
  writing style of, xxix–xxx
Ellsberg, Edward (uncle Ned), 157
Ellsberg, Gloria (sister)
  the Accident and, x, 29, 30–34,
    35, 38–39, 96, 119–20, 148,
    183, 223, 224, 271
  death of, 80, 203
  DE's "The Piano" and, 14–15
  mother's relationship with, 42
Ellsberg, Harry (father)
  the Accident and, xi, 29, 30,
    31–34, 37, 38–39, 96, 102,
    111, 119–20, 148–49, 183,
    203, 224
  as Christian Jew, 21, 26
  Christian Science and, xvi,
    21–27, 30, 31
  DE's childhood and, 4, 11–12,
    16, 37, 79–80, 89, 90
  DE's relationship with, 109, 120
  jokes told by, 42
  metaphysical arguments
    and, 26–27
  professional life of, 31–32, 42
  wife's relationship with, 32–34,
    42, 79–80, 90, 120
  World War II and, 157
Ellsberg, Harry (half-brother), 13,
  24, 25, 29–30, 37, 120, 157
Ellsberg, Mary (daughter), 10, 225
Ellsberg, Michael Gabriel (son)
  birth of, 100
  DE as father and, 42, 106
  on DE's influence, xxi–xxiv
  DE's unpublished writing and,
    xxxiii
  on DE's writing, xxvi, xxx
  editorial philosophy of,
    xxviii–xxx
  as writer, xxiv–xxv, xxviii
Ellsberg, Patricia (wife)
  on the Accident, 148
  on civil disobedience, 113
  DE's writing and, xxvi
  Ellsberg Notebooks and, 52, 61,
    97, 113, 123, 135, 146, 173
  on meditation, 85
  Pentagon Papers and, 40, 61, 303
  on people who know better do
    better, 230–31
  on spiritual values, 194
  on war, 303
Ellsberg, Robert (son)
  on DE, vii, xvii–xviii
  DE as father and, 10–11, 42, 90
  DE's writing and, xxvi

on moral vacuity, 95
Pentagon Papers and, 225
Ellsberg Notebooks
    ability of "good" people to do terrible things, xxxiv
    on the Accident, x–xi, 96, 102, 111, 119–20, 136, 147–49, 169, 183, 187, 202–3, 223–24, 271
    on accidental nuclear war, 49, 157–58
    on actualization, 83–84
    on The Advocate, 89
    on Afghanistan, 209
    on American Revolution, 52, 80–81, 239
    on antiwar movement, 67, 77, 188, 204
    on artificial intelligence, 262
    on atomic bomb, 95, 96, 102, 120, 128, 184, 193
    on authoritarian regimes, 123
    on authority, 131
    on axioms, 207
    on *The Bhagavad Gita*, 123–24, 170
    on bravery, 91
    breaking group solidarity, 212–13
    on brinksmanship, 144
    on bureaucratic morality, xxxiv
    on bureaucratic structures, 131–32
    on bureaucratized conscience, 152
    on capitalism, 193, 231
    on Cassandra, 230, 239
    on catastrophes, 214–15, 223, 233–34, 247
    on catastrophic situations, 153–54, 161, 211
    on chain of command, 67, 117
    on chain of resistance, 54
    on childhood, 79–80, 92
    on Christian Jews, 191–92
    on Christian Science, 92, 192, 204
    on cities, 85
    on civil disobedience, 62, 77, 107, 113, 139–40, 145–46, 153–54, 155, 160–61, 190, 194, 221, 227, 264
    on classified documents, 56
    on climate change, 68, 94, 227, 231, 259, 264, 270, 273, 274
    on Cold War, 150, 205, 212
    on colleagues' expectations, 165
    on command and control, 107, 130
    on community, 85, 86
    on compartmentalization of bureaucracies, 49, 121
    on compassion, 124
    on compulsiveness, 115–16
    on conformity, 50, 78
    on conscience, 192, 225
    on conscience within hierarchical organizations, xi, xxxiv, 62, 83
    on consequences, 67
    on conspiracy of silence, 161
    on contradictory views, 48
    on Contras, 158–59
    on cooperation in wrongdoing, 218
    on corruption of power, 48–49, 83
    on crises, 65, 82

Ellsberg Notebooks (*cont'd*)
   on Crisis Study, 76
   on cycle of conflict, 139
   on deadlines, 105–6
   on death, 91
   on decisions, 66–67, 76, 82, 102, 116, 131, 152, 213, 263, 271
   on democracy, 84, 225, 270
   on depression, 93, 97, 136–37, 148, 149
   on deterrence, 107, 138, 164, 184
   on documents, 213
   on ecological destruction, 150, 251–53
   on ecosystem, 99, 100, 108, 193
   on elites, 137–38, 143
   on elite universities, 90
   Michael Ellsberg on, xxviii, xxxiii
   on empathy, 96, 128, 256
   on empire, 108, 124, 159, 188, 193, 212, 220, 224, 232, 244, 255
   on enemies, 56, 128, 235
   on environment, 167, 244–45
   on escalation strategy, 129–30
   on Establishment, 90
   on ethics, 82–83, 92, 238, 261–62
   on evil, 57, 67, 82, 95, 96, 98, 99, 100, 109, 112, 113, 127, 146, 178, 192, 229, 235, 236, 244, 248–49, 261–62, 273
   on evolution of Earth, 86
   on expert witness testimony, 76
   on failures, 65, 66, 263
   on fascism, 232, 275
   on First Amendment, 65
   on forgiveness, 126, 132
   on freedom, 133, 136–37, 140–41
   on freedom of association, 65
   on gender identity, 132, 137
   on genocide, 162–63, 171–72, 229, 236
   on global cooperation, 242
   on global warming, 236, 242
   on "good death," 175
   on group behavior, 121–22, 127–28, 229–30
   on Harvard University, 65, 90, 115, 265
   on heurist biography, 217
   on hierarchical organizations, 106, 131, 132, 229
   on history, 86, 99, 248, 257
   on hope, 94, 103, 140, 231, 234
   on hopelessness and despair, 255–56
   on how to live one's life, 77–78, 84–85
   on humane imperialism, 244
   on human evolution, 68, 86, 247, 249, 269
   on human freedom, 84
   on humanism, 84
   on humanity, 68, 80, 84–85, 86, 94, 99, 128, 133, 141, 162, 201–2, 211, 214, 230, 242, 245, 249, 251–53, 256, 259, 272
   on human potential, 257
   on human survival, 84–85, 86, 94, 100, 103, 108, 272
   on Hurricane Katrina, 231
   on hypocrisy, 199, 255
   on hypothetical questions, 209
   on illegitimate war, 111
   on illusion, 80
   on immortality project, 52
   on information theory, 213

on integrative impulse, 161
on intellectual preoccupations, 169–70
on internal enemies, 171
on internal standards, 101
on Jews, 235
on karma, 249
on killing, 173
on lateness, 115–16
on leadership, 132
on limits, 92
on love, 68, 89, 99, 133, 185, 209
on loyalty conflicts, 111, 112, 128, 265
Joanna Macy's Gratitude Exercise, 252–53
on March on the Pentagon, 51
on Marines, 80, 89, 115, 137, 185, 197
on massacre, 116–17, 121, 224
on meditation, 85, 106
on meningioma, 217
on "Missile Gap," 120
on Monkey's Paw fable, 111, 169
on moral courage, 172, 264
on morality, 229–30, 233
on moralizing, 112, 125
on mother's death, 68, 187, 202–3
on Murphy's Law, 108
on Mutual Assured Destruction, 150
on "My Country, right or wrong," 106–7
on national defense, 65
on Nazis, 162–63, 178
on Richard Nixon, 66
on nonviolent non-cooperation, 256
on nonviolent resistance, 132, 272
on nuclear arms race, 45, 50, 107, 150, 151, 187–88
on nuclear first use, 211
on nuclear problem, 87
on nuclear reactors, 112
on nuclear war, 49, 94, 110, 112, 113, 117, 120, 123, 130, 139, 143–44, 150–51, 157–58, 179, 229, 236, 251
on nuclear weapons, 49, 92, 94, 95, 96, 107, 112, 115, 120–21, 128, 130, 135, 138–39, 141, 183–84, 185, 212, 230, 231, 235–36, 273
on nuclear winter, 236–37
on obedience, 62, 73–74, 78, 82, 83, 85, 98, 99, 106, 112, 117, 130–32, 148, 149, 158, 166, 169, 189, 192, 214, 272
on obstacles to public's enlightenment, 164–65
on oil consumption, 85
on oppression, 57
on oral histories, 214
on "others," 96, 128, 255, 267
on patriotism, 144–45, 188
on peace, 49, 129
on peacemaking, 138
on Pentagon Papers, xxiv, 47, 53–54, 56–57, 59–63, 66, 73–74, 77–78, 86–87, 92, 97, 116, 125, 126, 136, 154, 160, 188, 193–95, 202, 205, 207, 212
on Pentagon Papers trial, xxxiv, 60–61, 66, 69–72, 87, 97, 238
on Pentagon Papers trial jurors, 69–72

Ellsberg Notebooks (cont'd)
   on pessimism, 190
   on piano practice, 191
   on plausible denial, 144, 165–66
   on policy judgments, 137–38, 273
   on policy justifications, 92
   on popular sovereignty, 154
   on power-seeking, 94, 121, 163–64, 243
   on predictions, 50, 51
   on President's choices, 149, 151, 157, 179, 214, 248
   on President's culpability, 117
   on President's decision-making, 162, 206, 248
   on President's inaction, 199
   on President's power, 159
   on President's social pressures, 164
   on pre-traumatic stress syndrome, 263–64
   on problem-solving, 194
   on psychoanalysis, 203, 259
   questions for twilight years, 245, 249
   on quitting, 152–53
   on radioactive materials, 179
   on RAND, 115, 135, 188, 194
   on rational choice, 131
   on redemption, 126
   on religion, 226, 248–49
   on resilience, 178
   on responsibility, 67, 98
   on retirement, 92–93
   on right-wing coup, 166–67
   on risk-taking, 47, 54, 57–58, 62, 76–77, 78, 83, 149, 191, 238, 263
   on Rocky Flats, 103, 106, 107, 133
   on the Russell-Einstein Manifesto, 216
   on sacrifice, 98
   on safeguards against abuse, 74–75
   on scapegoating, 128
   on secrets, 56, 74–76, 81, 83, 96, 111, 116, 125, 127, 181, 189, 213, 244, 249
   on secularization, 85
   on John Seed, 220–21
   on self-defense, 139, 150, 159, 205
   on self-determination, 73–74, 75, 80–81, 124
   on self-sufficiency, 85
   on shame, 98, 99, 103, 107, 147–48, 192
   on silence, 173, 215
   on social change, 124, 141
   on social identities, 92–93, 96, 97, 103
   on societal values, 94
   on soldier training, 71, 198, 237–38
   on species awareness, 233
   on speeches, 215–16
   on stalemate policy, 55
   on the State, 97–98, 128
   on strategic bombing, 92, 150
   on strikes, 272
   on survivor guilt, 177–78, 224
   on teaching, 57
   on terrorism, 159–60, 208
   on "the end justifies the means," 230
   on thinking, 131

Jan Thomas and, xxix,
    xxxii–xxxiv
on traitor label, 61, 188, 208
on trauma, 177–78, 187,
    202, 232
on treason, 61
on trustworthiness, 67
on truth, 53, 54, 63, 78, 86–87,
    92, 96, 107, 116, 173–74, 215,
    227, 241, 248, 256, 267
on TV interview/lecturer
    personality, 92
on uncertainty, 102
on U.S. bombing, 135
on U.S. government, 109–10
on U.S. military
    intervention, 179
on U.S. policy myths, 159
on values, 91, 92, 94, 243
on vengeance, 218
on Veterans for Peace Event, 198
on Vietnam, 45, 49, 51, 52,
    54–55, 56, 59–60, 66, 69,
    73–74, 76–77, 81–83, 90–91,
    93, 115, 116, 125, 135–36,
    137, 138, 141, 151–52, 154,
    160, 179, 184, 187–88, 190,
    202, 204, 205, 208, 212,
    238–39, 274
on vigils, 77, 140, 154, 160, 264
on violence, 102–3, 129, 130,
    171, 198, 212, 218
on war, 96, 112, 128, 129, 130,
    137, 150, 153, 198, 244,
    247–48, 269, 271
on war resistance, 62, 95–96,
    124, 247
on whistleblowers, 161–62, 168,
    217, 227, 237, 239, 262

on willful ignorance, xxxiv
on writing block, 105–6, 241
on zen, 173
Enola Gay, 318–19
Erikson, Erik, 36, 102, 192, 232
Erikson, Kai, 231
evil
    DE on, xiii, xv, xvi, xxi–xxiii,
        xxxiv, 280, 281, 285, 287,
        291–96, 300
    Ellsberg Notebooks on, 57, 67,
        82, 95, 96, 98, 99, 100, 109,
        112, 113, 127, 146, 178, 192,
        229, 235, 236, 244, 248–49,
        261–62, 273
    Mohandas Gandhi on, 170

Falk, Dick, 216
Fanon, Frantz, 81
Fielding, Lewis, xxvii–xxviii
Flaubert, Gustave, 62
Floyd, George, 275
"43 Seconds" (DE), 317–20
Fox, Matthew, 219, 221
France, Vietnam policy of, xiii–xiv,
    59, 76
free will, 304–5
Freud, Sigmund, 177
Froemer, John, 113
Fulbright, J. William, 62

Galloway, George, 231
Gandhi, Mohandas
    on evil, 170
    on love, compassion, and
        nonviolence, 93
    on nonviolent actions, 219
    on Satyagraha, 93, 256
    on sitting, 146

Gandhi, Mohandas (*cont'd*)
  spiritual values and, 194, 202
  Vietnam war resisters and, xiv
  on violent struggle for
    justice, 124
  on war, 129
Garson, Greer, 22
Gelb, Leslie, 188
Geneva Conventions, 60
Genghis Khan, 294
George III (king of England), 237
Germany. *See also* Nazis
  reunification of, 170, 180
  World War II and, 284–85, 293
Ginsberg, Allen, 103
Gnostic Gospel of Thomas, 175
Gorbachev, Mikhail, 275
Grant, Ulysses S., 237
group behavior
  DE on, viii, 309–15
  Ellsberg Notebooks on,
    121–22, 127–28, 212–13,
    229–30
Gumbel, Bryant, 188

Hale, Nathan, 238
Halperin, Mort, 66, 136, 204
Hart, Gary, 164
Haushofer, Albrecht, 232–33
Hayden, Tom, 303
Hegel, Georg Wilhelm Friedrich, 68
Helfgott, David, 40–41
Henry V (king of England), 202
Heschel, Abraham, 190
Hitler, Adolf, ix, 157, 235,
  284–85, 293
Hoffman, Abbie, 51–52, 110
Holocaust, xi, 109, 226, 292–95,
  306, 315

Homer, *Iliad*, xi
hope
  DE on, xvii, xviii, xx
  Ellsberg Notebooks on, 94, 103,
    140, 231, 234
Housman, A. E., 198–99
Hubbard, Barbara Marx, 153
Hugo, Victor, 62
humanity
  DE on, viii, x, xi–xii, xxiii, xxv,
    52, 283–87, 303–4
  Ellsberg Notebooks on, 68, 80,
    84–85, 86, 94, 99, 128, 133,
    141, 162, 201–2, 211, 214,
    230, 242, 245, 249, 251–53,
    256, 259, 272
human survival
  DE on, viii, xi, xii, xviii, 50, 84,
    287, 303–4
  Ellsberg Notebooks on,
    84–85, 86, 94, 100, 103,
    108, 272
Humphrey, Hubert, 320
Hurricane Katrina, 231
Hussein, Saddam, 224, 286

"The Implications of the Twentieth
  Century for Theology"
  (DE), 303–7
India-Pakistan, 179
Indonesia, 97
Iraq, 218, 224, 231
Ireland, 179
Israel, 163

James, William, 117
Japanese people, U.S. concentration
  camps for, 95, 243
Jefferson, Thomas, 131

Jews
　Christian Jews, 21–27, 191–92
　Ellsberg Notebooks on, 163, 204, 226, 235
　DE on theology of Judaism, 306–7
Johnson, Lyndon, xv, 45, 301
Joint Strategic Capabilities Plan (JSCP), 183, 295
Joplin, Janis, 136
Judaism, 21, 25–26, 306–7

Kahn, Herman, 123, 144
Kahneman, Daniel, 152
Kehler, Randy, xiv, xix, 154, 202
Kennedy, John F., 144, 157, 301
Kennedy, Robert F., 272
Kenniston, Ken, 192
King, Martin Luther, Jr., xiv, 167, 174, 221
Kissinger, Henry, 59, 76, 82, 204
Klan members, 129
Klaver, Ellen, 133
Korea, 179
Korn, Dick, 126
Kottler, Mischa, 15–19, 37–39, 147
Kristofferson, Kris, 136

Lansdale, Edward, 157
Laos, 135
Lee, Barbara, 51
Lens, Sidney, 96
Leonard, Mrs., 79
Lifton, Robert Jay, 36, 68, 178, 192, 208, 232, 264
Livermore Lab, 145

MacArthur Foundation, xxvi–xxvii
Mack, John, 179
McNamara, Robert, 188

McReynolds, David, 167
Macy, Joanna, 51, 221, 252–53
Mahavira, 201
Mailer, Norman, 227, 235
Mandela, Nelson, 180
Manhattan Project, 193, 231
Mannebach, Margaret, 5–7, 14–16, 18
Manson, Charles, 123
Mao, Zedong, 294
March on the Pentagon (1967), 51
Marshall, Andy, 295
massacre
　DE on, 283–87
　Ellsberg Notebooks on, 116–17, 121, 224
"Massacre and Humanity" (DE), 283–87
Mejía, Camilo, 232
Milgram, Stanley, ix–x, 82, 98, 148, 214
Miller, Nancy, xxvii
Miller, Zell, 208
Missile Gap, 47
Mitchell, John N., 167
monotheism, 305, 306
Moorhead, William, 56
morality, ix, xiv, xxxiii, xxxiv, 229–30, 233, 307
Mussolini, Benito, 157
Muste, A. J., 49
"My Anguishing Secret" (DE), 297–302
My Lai massacre, 224

Næss, Arne, 220
Nagler, Michael, 112
Native Americans, 294
NATO, 151, 295

Nazis, ix, 95, 162–63, 178, 284, 292–94, 297
Neruda, Pablo, 41–42
Nhat Hanh, Thich, 185
Nicaragua, 158–59
Nietzsche, Friedrich, 264
9/11 terrorist attacks, xxii, 237, 282, 283, 287
Nixon, Richard
　aims and plans of, 47
　election of, 320
　Pentagon Papers and, xv, xix, 77, 172, 204
　"Plumbers" unit and, xix, xxvii–xxviii
　public interest and, 73
　resignation of, xix
　on right-wing coup, 167
　Vietnam escalation plans of, 66, 135
　Vietnam policy of, 136, 320
　Watergate conspiracy and, xix, 77
North Vietnam, 135
nuclear planning
　DE as defense analyst and, xii
　DE on, viii, xii–xiii, 76, 117, 175, 289–90, 292–96, 297, 298–302
　deterrence and, xii, 292–93
　nuclear war casualty estimates and, xiii, xxiii, 157
nuclear power plants, 153
nuclear weapons
　DE on first-use nuclear threat, 286
　DE on threat of, xiv–xvi, xvii, 289–90, 291, 292, 317–20
　development of, 304

Ellsberg Notebooks on, 49, 92, 94, 95, 96, 107, 112, 115, 120–21, 128, 130, 135, 138–39, 141, 183–84, 185, 212, 230, 231, 235–36, 273
nuclear winter, xiii, 236–37, 291, 304

Obedience to Authority (Milgram), ix–x
Oppenheimer, J. Robert, 49
Orwell, George, 63, 78

pacifism, 281
Paine, Thomas, 121, 188
Papers on the War (DE), xxi, xxvi
Pascal, Blaise, xii
Pentagon Papers
　DE's proposed title for, 46
　DE's reading of, xiii–xiv, 136, 205
　DE's release of, ix, xv, xix, xxxiii, 40, 53–54, 56, 57, 60, 172
　DE's research on, 76
　DE's *Secrets* and, xxix
　Ellsberg Notebooks and, xxiv, 47, 53–54, 56–57, 59–63, 66, 73–74, 77–78, 86–87, 92, 97, 116, 125, 126, 136, 154, 188, 193–95, 202, 205, 207, 212
　Richard Nixon and, xv, xix, 77, 172, 204
Pentagon Papers trial (1973)
　DE's intellectual explorations following, ix, xxiii
　Ellsberg Notebooks and, xxxiv, 60–61, 66, 69–72, 76, 87, 97, 238
"The Piano" (DE), 15–19
　DE's childhood and, xxvii, 3–11

DE's fear of losing mother's love
and, 13–15, 19
DE's marriage counseling and,
3–4, 14–15
piano lessons and, 15–16
piano practice and, 3–8, 10–11,
13–14, 17–19
piano recitals and, 8–10, 14,
15, 17
Piers, Maria, 46
Pol Pot, 286, 294
Proust, Marcel, 62

Quakers, 57

Rachmaninov, Sergei, 5, 40, 42
RAND Corporation
DE as defense analyst for, xii, xiii,
xvii, 72, 76, 97, 115, 135–36,
185, 197, 204, 295
Ellsberg Notebooks on, 115, 135,
188, 194, 197, 204, 207
Reader's Digest, 9
Reagan, Ronald, xxxii, 144, 158,
208, 298
Reifer, Tom, xxvi, 293
"The Responsibility of Officials in a
Criminal War" (DE), ix
revealed preference, xxiii
"Revolutionary Judo" (DE), 274
Rilke, Rainer Maria, 264
Risk, Ambiguity and Decision (DE),
xxvi, 116, 274
risk
DE on, xi, xxvi, 116, 274,
299, 300
Ellsberg Notebooks on, 47, 54,
57–58, 62, 76–77, 78, 83, 149,
191, 238, 263

Rockefeller, John D., 73
Romans, 294
Roosevelt, Franklin Delano, 76,
95, 136
Rostow, Walt, 183
Rotblat, Joe, 231
Rowen, Harry, 183, 188
Rwanda, 294

Sartre, Jean-Paul, 62
Schumann, Robert, 16
Science and Health, 22–24, 25, 26, 42
Secrets (DE), xxi, xxvi, xxviii–xxix
Seed, John, 220–21
Shakespeare, William, 257
SIOP (Single Integrated Operational
Plan), 47, 175, 291, 293,
294–95
Smith, Huston, 219
Smithsonian Institution, xxviii
Snyder, Gary, 83
Socrates, 215
Soleimani, Qasem, 272
South Africa, xviii, 133, 180,
199, 244
Soviet Union
as authoritarian regime, 123
changes in, 244
global warming and, 242
nuclear arms race and, 107
nuclear war plans and, 143,
157, 236, 289, 294, 295, 298,
300, 301
U.S. nuclear weapons and, 128
Speer, Albert, ix, 55, 97, 285
splitting of atom, perils of, xi
Stalin, Joseph, 95, 294, 297
Stendhal, 62
Stephanopoulos, George, 199

Suharto, 294
Swimme, Brian, 220

Tamerlane, 294
Tau Beta Pi Magazine, 138
Temple, Shirley, 22
Terkel, Studs, 66
terrorism
    DE on, xxii, 279–82, 285, 286–87
    Ellsberg Notebooks on, 159–60, 208
theology, 303–7
Thieu, Nguyen Van, 320
Thomas, Dylan, 36
Thomas, Jan R.
    as DE's assistant, xxvi, xxxi–xxxii
    DE's handwriting and, xxix
    DE's reading and note taking and, xxiv
    DE's unpublished writing and, xxviii, xxx, xxxii, xxxiii
    DE's writing and, xxvi, xxxii
    Ellsberg Notebooks and, xxix, xxxii–xxxiv
Thomas, Lowell, 8
Thoreau, Henry David, 146, 167
Titanic, xii, 105, 107, 150, 213, 272
Tito, Josip Broz, 305
Tolstoy, Leo, 62, 178
Tomlin, Lily, 264
Touchard, Peter, xxxii
Tran, Ngoc Chau, 77
Truman, Harry, 76, 301
Trump, Donald, 267
Truth, Sojourner, 187
Tschannerl, Janaki, 51, 137, 160, 167, 168, 170, 201–2

Tuchman, Barbara, 247
Tversky, Amos, 152

UN Charter, 60
United Kingdom, 291, 292
University of Massachusetts, Amherst, xxv, xxxii
Ustinov, Peter, 231

Vann, John Paul, 191
Vietnam (1965–67)
    DE on body counts, 46
    DE on ending of, 54, 320
    DE on policy of, ix, xiii–xiv, 51
    DE's encounter with war resisters and, xiv, xix–xx
    DE's writings on, xxi, xxix
    Ellsberg Notebooks on, 45, 49, 51, 52, 54–55, 56, 59–60, 66, 69, 73–74, 76–77, 81–83, 90–91, 93, 115, 116, 125, 135–36, 137, 138, 141, 151–52, 154, 160, 179, 184, 187–88, 190, 202, 204, 205, 208, 212, 238–39, 274
    Tom Hayden on, 303
    Richard Nixon's resignation and, xix
Vonnegut, Kurt, 249

Wagner, Jane, 264
Wallace, George, 167
Wallis, Jim, 233, 234
War Resisters' International, xix, 62, 137, 154, 160
Wellfleet gatherings, 192, 224, 227, 239, 259
whistleblowers

DE as, xi, 125, 161–62
Ellsberg Notebooks on, 161–62,
    168, 217, 227, 237, 239, 262
  terrorism and, 282
White, Katherine, 98
White Train trial, 140
Wilber, Ken, 149
Wilber, Treya, 153
Williams, Forrest, 103
Wohlstetter, Albert, 136,
    154, 295

Wolff, Leon, 123
World War I, xi, 123, 150
World War II, 157, 205, 284–85, 286,
    291–92, 294
Wren, P. C., *Beau Geste*, 62, 300

Yippies, 51
Yugoslavia, 294, 305

Zimmer, Heinrich, 123–24
Zinn, Howard, 102–3, 244

A NOTE ON THE AUTHOR

Daniel Ellsberg (1931–2023) was a lecturer, a writer, and an activist on the dangers of the nuclear era, wrongful U.S. interventions, and the urgent need for patriotic whistleblowing. He began his career as a strategic analyst at the RAND Corporation and consultant to the Defense Department and the White House, specializing in problems of the command and control of nuclear weapons, nuclear war plans, and crisis decision-making.

He transferred to the State Department in 1965 to serve two years at the U.S. Embassy in Saigon, evaluating pacification in the field. On return to the RAND Corporation in 1967, Ellsberg worked on the top-secret McNamara study of U.S. decision-making in Vietnam from 1945 to 1968, which later came to be known as the Pentagon Papers.

In 1969, he photocopied the seven-thousand-page study and gave it to the Senate Foreign Relations Committee; in 1971 he gave it to the *New York Times*, the *Washington Post*, and seventeen other newspapers. His trial, on twelve felony counts posing a possible sentence of 115 years, was dismissed in 1973 on grounds of governmental misconduct against him, which led to the convictions of several White House aides and figured in the impeachment proceedings against President Nixon.

Ellsberg then returned to his central concern prior to 1964: reducing the risk of nuclear war. For the remaining fifty years of his life, he lectured, wrote, organized, and participated widely in antinuclear and anti-interventionist actions as a voice of moral conscience.

Ellsberg earned a BA and a PhD in economics from Harvard University. He was the author of *The Doomsday Machine: Confessions of a Nuclear War Planner* (2017), *Secrets: A Memoir of Vietnam and the Pentagon Papers* (2002), *Risk, Ambiguity and Decision* (2001), and *Papers on the War* (1972). His 1961 article, "Risk, Ambiguity and the Savage Axioms," is widely considered to be a landmark in decision theory and behavioral economics.

A NOTE ON THE EDITORS

MICHAEL ELLSBERG, Daniel's son, is the author of three previous books. His writing has been featured in the *New York Times*, the *Washington Post*, and on *The Daily Beast*. He lives in Berkeley, California. Find him on the web at www.ellsberg.com.

JAN R. THOMAS was Daniel Ellsberg's assistant in the 1980s and for the last four years of his life. While preparing his papers for his archive, she recognized the significance of his unpublished notebooks, which became the impetus for this book. Jan is a facilitative editor, environmental activist, interfaith minister, and spiritual director residing in the San Francisco Bay Area.